"People are visual and auditory creatures l
the arts and humanities have a path straighı
nels are tailor-made for deep connection anı
process expresses so much of the individual'ı
This book offers so many approaches to enh
communicate, connect, and understand the c

Mandy Seligman, *Fine Arts Photographer, Psychologist and Founder of SeeingHappy.org*

"Coaching is a creative process, and unsurprisingly creative approaches have blossomed in coaching over the past decade, from the use of visual images to sound, from collage to poetry and from improv to dance. This book brings together a kaleidoscope of contribution and with each twist of the page, opens up new possibilities for working with clients. For those who want to coach in the full array of colours, Arts-Based Coaching: Using Creative Tools to Promote Better Self-expression is a fantastic contribution to the library of coaching psychology."

Prof Jonathan Passmore, *Henley Business School, UK & Senior Vice President EZRA Coaching*

"In a world of cognitive overload, this is a timely book, which reminds us of the power of creativity in coaching. It invites us to consider the richness and depth of arts-based practices. Wonderful things can happen when we engage not only our minds but also our senses, body and heart. Highly recommended."

Dr Ana Paula Nacif, *University of East London, UK*

"In a world that is evolving at astonishing speed, coaches can greatly benefit from fresh, innovative ways of connecting with clients. This is a wonderful, colourful and richly textured account of a transformative approach to development that integrates art-making with coaching. I really appreciated the range of artistic approaches explored, from photography, poetry, and dance to sand-tray coaching. I highly recommend this book to coaches and coaching psychologists who wish to expand their repertoire of offerings to clients."

Iain McCormick, *PhD, Author, Award Winning Schema and Executive Coach*

"*Arts-Based Coaching* puts both the art and science into coaching. Its chapters will appeal to coaches who hunger for expressive tools to foster client reflection and deepen conversations. This book is full of practical advice, including case studies, cultural and ethical considerations, and recommendations."

Dr. Robert Biswas-Diener, Author of *Positive Provocation*

Arts-Based Coaching

This book, written in an accessible way by leading experts in the field, offers a comprehensive exploration of arts integration in coaching through the lenses of positive and health psychology.

Drawing together international experts and interdisciplinary perspectives, including health and neuroscience, the book explores the intersection of positive psychology and the arts, offering insights and strategies for using art to promote personal growth. The chapters in this book weave theory into practice, condense research and theoretical concepts into straightforward frameworks, and offer easily understandable ideas and examples. It provides a theoretical rationale for various art forms, including poetry, music, visual arts, dance, cinema, and photography. Each chapter includes case studies to present practical ways in which arts can enhance coaching conversations.

Arts-Based Coaching is a practical guide that will interest coaching psychologists, coaches, dual practitioners offering therapeutic coaching, leaders, educators, and other professionals using coaching in their professional practice, as well as course leaders and students in coaching and coaching psychology.

Andrea Giraldez-Hayes is a chartered psychologist, executive coach, supervisor, psychotherapist, and consultant with a remarkable track record in academia and professional practice. She is the course director for the MSt in coaching at the University of Cambridge. Andrea has written several books and articles and is an Associate Editor for prestigious publications such as *Coaching: An International Journal of Theory, Research and Practice* and the *International Coaching Psychology Review*.

Max Eames is a chartered psychologist, senior accredited psychotherapist, and registered applied psychology practitioner supervisor in private practice. As an Associate Fellow of the British Psychological Society and a member of the British Association for Counselling and Psychotherapy, he has extensive teaching, clinical, and supervisory experience in both private-sector and National Health Service-affiliated settings.

Coaching Psychology

Series Editor: Stephen Palmer

Coaching psychology is a distinct branch of academic and applied psychology that focuses on enhancement of performance, development and wellbeing in the broader population. Written by leading experts, the **Coaching Psychology** series will highlight innovations in the field, linking theory, research and practice. These books will interest professionals from psychology, coaching, mentoring, business, health, human resources and management as well as those interested in the psychology underpinning their coaching and mentoring practice.

Titles in the series:

Coaching Psychology: Constructivist Approaches
Jelena Pavlović

Introduction to Coaching Psychology
Siobhain O'Riordan and Stephen Palmer

Coaching Psychology for Mental Health: Borderline Personality Disorder and Personal Psychological Recovery
Martin O'Connor and Hugh O'Donovan

Neurodiversity Coaching: A Psychological Approach to Supporting Neurodivergent Talent and Career Potential
Nancy Doyle and Almuth Mcdowall

Schema Coaching: Overcoming Deep-seated Challenges
Iain McCormick

Arts-Based Coaching: Using Creative Tools to Promote Better Self-expression
Andrea Giraldez-Hayes and Max Eames

https://www.routledge.com/Coaching-Psychology/book-series/COACHPSYCH

Arts-Based Coaching

Using Creative Tools to Promote Better Self-Expression

Edited by Andrea Giraldez-Hayes and Max Eames

Routledge
Taylor & Francis Group

LONDON AND NEW YORK

Designed cover image: ©Getty Images

First published 2025
by Routledge
4 Park Square, Milton Park, Abingdon, Oxon OX14 4RN

and by Routledge
605 Third Avenue, New York, NY 10158

*Routledge is an imprint of the Taylor & Francis Group, an informa
business*

© 2025 selection and editorial matter, Andrea Giraldez-Hayes and
Max Eames; individual chapters, the contributors

The right of Andrea Giraldez-Hayes and Max Eames to be
identified as the authors of the editorial material, and of the
authors for their individual chapters, has been asserted in
accordance with sections 77 and 78 of the Copyright, Designs and
Patents Act 1988.

All rights reserved. No part of this book may be reprinted or
reproduced or utilised in any form or by any electronic,
mechanical, or other means, now known or hereafter invented,
including photocopying and recording, or in any information
storage or retrieval system, without permission in writing from the
publishers.

Trademark notice: Product or corporate names may be trademarks
or registered trademarks, and are used only for identification and
explanation without intent to infringe.

British Library Cataloguing-in-Publication Data
A catalogue record for this book is available from the British
Library

ISBN: 978-1-032-59189-6 (hbk)
ISBN: 978-1-032-59190-2 (pbk)
ISBN: 978-1-003-45343-7 (ebk)

DOI: 10.4324/9781003453437

Typeset in Times New Roman
by SPi Technologies India Pvt Ltd (Straive)

Contents

Figures

Editors

Andrea Giraldez-Hayes, PhD, is a chartered psychologist, executive coach, supervisor, psychotherapist, and consultant with a remarkable track record in academia and professional practice. With an enduring commitment to continuous learning and professional development, Andrea has cultivated a diverse skill set over her 35-year career.

Having served as Senior Lecturer at the University of Valladolid (Spain, 1993–2013), Programme Director for the MSc in Applied Positive Psychology and Coaching Psychology and Co-director of the Wellbeing and Psychological Services Centre at the University of East London between 2018 and 2024, she is currently the course director for the MSt in coaching at the University of Cambridge.

She has contributed to the development of the coaching profession, serving in different roles at the European Mentoring and Coaching Council (EMCC) and the British Psychological Society (BPS), including her current role as Chair of Coaching Psychology at the British Psychological Society's Partnership and Accreditation Committee (PAC).

Andrea is passionate about how research evidence can inform practice. She has published many books, chapters, and peer-reviewed articles. She is also the Associate Editor for prestigious publications such as *Coaching: An International Journal of Theory, Research and Practice*, the *International Coaching Psychology Review*, and the *International Journal of Coaching*.

Throughout her career, Andrea has served as the Director of the Arts Education, Culture and Citizenship postgraduate course for the Organization of Ibero-American States for Education, Science and Culture (OEI), guest lecturer, and community arts consultant in multiple countries, including Spain, the United Kingdom, Australia, Italy, Mexico, the Dominican Republic, Ecuador, Costa Rica, Panama, Peru, Chile, Uruguay, and Argentina.

Max Eames, PhD, is a chartered psychologist, senior accredited psychotherapist, and registered applied psychology practitioner supervisor in private practice. As an Associate Fellow of the BPS and a member of the British Association for Counselling and Psychotherapy (BACP), he has extensive teaching, clinical, and supervisory experience in both private-sector and National Health Service-affiliated settings. Max is past Clinical Director of a university-based well-being and psychological services centre, heading its counselling and psychotherapy services activities. He now serves as Deputy Head of the London School of Economics' counselling service whilst supporting his alma mater, the University of East London, as a Visiting Senior Lecturer. A fellow of the Higher Education Academy, Max is also an accredited mental health first aid (MHFA) instructor, a trainer and facilitator certificated by the Institute of Leadership and Management, and an experienced academic. His teaching extends across a range of subjects and disciplines at both undergraduate and postgraduate levels, whilst his research examines the therapeutic use of metaphors, imagery, metacognitive rationales, and other conceptual frames in encouraging mindful and adaptive understandings of psychological distress. Max grew up in California but settled in the United Kingdom, where his varied career has included work as a chartered architect, a restaurateur, and a business-turnaround consultant.

Contributors

Alexandra Baybutt, PhD, CMA – Certified Movement Analyst, RSME – Registered Somatic Movement Educator, works as an artist, educator, and researcher. Her professional experiences include dancing, choreographing, movement directing, teaching, analysing, dramaturgy, and researching since 2004. Since 2010, she has been teaching Laban/Bartenieff Movement System on modular programmes in Europe, including for EMove Institute (NL) and Choronde (IT). Alexandra is a module convenor of performance practice with a BA in creative arts and humanities from UCL (United Kingdom). Her research interests concern space: cellular, kinespheric, and political.

Stephen Brown is a professional coach, consultant, and creative. He is also a coach educator and is accredited with the EMCC at the Senior Practitioner level.

Doreen Fleet, PhD, is a chartered psychologist (BPS) and a BACP-accredited therapist. She began private practice in 2006 and was a senior lecturer between 2008 and 2020. Currently, she is a visiting lecturer and a PhD research supervisor for Chester University in the United Kingdom. She has had several research papers published in academic journals, and in 2022, her book on pluralistic sand-tray therapy was published by Routledge.

Julie Flower is a leadership and team development practitioner working internationally with a background in public service and third-sector leadership. She is also an External Tutor in Coaching at Henley Business School and a co-editor of Passmore, J. et al. (eds.) (2021, 2022, 2023) *Coaching Tools*, Volumes 1, 2, and 3. Julie is an experienced and award-winning improvised comedy performer who can regularly be seen making things up on stage at festivals, including at the Edinburgh Fringe.

Neil Gibson, PhD, is a qualified social worker and academic specialising in the therapeutic use of photography. He is the author of *Therapeutic Photography: Enhancing Self-Esteem, Self-Efficacy and Resilience* and the creator of the world's first academic course on these techniques.

Meirion Jones is an experienced coach, business trainer, and management consultant. He works with leaders in the digital, arts, and professional services sectors, supporting individuals and teams on topics such as purpose, behaviour change, leadership and communication, and creativity. He trained in illustration and art history at a leading London art college before moving into journalism, followed by publishing, management consultancy, and a series of in-house strategy planning roles. Coaching enables him to bring these different strands of experience together to serve his clients.

Adrian Machon has spent over 30 years studying and supporting human growth and development. In the last 15 years, he has coached and facilitated personal transformation and development within major global businesses. His coaching utilises a wealth of validated scientific, psychological, and leadership thinking to enrich performance and personal fulfilment. Adrian's style combines a deeply spiritual inclination, creative design, and practical, enduring outcomes. Three main intentions have shaped and motivated his life: alleviating suffering, promoting life, and realising potential.

Andrew Machon is both a scientist and an artist dedicated to the development of masterful practitioners. Though initially a biochemist, he specialises in change through cultivating senior leadership in major multinational organisations worldwide. He is a qualified Psychotherapist, Master Coach, and experienced coaching supervisor dedicated to inspiring the next generation of coaches. Through coaching retreats, he explores how we can unlock the secrets to mastery, a topic illuminated by several of his own books and artwork.

Auriel Majumdar is a creative coach, supervisor, and educator specialising in professional and personal development in the creative and cultural sectors. An EMCC-accredited Master Practitioner Coach and EMCC-accredited Coach Supervisor, Auriel has a BSc. in psychology from Durham University; an MSc. in Coaching and Mentoring from Sheffield Hallam University, where she was latterly Course Leader for the Master's in Coaching and Mentoring; and a Professional Certificate of Advanced Study in Coaching Supervision from Oxford Brookes University.

Beth McManus is a coaching psychologist, artist, and researcher who lives in Manchester, United Kingdom, with her partner, James, and their two Devon Rex cats, Peanut and Pickle. She is an EMCC-accredited Coach and works as a Coaching Supervisor, with specialisms in supporting coach well-being and ethical awareness. Her PhD, exploring the role of arts-based approaches in coaching supervision, commenced in September 2023. Her best work happens at the intersection of psychology, coaching, and creativity.

Nefeli Soteriou has a background in film and media arts, behavioural coaching for mental health, creativity coaching, and education. She has real-world experience as a life coach and filmmaker. Nefeli specialises in helping film-makers with every aspect of filmmaking, from completing unfinished films to handling the stresses and pressures they face.

Patricia Sotomayor is an ICF-certified Master Executive Coach specialising in systemic-team coaching and neuroscience. As a Global Advisor to various tech companies' Global Inclusion Councils, she champions diversity and inclusion. With over 18 years of corporate experience in Spanish multina-tionals, she excels in results-driven projects and multicultural team leader-ship. She holds a master's degree in contemporary photography and visual arts and founded FOCCUS.ES in 2016, where she integrates photography into her work through portraiture. She teaches at Madrid business schools and consults internationally on visual narrative, pioneering the Photo Coaching® methodology.

Andréa Watts founded UnglueYou®, her arts-based, creative coaching practice, in 2012. She is the author of *Collage as a Creative Coaching Tool: A Comprehensive Resource for Coaches and Psychologists* (Routledge 2022). Her clients include Google Health, Imperial College London, and the US Air Force.

Gill Westland is the founding Director of the Cambridge Body Psychotherapy Centre, where she trains body psychotherapists. She also teaches the MA in body psychotherapy at Anglia Ruskin University, Cambridge, United Kingdom, and is the author of *Verbal and Non-verbal Communication in Psychotherapy*.

Wendy-Ann Smith is a coaching psychologist and founder of the Coaching Ethics Forum, Journal of Coaching Ethics, and ETHICAL EDGE Insights. Her research focuses on coach development, ethics, and wellbeing. Wendy-Ann supports coaches through one-to-one coaching and workshops, inte-grating coaching and positive psychology to enhance ethical awareness and practice. She enjoys fostering growth in others and approaches life with curiosity and passion.

Foreword

Since 2000, the fields of coaching and coaching psychology have developed into areas of practice beyond just using simple frameworks or models. This may reflect the shift in training originally involving just short courses or workshops to master's- or doctorate-level programmes which involve learners undertaking research and sharing their findings with colleagues at conferences or publishing their results in journals.

No longer are practitioners working in silos in consultancy companies promoting one particular in-house framework. Many practitioners are members of professional coaching or psychology bodies having to undertake regular professional development as part of maintaining accreditation as a coach or coaching psychologist. This is in harmony with the need to expand one's knowledge of the field to enhance understanding and skills which could help to facilitate coachee insight and goal achievement.

Professional and personal development can take many forms, including reading books and *Arts-Based Coaching: Using Creative Tools to Promote Better Self-Expression* is no exception. It is one of those rare, innovative, practical guides that provide the reader with a comprehensive introduction to a new, exciting area of practice. It brings together and integrates art therapy, therapeutic arts, and arts in psychotherapy into what has been termed by the co-editors, Dr Andrea Giraldez-Hayes and Dr Max Eames, as arts-based coaching. The chapters are written by leading authors in the field and include topics such as the visual arts, collage, sand-tray coaching, poetry, photography, music, or dance. With any pioneering approach to coaching, ethical practice is always paramount, and this is covered, too, as the last chapter explores ethical considerations in using arts-based tools and approaches in coaching.

This insightful book includes useful case studies, discussion points, and suggested resources to aid reflection and further study. As a practical guide, it will interest and may inspire coaches, coaching psychologists, and other practitioners interested in integrating arts-based coaching into their professional practice.

Professor Stephen Palmer, PhD FISCP
Series Editor, Coaching Psychology

Acknowledgements

As members of various academic and professional communities, we remain inspired and informed by those who have enthusiastically participated in our seminars, lectures, workshops, and supervision sessions. Their willingness to challenge us by asking questions prompted a deeper enquiry into what would be of interest to coaches who wish to embrace arts-based interventions in their coaching practice.

We are grateful to Professor Stephen Palmer for his enthusiasm and encouragement to add this book, the product of that process of enquiry, to his prestigious Coaching Psychology collection.

We also express deep gratitude to the team at Routledge and, in particular, to Katie Randall as our editor. Her support and guidance throughout this book's journey made the many weeks and months a pleasure. Overall, the team at Routledge reflects the professionalism and integrity that makes them a leader in psychology and mental health publishing.

In turn, our chapter authors infused this book enthusiastically and with many actionable ideas for enhancing coaching conversations. Each contributor was extremely patient with us as we balanced the various personal and professional commitments which comprised our day-to-day lives. Rather than impatience, they consistently expressed understanding and good grace when life's challenges seemed to interfere with our speed of pace. We are fortunate to have worked with many talented and creative individuals throughout this project.

Andrea Giraldez-Hayes: I am profoundly grateful for the time and learning I have shared with students, teachers, artists, and colleagues who have been integral to my personal and professional journeys. Whilst it is impossible to include everyone, I must name some of them. Firstly, I sincerely thank Maestro Herbert Diehl for igniting my passion for music. Additionally, I owe a debt of gratitude to Carmelo Saitta, Silvia Malbran, Lucina Jimenez, Evangelos Himonides, and my esteemed friend, colleague, and co-author, Maravillas Diaz.

Furthermore, I am indebted to many colleagues in the fields of coaching psychology and positive psychology, including Professor Martin Seligman and Mandy Seligman, for their enthusiasm for exploring the avenues of well-being arts, and Jonathan Passmore, Piers Worth, Jolanta Burke, and Ana Nacif for their trust and unconditional support.

There are not enough words to express my gratitude to my co-editor, Max Eames, for his unwavering friendship and illuminating conversations.

Lastly, I express my profound appreciation to my daughters, Maise and Pilar, for being beacons of light in my life. Their presence is a constant reminder of the importance of kindness, perseverance, and love amidst life's challenges; they are the present and the future.

Max Eames: Andrea's willingness to challenge me professionally in our various collaborations has always been greatly appreciated. As a mentor, colleague, and friend, she has done much to help me define my career as a psychologist. Along with my colleagues at the London School of Economics and the University of East London, she continues to push me to grow professionally as well as personally. Others have nudged me far beyond my comfort zone for a great many years and, again, their role in my development is considerable. Christine A. Padesky, Kathleen Mooney, and Helen Kennerley have generously shared their passion for discovery-based interventions, which encourage client creativity and curiosity. They have done more than anyone else to shape my thinking and challenge me to be a better practitioner. Lastly, it certainly would not have been possible to achieve much on a practical level without the steadfast and good-natured support, wisdom, and perspective of my partner, Angel Correa, who continues to find ways of reminding me not to take myself too seriously.

Preface

Over the past years, there has been a rise in the exploration of arts-based approaches within the field of coaching and coaching psychology, attracting the attention of a gradually increasing number of researchers and practitioners. This burgeoning field, which we have named arts-based coaching, draws from a rich tapestry of disciplines, including art therapy, therapeutic arts, and arts in psychotherapy. Grounded in the evidence of creative expression as a potent catalyst for personal growth and transformation, arts-based coaching pioneers, many invited to contribute to this book, harness the power of various artistic modalities, including music, visual arts, poetry, photography, or dance. The courageous exploration of unconventional approaches and techniques not only enriches the coaching experience but also pushes the boundaries of traditional coaching paradigms, inspiring other coaches to evolve and continually adapt in their practices.

This book contains a wealth of theoretical and experiential knowledge. Each chapter, authored by experts in their respective fields, presents a unique and innovative approach, offering the theoretical basis that underpins practice and practical strategies for integrating arts-based interventions into coaching sessions whilst addressing the ethical considerations intrinsic to such profoundly personal work. It was only possible to create the breadth and depth of exploration with the wisdom and creativity of our contributing colleagues. We are grateful for their generosity and dedication in sharing their knowledge and expertise. Their contributions have made this book a valuable resource for coaches, researchers, and anyone interested in the intersection of coaching and the arts.

We encourage you to approach this book with an open mind and a curious heart, letting the diverse perspectives and case studies inspire you to explore new territories in your own coaching practice and your clients' work and to find options and motivation as they navigate aspirations and challenges with curiosity, creativity, and courage.

Andrea Giraldez-Hayes
Max Eames

Introduction

The science of arts-based practices in coaching

Max Eames and Andrea Giraldez-Hayes

Introduction

The integration of arts-based practices into coaching has gained increasing attention in recent years as practitioners and researchers alike seek to explore innovative approaches to facilitating personal and professional growth. Whilst coaching theory often draws from the many theoretical orientations found in the literature of art therapy and psychotherapy, the incorporation of arts-based practices in coaching offers a unique and complementary perspective. As such, the first aim of this introduction is to consider, even if briefly, the science behind arts-based practices in coaching.

Providing a solid foundation for coaching theory

Coaching theory has long been influenced by various psychological disciplines, including cognitive-behavioural therapy (CBT), solution-focused brief therapy (SFBT), and positive psychology (Palmer & Whybrow, 2018). These evidence-based approaches provide a solid foundation for coaching interventions, focusing on goal setting, problem-solving, and the cultivation of strengths and resilience. The psychodynamic perspective, which explores the influence of unconscious processes on behaviour, offers another theoretical foundation for the application of arts-based practices in coaching. By engaging with art and creativity, clients can access and explore latent thoughts and emotions, offering a pathway to understand and integrate various aspects of the self into conscious awareness (Rubin, 2005).

Throughout this book, it is argued that the integration of arts-based practices in coaching can offer a creative and experiential approach which tends to enhance both the coaching process (Whitelaw, 2020) and its likely outcomes. When integrating arts-based practices into coaching conversations, it is considered that doing so taps into a client's non-verbal, symbolic expressions, enriching personal narratives with deeper, often unarticulated insights into clients' thought processes and emotional states (Kaufman & Gregoire, 2014). Such processes can reveal underlying patterns and conflicts, facilitating both personal growth and emotional freedom.

DOI: 10.4324/9781003453437-1

Drawing on a wide range of creative and scientific modalities

Even if your preference were to adopt an entirely atheoretical approach, this book sets out to make it clear that arts-based practices draw upon a wide range of creative modalities, such as visual arts, music, dance, drama, and creative writing. Whilst not demonstrably 'scientific' in the traditional sense, each of these practices is said to be grounded in the principles of expressive arts therapy, which proposes that the creative process itself is inherently therapeutic and can facilitate self-expression, insight, and transformation (Malchiodi, 2019). By engaging in various arts-based activities, clients are said to be well-positioned to find various means of accessing and exploring their thoughts, feelings, and experiences in a non-verbal and symbolic manner (Levin, 2018), bypassing the limitations of language and conscious reasoning.

Perhaps the science behind arts-based practices in coaching can most convincingly be understood through the lens of neuroscience and embodied cognition. Research has shown that engagement in creative activities activates multiple brain regions, including those associated with emotion, memory, and self-reflection (Bolwerk et al., 2014). The heightened neural activity accompanying such engagement is said to facilitate the integration of cognitive, emotional, and sensory experiences (King, 2019), leading to new insights and perspectives. Moreover, many arts-based practices involve the body and movement, tapping into the concept of embodied cognition. As such, it is considered that our thoughts, feelings, and behaviours are deeply intertwined with our physical experiences (Herman & Behm, 2020).

The place of personal interpretation and constructed meanings

The constructivist theory further supports the use of arts-based practices in coaching by emphasising the role of personal interpretation and meaning-making in human development. Constructivist approaches to coaching, akin to their psychotherapeutic counterparts, view learning and change as a process of constructing personal knowledge from experiences (Mahoney, 1991). Arts-based interventions align with this view by facilitating experiential learning and allowing clients to reframe their personal narratives and histories in novel, creative ways (Allen, 2005).

Empirical evidence increasingly supports the effectiveness of arts-based practices in coaching. For example, a study by Whitelaw (2020) found that the use of visual arts in coaching sessions enhanced clients' self-awareness, creativity, and problem-solving skills. Participants reported gaining new insights into their challenges, all through the process of creating and reflecting on their artwork. Similarly, a qualitative study by Levin (2018) explored the experiences of coaches and clients engaged in expressive writing exercises. The findings indicated that the writing process itself facilitated deeper self-exploration, emotional catharsis, and the reframing of various personal narratives, leading to positive shifts in perspective and behaviour.

The invitation being made throughout this book

The authors featured in this book invite you, through various means, to reflect on the application of arts-based practices in your practice, given that coaching, by its nature, is diverse and adaptable to various contexts and client needs. For example, a coach working with a client on career transitions might facilitate the creation of a collage representing a desired future using images, words, and symbols. The very process of selecting and arranging the elements can uncover hidden desires, values, and obstacles, providing a tangible representation of the client's aspirations (Herman & Behm, 2020). Equally, a coach supporting a client with stress management might co-create a mindful drawing exercise, encouraging a focus on the sensory experience of mark-making and colour choice. Such a practice is considered to promote relaxation, self-regulation, and the development of various coping strategies (King, 2019).

The ethical considerations involved in integrating arts-based practices into coaching broadly mirror those in psychotherapy, emphasising confidentiality, informed consent, and competence. Coaches utilising arts-based methods must ensure they are appropriately trained and sensitive to the potential emotional vulnerabilities such practices may evoke. Meantime, it is argued that the integration of arts-based practices in coaching will continue to be supported by a robust scientific foundation that intersects with psychological principles and therapeutic methodologies.

The present and future of arts-based interventions

Arts-based interventions offer unique and powerful tools for facilitating personal growth, emotional intelligence, and transformative learning, enriching the coaching experience beyond traditional verbal interactions. As the field of coaching continues to evolve, further research is needed to explore the full potential and limitations of arts-based practices, ensuring they are applied ethically and effectively to support client development.

By augmenting the practices and theoretical orientations of psychotherapy, it is argued throughout this book that we can facilitate various transformations using arts-based and creative interventions. As research in this area continues to evolve, it seems helpful for us as coaches to stay curious about the latest empirical findings and to engage in ongoing training to ensure the ethical and competent integration of arts-based practices into our coaching practice.

Chapter summaries: Insights at a glance

What follows is a chapter-by-chapter resume of each of the practices and interventions presented throughout this book. This resume is, of necessity, concluded with a reminder that there is a need to be aware at all times of the potential emotional responses triggered by arts-based and creative endeavours. As such, a robust ethical stance means that more attention generally needs to be given to the various practices likely to be involved in each of the invitations being made by the book's authors.

Chapter 1 examines the significance of both verbal and non-verbal communication in coaching. It emphasises that non-verbal communication, conveyed through body language, tone, and paralanguage, accounts for a substantial part of human interaction. The author argues that understanding the neurological foundations of communication, including the roles of the left and right brain hemispheres and the autonomic nervous system, can enhance our ability to interpret and respond to the implicit messages of our clients. This chapter also explores the importance of embodied awareness, mindfulness, and attending to one's bodily sensations whilst engaging in a coaching conversation. Techniques such as shifting attention between verbal and non-verbal cues, inviting clients to connect with their inner experiences, and moving away from solely "talking about" issues towards direct bodily exploration are recommended. Moreover, it is convincingly argued that each will tend to enrich the coaching process and facilitate greater self-awareness on the part of clients.

Chapter 2 considers the power of imagery and metaphors in coaching interventions, either in arts-based coaching or in general. In so doing, it examines the role of mental imagery in shaping our experiences, memories, and emotions. Metaphors are presented as linguistic expressions that help conceptualise abstract experiences, offering clients new perspectives and insights. The chapter explores the dual nature of imagery, its potential challenges, and the importance of considering individual differences and cultural values when using metaphors. It also emphasises the collaborative process of co-creating metaphors with clients and refining their serviceability. Case studies illustrate the practical application of imagery and metaphors in addressing various coaching goals, such as career transitions, performance anxiety, resilience, and work – life balance. Overall, the chapter advocates for the strategic use of imagery and metaphors as powerful tools in coaching to facilitate personal growth and change.

Chapter 3 explores the use of photography as a therapeutic tool for self-exploration in coaching. It discusses theoretical frameworks, such as Bronfenbrenner's socio-ecological model and Winnicott's concepts of the *True Self* and *False Self*, which can greatly inform the interpretation of photographic self-portraits. The chapter outlines various practical exercises, including taking self-portraits to capture positive aspects of oneself and creating two photographs representing "how I see myself" and "how others see me." These exercises aim to enhance self-efficacy, self-esteem, and empowerment by facilitating self-reflection, emotional connection, and social learning. The author argues that the familiarity and accessibility of photography, combined with its ability to evoke emotional responses (the "Punctum"), make it a potentially valuable tool for exploring identity and fostering personal growth within a safe and controlled environment.

Chapter 4 presents a robust case for the use of portrait photography and body language as a coaching tool. The Photo Coaching® methodology, arising from the author's experience as a portrait photographer and executive coach, allows individuals to gain valuable insights by becoming external observers of themselves. This is partly a story of the author's professional development, whereby early portraiture focused on capturing subjects' personalities and inner selves. Since those early endeavours, the approach has been deployed therapeutically to explore moments of transition and raise self-awareness. The author considers that reflecting on one's own portraits and gestures can reveal deeply rooted beliefs and facilitate personal growth. The process involves capturing portraits, viewing them with a coach, and exploring their meaning and coherence with various thoughts and accompanying emotions. Case studies demonstrate how Photo Coaching® can help individuals set goals, measure progress, and celebrate achievements. The chapter thus highlights the power of photographs in enriching the coaching process and enabling in-depth exploration of one's identity and values.

Chapter 5 explores how coaches can access their innate creativity to facilitate deeper, long-lasting personal development and change. The authors emphasise the importance of nurturing a co-creative relationship between coach and client, where both can tap into their creative potential. The authors introduce four essential inner tools: the *Spirit Level*, which helps centre and balance; the *Compass*, which activates the inner artist and guide; the *Mirror*, which encourages reflection and noticing; and the *Wand*, which invites the skilled use of imagination. These tools collectively enable coaches to create a space for creative learning and growth, fostering resourcefulness, creative expression, and co-creative relationships. The authors argue that combining competency frameworks with creative explorations into the nature of coaching offers a more wholesome vision of what it means to coach at one's best.

Chapter 6 introduces what is referred to by the authors as Illustrated Coaching, a method which captures the themes of a coaching conversation. This takes shape in the form of powerful illustrations as co-created by the coach and client. By drawing out the client's inner psychological landscape, or 'inscape', the coach helps the client explore key themes: interests, aspirations, and concerns. Such a process triggers insightful responses and realisations, potentially leading to expanded self-awareness. The effectiveness of Illustrated Coaching relies on the coach's illustrative skill and ability to authentically capture the client's imagery. The co-creative approach is critical, as the power resides with the client to inform and guide the image-creation process. The authors consider that Illustrated Coaching has the potential to inspire clients to take charge of their own creative expression and personal growth through various art forms, allowing for deeper reflection and learning.

Chapter 7 explores the potential for working with music within a coaching context, drawing on research from music therapy and the use of music in psychotherapy. The author considers the likely rationale for the universal appeal of music and its profound impact on emotions, thoughts, and behaviours. In doing so, she delves into the practical applications of listening to music in coaching, offering techniques such as grounding exercises, using soundtracks to explore emotions, and creating personalised playlists. Ethical considerations, such as cultural sensitivity and the subjective nature of music, are also considered, whereby emphasis is placed on the importance of obtaining informed consent and adhering to ethical guidelines when incorporating music into coaching. An indicative case study illustrates how jazz improvisation can be used as a metaphor to help coaches develop attunement, responsiveness, and spontaneity in their practice. The author concludes by acknowledging the potential of music as a versatile tool in coaching whilst also calling for further research to examine its efficacy in this context.

Chapter 8 explores the potential of using art galleries and public buildings as creative spaces for coaching and reflection. Drawing on research linking museums and galleries to well-being outcomes and human flourishing, the author proposes that such environments can serve as more than just a setting for coaching but as a substitute coach. What is outlined involves a three-part coaching process comprising an initial dialogue, a period of client reflection in the gallery space, and a process of reconnection to discuss insights and realisations. The author emphasises the importance of contracting, client safety, and the coach's accountability in managing the unpredictable nature of public spaces. A useful case study illustrates how the gallery environment can stimulate metaphorical thinking, self-awareness, and new perspectives for the client. The author concludes by inviting us as coaches to experiment with her approach in our own reflective practice and client work, all whilst considering our coaching philosophy and the unique challenges involved in working in public spaces.

Chapter 9 explores the concept of sand-tray therapy and its applications in coaching. Sand-tray therapy involves using a tray filled with sand and symbolic objects to help clients explore instances of emotional and psychological distress. Various theoretical approaches have adopted sand-tray therapy, each adapting it to their specific underpinning theory. The author explores some of the important distinctions between psychotherapy and coaching, noting that coaching tends to focus on the present and future concerns of the client, whilst psychotherapy may delve more deeply and deliberately into past issues. She also draws similarities between the pluralistic *therapeutic* approach and that which can be used in coaching, emphasising collaboration, goal setting, and the belief in the client's inner resources. In doing so, the author presents an introduction to what she refers to as Pluralistic Sand-Tray Therapy (PSTT), as well as a means of adapting its principles to coaching. As a form of arts-based coaching, structured sand-tray sessions can be used to address specific issues such as workplace conflicts, low self-esteem, and the pursuit of happiness. The examination of both symbolism and metaphorical expression in sand-tray coaching can facilitate instances of deep exploration and insight. As such, this approach potentially affords our clients a set of unique benefits, particularly when compared to talk therapy approaches.

Chapter 10 introduces what the author refers to as creative movement coaching, a person-centred approach which draws on somatic movement education, dance, and the *Laban/Bartenieff Movement System* (LBMS). The approach itself emphasises the client's agency, sensitivity, and creativity, with the coach guiding and responding to specific aims and interests. It does so through various movements attended by reflective dialogue. Movement coaching respects the creative capacity of both client and coach, adapting to individual needs and goals. LBMS supports the observation and experience of movement, helping coaches identify patterns, durations, and frequencies in what is termed a client's *movement signature*. The author examines the importance of bodily co-presence, observation, and affect in the learning process, doing so on the part of both client and coach. She argues that creative movement coaching should remain a frame through which to view a plural field of interpersonal movement practices and creative learning, all whilst acknowledging the specific methods, goals, and desired outcomes of our clients.

Chapter 11 explores the potential of improvisation (i.e., improv) as a means of arts-based coaching, drawing parallels between the spontaneous, collaborative nature of improv comedy and the dynamic, co-creative coaching process. The author examines how improv principles and exercises can support coaches in developing presence, flexibility, and comfort with uncertainty whilst also offering practical tools for what amounts to an eclectic coaching approach. Emerging evidence suggests that engaging in improv exercises can lead to heightened awareness, positive affect, flashes of insight and creativity, and better interpersonal skills. The author argues that improv training can enhance the interested coach's development by promoting self-awareness, empathy, and rapport-building, as well as providing opportunities for use in coaching sessions. She emphasises the importance of personal and professional reflection in translating experiential learning from improv exercises into actionable insights. This chapter concludes by encouraging coaches to experiment with improv techniques as a discovery tool, holding promise of both strengthening the coaching relationship and articulating the needs and aspirations of the client.

Chapter 12 introduces film in coaching, a technique derived from cinematherapy, whereby coaches select commercially successful narrative films relevant to a client's areas of concern. Narrative films tend to resonate with human nature, inspiring both meaningful insights and action steps. The chapter explores the history of cinema and its impact on various fields, including the emergence of film analysis as an academic discipline. The author emphasises the importance of understanding a film's stylistic elements – narration, setting, costume, makeup, lighting, staging, editing, and sound – to engage in meaningful conversations with clients. A helpful case study illustrates how discussing films can build trust and inspire personal growth. This chapter concludes by advancing the argument that integrating film into a coaching conversation can prove to be a dynamic approach to self-discovery, harnessing the power of storytelling to cultivate self-awareness and foster positive change. Discussion points bring us as readers into the argument in that we are encouraged to relate one or more favourite films of our own, mapping them to a set of potential clients' journeys.

Chapter 13 explores the integration of environmental psychology and arts-based coaching, emphasising the profound influence of space and place on human thoughts, feelings, and actions. Drawing on findings from psychological enquiry, the author argues that coaches should carefully select, adapt, or transform coaching environments to align with their clients' specific needs and objectives. The chapter introduces various core concepts from environmental psychology, such as the restorative benefits of certain environments and the symbolic significance of settings. What follows is an invitation for coaches to assess environmental influences on clients, adapt their coaching strategies to various settings, and consider the logistical details of arts-based interventions. The practical application of arts-based interventions is discussed, including transcending the constraints of verbal communication, aligning settings with coaching objectives, exploring complex emotions, and fostering collaboration. Case studies demonstrating the use of natural and urban settings in coaching are presented. They provide the reader with a sense of how emphasising the potential for well-configured settings can enhance the effectiveness of arts-based and creative activities in coaching.

Chapter 14 explores the potential of integrating poetry into coaching practice. Drawing on the ancient roots of poetry and its therapeutic applications, the author argues that the expressive nature of poetry can deepen self-reflection, spark insight, and enhance the coaching experience. The chapter presents theoretical notions underpinning the introduction of poetry into coaching, including its ability to transcend conventional prose, evoke emotions, and convey condensed meanings. As a poet herself, the author offers practical guidance on using poems in coaching, drawing on Palus' *Artful Coaching Framework*. Such guidance is grounded in a case study illustrating the transformative power of poetry in addressing a set of existential questions. The chapter concludes with a reflective poem accompanied by a reminder of various matters for coaches to consider when incorporating poetry into their practice. The reader is thus invited to reflect on the need for careful contracting, tending to one's own creative capacity, and immersing oneself in poetry to harness its potential wisely in service of our clients.

Chapter 15 explores the impact of the 2020 global pandemic on the coaching industry, which led to a significant shift towards online platforms. The author delves into the various means by which creative coaches have adapted their methodologies to thrive in the digital realm, embracing technological advancements and innovative approaches which are tailored for digital delivery. In what is offered to the reader as a personal reflection, the author also at times shares his experiences in navigating the digital terrain and presents case studies that illustrate the intricacies of coaching in the virtual sphere. In so doing, he helpfully distinguishes between analogue and digital creative products, encouraging coaches to adapt their favoured creative approaches for online work whilst exploring various fully digital solutions. Importantly, the author also invites us to reflect on the need to attend to various matters, such as ethical considerations, data security, and professional standards when working with digital tools. This chapter concludes by providing a set of practical insights and strategies for those of us seeking to harness the power of digital platforms, offering a comprehensive guide to elevating our practice in an increasingly online world.

Chapter 16 emphasises the importance and value of using collage to enable clients to access and explore all aspects of the self, promoting better self-expression and self-awareness simultaneously. In so doing, it provides an overview of the three-stage *Collage Coaching Technique ™* (CCT) developed by the author herself. The reader is thus presented with an overview of Gathering, Creating, and Storytelling endeavours, all of which are central to the technique. The core principles inherent to the various stages involved in using this technique – such as the hand and mind connection, working with the unconscious, and the power of narrative storytelling – are examined in detail. The author highlights the multiple modalities of expression available when coaching with collage, examining how they can facilitate powerful instances of client self-awareness. The role and behaviour of the coach are emphasised for best practice, and a client reflection is presented which illustrates the CCT's theory in practice. This chapter concludes by advancing the argument that the CCT forms the basis of a set of arts-based interventions in which clients can express themselves authentically in a safe place, potentially leading to both deeper self-awareness and enhanced personal growth.

Chapter 17 explores some of the ethical considerations of using arts-based tools and approaches in coaching. Whilst the use of art and creativity in coaching has gained popularity, the authors argue that more attention needs to be given to the ethical implications of the various practices likely to be involved. They examine the potential for unintended harm and the importance of informed consent, voluntary participation, confidentiality, and the coach's competence as essential factors in facilitating art-based interventions. The authors invite us to consider and reflect on various ethical issues, drawing from the experience of arts-based and creative psychotherapy, as well as what is referred to as art therapy, to advance the arguments for the development of an ethical framework for arts-based coaching. The authors emphasise the need for coaches to be aware of the potential emotional responses triggered by art and to operate within their scope of competence. This chapter concludes by reminding us of the importance of integrating ethics into coach education and into our various reflexive endeavours. To underscore this message, a set of case studies illustrate various ethical challenges related to the responsible use, display, archiving, publishing, and ultimately ownership of arts-based and creative specimens in what can prove to be an exciting way of working for coaches and clients alike.

References

Allen, P. B. (2005). *Art is a way of knowing*. Shambhala Publications.

Bolwerk, A., Mack-Andrick, J., Lang, F. R., Dörfler, A., & Maihöfner, C. (2014). How art changes your brain: Differential effects of visual art production and cognitive art evaluation on functional brain connectivity. *PLoS One, 9*(7), e101035.

Herman, A., & Behm, L. (2020). Embodied cognition and the arts: A new perspective on coaching. *Coaching: An International Journal of Theory, Research and Practice, 13*(1), 3–15.

Kaufman, S. B., & Gregoire, C. (2014). *Wired to create: Unravelling the mysteries of the creative mind*. Perigee Books.

King, N. (2019). Creativity in coaching: Using arts-based practices to enhance coaching outcomes. *International Coaching Psychology Review, 14*(2), 6–17.

Levin, S. K. (2018). Writing the self: Using expressive writing in coaching. *Coaching: An International Journal of Theory, Research and Practice, 11*(2), 171–185.

Mahoney, M. J. (1991). *Human change processes: The scientific foundations of psychotherapy*. Basic Books.

Malchiodi, C. A. (2019). Expressive arts therapy and the science of creativity. In C. A. Malchiodi (Ed.), *Handbook of art therapy and digital technology* (pp. 21–37). Jessica Kingsley Publishers.

Palmer, S., & Whybrow, A. (Eds.). (2018). *Handbook of coaching psychology: A guide for practitioners* (2nd ed.). Routledge.

Rubin, J. A. (2005). *The art of art therapy: What every art therapist needs to know*. Brunner-Routledge.

Whitelaw, A. (2020). Integrating visual arts in coaching: Enhancing creativity and insight. *Coaching: An International Journal of Theory, Research and Practice, 13*(2), 209–223.

Chapter 1

Verbal and non-verbal communication in coaching

Gill Westland

Introduction

Cognitive psychologists describe verbal and non-verbal communication as explicit and implicit. Explicit communication is conveyed in spoken language, whereas implicit communication is conveyed physically and not symbolised in words. A person's body physically expresses a wide range of non-verbal communications and receives messages directly from within the body itself. Such implicit communications, which are picked up continuously, should be registered at a conscious level. Both verbal and non-verbal communication are two-way, with clients simultaneously expressing and receiving a vast array of information. In the context of an in-session exchange between client and coach, it must be remembered that coaches are undergoing the very same phenomena.

This means that there is much going on simultaneously – which begs the question: how and why is a better understanding of this phenomenon a gift to the interested coach? In turn, how can we, as coaches, decipher all this information, given that communication entails verbal and non-verbal elements running alongside each other? Whilst what people say tends to be noticed more, it has been estimated that roughly 90% of communication is non-verbal, and only 10% is verbal (McGilchrist, 2009b). This suggests that neglecting the non-verbal elements of communication will likely reduce the potency of our work with our clients.

Much of this chapter is adapted from *Verbal and Non-Verbal Communication in Psychotherapy* (Westland, 2015). It applies to coaching as the ability of any coach to enquire and facilitate will arguably be enriched by developing the capacity to give more attention to the non-verbal elements of our interactions with clients. Doing so invites a deeper level of self-awareness with a fuller understanding of coach – client interactions. It is likely to engender more profound moments of interaction with any client and signal an array of identifiable shifts indicative of change. In these moments, it is argued that the body's tissues re-organise themselves in alignment with newfound and hopefully enduring transformations (Westland, 2018).

DOI: 10.4324/9781003453437-2

As you read this chapter, I suggest you pause and notice what is happening in your body every so often. Are you comfortable with the way you are sitting? Are you feeling tense anywhere? What happens when you notice that? This will support your reading and bring more awareness to other, perhaps more implicit, aspects of your experience.

Communications

Non-verbal communications are carried by the body in the form of postures (e.g., chest puffed up, shoulders rounded, commanding the room) and movements (e.g., heavy/light footsteps, slow/quick walking into the room, manner of sitting down/getting up), gestures (e.g., quick outward arm movements, lack of gesture), self-sensing (e.g., rubbing arm, stroking hair, clutching the hands tightly together), gazing and looking (e.g., close/distant, out of the window, at the coach or not), facial expressions (e.g., lively and alert, immobile), eyes (e.g., full of longing, no-one at home, watchful, or perhaps the eyes and mouth conveying different messages) and personal mannerisms. Non-verbal communication also includes changes in breathing (hardly noticeable, slow with sighs, irregular, fast), changes in skin colour and its hues (for example, blushing or going paler in the face), and involuntary movements such as shivering with cold, fatigue or fear.

Non-verbal communication also includes how someone speaks, how loud and fast they speak, the tone of their voice, and which words or phrases they tend to emphasise. The rhythms of the speech, where someone makes pauses, and the length of those pauses create a musical feel to the spoken sentences. Words – verbal communication – provide information and content, but the way the words are spoken carries various emotional meanings. This non-verbal communication of emotions is known as *paralanguage*. Paralanguage also includes sounds such as ums, sniffs, and sighs because these sounds often convey emotions in their intonation, pitch, and rhythms.

Neurological foundations for understanding communication

Understanding how the brain functions and how the body processes information can help us understand clients whilst serving as a guide to choosing between a non-verbal, exploratory focus or a verbal explanation. The part of the brain known as the *cerebral cortex* organises experiences from the environment and manages conscious thoughts, memory, and planning, but it needs to be in overall control of bodily activities (Cozolino, 2017). The cerebral cortex is divided into two hemispheres, the left side and the right side, each with different functions. It is considered that the left and right sides of the brain process information from the world differently, communicate with each other, and are both involved in any form of activity, albeit with some degree of specialisation on each side.

The left side of the brain is understood to be concerned with the following:

- Verbal communication – e.g., naming objects, vocabulary, spelling, reading, writing, and comprehension
- Selective, focused attention, parts of things, and one's focus on things/objects
- Analytical and mathematical thinking
- Serial information and sequencing
- Narrative memory – e.g., descriptions of autobiographical events

It is understood that the right side of the brain is concerned with the following:

- Non-verbal communication
- Whole-global attention in context – e.g., being able to infer things
- Shared meanings – e.g., intersubjectivity
- Empathy, intuition, humour, and creativity
- Implicit memory – i.e., in one's body and not conscious
- Social and emotional intelligence
- Regulation of stress and emotional arousal (McGilchrist, 2009a)

We can think of the left hemisphere as the *what* and the right hemisphere as the *how* of communication (McGilchrist, 2009a). The client, relating more from within what are considered to be the concerns of the left hemisphere, asks, "Why do I feel like this?" The coach can give an explanation. That can be helpful in the sense that this is the so-called *what*. Meanwhile, the same client is also likely to want to feel that the coach "gets them" by how they are with them and not solely from what is said. This is the so-called *how*. That said, emotional health arguably depends on both sides of the brain working synergistically together.

Your own everyday engagement with the written word would be one such example of the notion of left and right-brain synergy. As you read this page, it is considered that the left side of the brain processes the words on the page, whilst the right side of the brain is simultaneously gathering information about how you feel about what you are reading, how you are sitting, and so on. Pausing to ask yourself how you feel about the content you have just read gives a sense of the manner in which the left and right sides of the brain can be understood to work together.

The *peripheral nervous system* is divided into the *somatic nervous system* and *the autonomic nervous system*. The somatic nervous system allows the body to interact with the environment and sense what is happening. The body can react to this information coming in and residing out of one's conscious awareness. The autonomic nervous system regulates physiology as well as our level of arousal (e.g., stimulated/calm) and feelings. For those unfamiliar with physiology, I recommend Stauffer's work (2010), which is intended to provide an understanding of anatomy and physiology to psychotherapists.

Emotions and physiology

Emotional and physiological regulation are understood to be closely linked (Porges, 2011). Some feelings, such as excitement, joy, irritation, anger, and fear, are associated with aroused physiology and dominance of the sympathetic branch of the autonomic nervous system. Feeling satisfied, calm, being at peace, sadness, grief, and love are thought to be indicative of less arousal and the dominance of the parasympathetic branch of the autonomic nervous system (Reich, 1983). A client's words may convey a certain flatness of mood and low physiological arousal, or at another time, higher arousal, which goes with feeling frustrated. For that same client, tapping the arm of a chair may be a sign of discharging anxiety and lowering levels of stress. Similarly, the relaxed coach will convey tranquillity through slower speech and body movements.

It is reasonable to assume that some degree of understanding of the autonomic nervous system can also assist with the pacing of sessions. For example, recognising when a client is becoming calmer as they discuss a topic or appear to be getting overwhelmed indicates what might be required from the coach in the next sequence of interactions. In moments of exchange, a client becoming overwhelmed by their feelings may benefit from a question such as, "How long have you felt like this?" to engage their thinking more fully.

Child development

The brain develops in early baby – carer interactions, and the quality of the interactions is crucial for optimum brain development (Schore, 1994; Siegel, 1999). It is considered that the development of the right side of the brain is particularly significant in the first 15 months and for the first three years of life. As language develops, the left side of the brain becomes more important. Where there have been problems in early child and primary carer interactions, research has indicated that the impact of impaired early interactions is that the brain may not have developed optimally (Trevarthen and Aitken, 1994; Schore, 2003).

An important aspect of early child development is that of learning how to regulate feelings and physiology in the context of baby – carer interactions. At birth, babies have some capacity to comfort and calm themselves (i.e., to self-soothe), but they require a sensitive carer to tune into their bodily communications and to adapt their interactions in pursuit of either soothing or stimulating the baby. In this interactive dance, referred to as *interactive regulation*, baby and carer concurrently influence and are influenced by each other. They are simultaneously regulating each other and their individual physiology, feelings, and energy levels (Beebe and Lachmann 2002). However, a baby may have been inadvertently stimulated when they are becoming drowsy and moving towards sleep. Perhaps this is because the carer misses the baby's cues, or perhaps the carer's own needs are required to take precedence. These moments of missing the baby's communications are part of daily life and can be repaired. However, if there are repeated out-of-synch interactions, the baby might develop into an adult who cannot regulate their feelings and physiology. They may function quite well at work but at a tremendous cost to themselves as their over-aroused autonomic nervous system makes them irritable and tired, and they cannot unwind. Or perhaps they develop into someone who underachieves, or does not tend to know how they feel and what they want (Schore, 2003).

Being and doing

In today's society, there is a general tendency to "do" or take action rather than simply "be" and give time for considered reflection. It is perhaps, therefore, not surprising that this is also highly evident in the therapy world. However, Schore (2011) argues,

> At the most fundamental level, the work of psychotherapy is not defined by what the therapist explicitly, objectively does for the patient, or says to the patient. Rather, the key mechanism is how to implicitly and subjectively be with the patient, especially during affectively stressful moments when the "going on being" of the patient's implicit self is dis-integrating in real time.
>
> (Schore, 2011, pp. 94–95)

Schore's notion of real-time disintegration is arguably applicable to the mechanisms involved in coaching, as well. Including more elements of non-verbal communications in coaching requires *embodied relating* with a focus on being with – in other words, being to being. Embodied relating is being "in" your body with direct, subjective experience of how it is uniquely experienced. It is a moment-by-moment process of change, representing shifts in one's level of consciousness whilst being able to tune into those shifts at any given moment. Embodied relating is not the same as thinking about your body or indeed having a body (Westland, 2019).

Cultivating embodied awareness

The starting point for embodied relating is that of noticing your own body. *Awareness and mindfulness practices* are central to this endeavour. Mindfulness is being mindful of the nuances and details of experiences arising in the immediate moment (i.e., being "in the now") whilst being present to such phenomena. Awareness is being cognisant of oneself within a wider perspective, of having a broader sense of things (Wegela, 2014). Such practices are anchored in the body in the form of "embodied self-awareness" (Fogel, 2009). Repeated mindfulness practice can help to slow us down, become more present, and receive more detailed information from our bodies – as well as from our clients and the wider environment. It is possible to group instances of embodied self-awareness into three zones of awareness:

- Inner awareness of subjective experiences – physical sensations such as itches, tensions, tingling, pressure, and movements (i.e., interoception).
- Outer awareness – sense impressions perceived from the environment through seeing, hearing, smelling, touching, and tasting (i.e., exteroception).
- Awareness of "fantasy" – processes which tend to take us out of the present moment of sensory experiencing into imaginings, explaining, planning, and thinking.

Information gathered in each zone can serve to guide us in how to proceed, and none of the zones is more valid than any other.

Embodied awareness with clients

Prior to meeting with a client, preparation of yourself is essential and involves tuning into your body. As you tune into yourself, ask yourself the following:

- What am I sensing in my body – e.g., hot/cold parts, tension, aches, tiredness?
- What am I feeling – e.g., excited, anxious, bored, rushed, relaxed?
- What am I thinking – e.g., the content and the quality of my thinking?
- What am I imagining – e.g., the journey home, getting shopping, the weekend?

The key thing is to simply note the various sensations, feelings, thoughts, and imaginings without trying to make rational sense of them. The idea is to capture information about yourself in the present moment and to explore how it changes as different phenomena come into your awareness.

When your client walks into the room and during the session, you can sometimes gather information about your client – coach interactions by turning your attention inward and quietly asking the same questions.

Shifting attention

What is spoken about tends to be in the foreground of our awareness, but if we widen our awareness, then background information from bodily communications comes more into focus. What this means in practice is learning to shift our attention away from the content of the client's words by lightly registering it and letting it float by you. As you practise this, simultaneously tune into your experience of yourself whilst observing the client's posture, gestures, way of speaking, and movement. Let your attention shift backwards and forwards from quiet, unobtrusive observation of the client to your own experience. As a rule of thumb, give about 50% attention to yourself and 50% to the client; although in practice, this will vary depending on what is being discussed.

Throughout the coaching session, it can be helpful to also let yourself tune in and gather up more subliminal information in the interactions between you and the client. Such information is likely to guide you in the various interactions with your client, helping you with making informed choices, and suggesting how to go on. For example, perhaps the client is saying something, and yet you are picking up in your own body that the words and feelings being communicated are implicitly at odds. Perhaps the words and feelings are in harmony, but you harbour a sense that the depth of feeling is not being adequately expressed in the client's words.

Enhancing client self-awareness

Sometimes, simply slowing yourself down, tapping into the non-verbal communications, and listening deeply to the interactions between yourself and a client will invite that client towards a fuller experience of themselves. For example, the client may spontaneously come to a deeper perception and understanding about what is holding them back or may realise the enormity of the problems being discussed. Equally, many clients may benefit from learning more about their inner experiences in a more guided exchange. One way to initiate this process would be to ask the client to pause at a suitable moment and then explain that it is possible to gather information by attending to what their body may know about the issue being discussed. It tends to be helpful to ask, "As you are speaking/thinking about this issue, what are you noticing in your body?" You can prompt with, "In your shoulders? Are they stiff, loose, tense, achy?" The focus is best placed on body sensations, as these tend to guide the client toward including more of the various messages of their body as a means of enhancing overall self-awareness.

Depending on the client and the client's in-session story (for example, a workplace challenge or conflict), you can *talk about* how the topic of discussion may be connected with a pain in the upper back. Of course, it could be an existing back problem or related to sitting for long periods in poor office furniture. However, if the question somehow speaks to the client, it might point towards a particular person on the client's workplace team who triggers "backache" as they are so frustratingly slow and are not pulling their weight. In this instance, the client has begun to consider what might well prove to be a useful explanation. However, with a client who is willing to continue the exploration through body awareness, you can stay with more body-based experiencing and reflecting. Then any talking arises *from the experience* rather than solely from thinking about the problem. You might, for example, suggest that the client move their shoulders and upper back and, as they move, notice how they feel.

There is no particular goal to this form of enquiry, but it is likely to bring to light other dimensions of the problem. For example, as the client's shoulders move, they might well feel sad and thus make useful connections. Perhaps the client regrets not acting a year ago with this member of staff, as at one stage, he felt sorry for them. Perhaps the client's partner had cancer, and there are parallels to be drawn to their father dying when they were a child. As a child, the client may have been bewildered, angry, and sad. It may have been the case that Dad went off to hospital and never came home, and the client simply learned to shoulder the burdens in the family and not make a fuss.

Sometimes clients may feel too self-conscious to move in front of you, and so you might ask if there is an image for the shoulder ache. This will be another entry point for some clients to explore various issues more experientially. You might ask, "As you have that image, what are you experiencing in your body?" Again, you can facilitate such an exploration by offering various prompts.

Putting it all into practice

Bringing in more implicit information into your sessions with clients involves an awareness of the following:

- Cultivating embodied relating
- Being with yourself whilst being with the client
- Observing the client's body and what appears to be happening to the client
- Inviting the client to connect with their inner life through body awareness
- Shifting the focus of the session away from *talking about* and towards *direct experiencing* of the body's various messages

Discussion points

- What do you think, and how do you feel about what has been presented in this chapter?
- What are you going to do about it? Your curiosity may lead you to further reading or an activity that will enhance your body awareness in daily life.
- How might you apply what you have read in your coaching practice? What might hold you back?

Suggested resources

Navarro, J. (2020). *The Power of Nonverbal Communication*. TEDx. Retrieved from https://www.tedxmanchester.com/speakers-2020/joe-navarro
Sutton, J. (2022). *How to Read Nonverbal Communication Cues: 5 Techniques*. Retrieved from https://positivepsychology.com/nonverbal-communication-cues

References

Beebe, B. and Lachmann, F. M. (2002). *Infant Research and Adult Treatment, Co-constructing Interactions*. London: Analytic Press.

Cozolino, (2017). *The Neuroscience of Psychotherapy. Building and Rebuilding the Human Brain* (3rd ed.). New York: W. W. Norton.

Fogel, A. (2009). *The Psychophysiology of Self-Awareness. Rediscovering the Lost Art of Body Sense*. New York: W. W. Norton.

McGilchrist, I. (2009a). *The Master and his Emissary. The Divided Brain and the Making of the Western World*. New Haven: Yale University Press.

McGilchrist, I. (2009b). The Divided Brain and the Making of the Western World. *Network Review*, Winter 2009/2010, 3–6.

Porges, S. (2011). *The Polyvagal Theory. Neurophysical Foundations of Emotions, Attachment, Communication, and Self Regulation*. New York: Norton.

Reich, W. (1983). *The Function of the Orgasm*. London: Souvenir Press.

Schore, A. N. (1994). *Affect Regulation and the Regulation of the Self: The Neurobiology of Emotional Development*. Hillsdale, NJ: Lawrence Erlbaum Associates.

Schore, A. N. (2003). *Affect Dysregulation and Disorders of the Self*. New York: W. W. Norton.

Schore, A. N. (2011). The right brain implicit self lies at the core of psychoanalytic psychotherapy. *Psychoanalytic Dialogues*, 21, 75–100.

Siegel, D. J. (1999). *The Developing Mind: How Relationships and the Brain Interact to Shape Who We Are*. New York: Guilford Press.

Stauffer, K. A. (2010). *Anatomy and Physiology for Psychotherapists. Connecting Body and Soul*. New York: W. W. Norton.

Trevarthen, C. and Aitken, K. J. (1994). Brain development, infant communication, and empathy disorders: Intrinsic factors in child mental health. *Development and Psychopathology*, 6, 597–633.

Wegela, K. Kissel. (2014). *Contemplative Psychotherapy Essentials. Enriching Your Practice with Buddhist Psychology*. New York: Norton.

Westland, G. (2015). *Verbal and Non-Verbal Communication in Psychotherapy*. New York: W.W. Norton.

Westland, G. (2018). A study of significant moments of change in body psychotherapy. *Body, Movement and Dance in Psychotherapy*, 13:1, 17–32.

Westland, G. (2019) Relating through the body – self, other, and the wider world. In. Fuchs, T., Koch, S., Payne, H., Tantia, J., (Eds.). *The Routledge International Handbook of Embodied Perspectives in Psychotherapy: Approaches from Dance Movement and Body Psychotherapies*. (Routledge International Handbooks) London: Routledge.

Chapter 2

Landscape of the mind
Using imagery and metaphors in arts-based coaching

Max Eames

Introduction

The interplay between imagery, its content, and various beliefs about what is imagined has a direct bearing on all our day-to-day experiences. That said, it is not uncommon for the matter to remain largely unexamined in a coaching session. This chapter provides a brief induction to the multifaceted nature of imagery and metaphors.

In what is often a highly constructive form of engagement with a client's mental landscape, coaches can use imagery and metaphors to offer a fresh means of understanding an array of psychological challenges. At their best, coaching interventions which incorporate the use of imagery and metaphors can facilitate profound changes in perception, mood, and self-efficacy. They do so by exploring not only the *content* of imagery but also various *attitudes* towards the images themselves. By the end of this chapter, it is hoped that the interested reader will have contemplated the use of imagery and metaphors within arts-based and other coaching interventions, considered some of the potential challenges to remain aware of, and reflected on likely future directions for coaching practice and research.

The place of imagery in our past, present, and future

Whenever we reflect on our past or contemplate our future, imagery is at play. In fact, imagery influences the formation of our memories, our goals and wishes, and our emotional responses. As such, in a great many of our thought processes, imagery tends to predominate over both abstract reasoning and 'talking to oneself' with words (Padesky & Holmes, 2023). This notion runs counter to received wisdom in that most people's tendency is to pay a great deal of attention to their 'self-talk'.

So, what would serve as a working definition for this important form of thinking? A succinct and relatable definition is provided by Padesky and Holmes (2023). They propose that "mental imagery refers to sensory processing in the absence of sensory stimuli" (p. 196). Such a definition also makes a

DOI: 10.4324/9781003453437-3

distinction between mental imagery and perception, whereby the latter refers to a response to actual stimuli. Several further distinctions need to be made, some of which are outlined in the following sections.

Mental imagery as so much more than 'images'

It is not uncommon to wrongly assume that imagery refers solely to 'images' arising from the mind's eye. It stands to reason that mental imagery may comprise *any number* of sensory modalities (e.g., sound, temperature, and smell), transcending mere verbal or abstract mental activities (Kosslyn et al., 2001). For example, if you were to imagine biting into a hot slice of your favourite pizza whilst reading this sentence, the so-called imagery is likely to be multimodal, incorporating several sensory modalities at once.

Padesky and Holmes' definition captures the essence of imagery as a mental representation which is not *perceived* but, rather, recalled or imagined. Such an understanding complements Kosslyn et al.'s (2001) depiction of imagery as information accessed *from memory*, reminding us of the synergy between imagery, memory, and perception. It also lends us a hand in understanding why the distinction between imagery and memories is often blurred, given that both involve information drawn from past experiences.

That said, such blurring is important and ultimately helpful. We use mental imagery to recall memories (e.g., "Where did I put my car keys?") or to anticipate and even problem-solve future challenges (e.g., "If we drive to London, I'd prefer to park the car in the outskirts of town and then use public transport"; Norem, 2001; Schacter et al., 2007). Such everyday examples serve to remind us of the practical uses of imagery when constructing a sense of something which may never have been perceived.

The dual nature of imagery

Few of us would deny the occasional tendency to place a great deal of focus on negative, intrusive imagery associated with instances of conflict and struggle. Such a tendency is a reminder of the dual nature of imagery (Hackmann et al., 2011b). On the other end of the spectrum, imagery has the potential to simulate adaptive experiences and outcomes in the mind's eye. In that sense, such potential warrants our equal attention as coaches. Deliberately constructed positive imagery, as discussed by Taylor et al. (1998), Wells (2000), and Gilbert (2005), can help us to envisage new possibilities, prepare for future events, and foster adaptive emotional and behavioural responses.

The power of mental imagery to evoke either positive or negative emotion, facilitate insight, and catalyse change is well-documented in psychological research (Holmes & Mathews, 2005; Blackwell, 2019). For example, the emotional resonance of imagery can impact a person's mood state, influencing both beliefs and behaviours (Baddeley & Andrade, 2000; Brewin et al., 2010). In a typical coaching conversation, imagery can help clients visualise goals, explore alternative outcomes, and rehearse strategies for dealing with challenges.

The place of metaphors in our conceptual framing

Turning now to metaphors, it was Lakoff and Johnson's (1980, later 2003) seminal work which introduced the notion that metaphors are foundational to our conceptual framing. Their findings advance the argument that metaphors tend to define how we think, speak, and act – despite doing so largely at an unconscious level. Through conceptual metaphors such as "life is a journey", Lakoff and Johnson hold that our understanding of abstract concepts is implicitly structured by metaphorical mappings, deeply influencing both cognitive processing and perception.

Metaphors can serve as a versatile tool in coaching conversations, facilitating a shared understanding of the client's experience. By drawing parallels to a relatable metaphor, clients are often able to embody alternative perspectives. Whether in arts-based or other coaching contexts, such collaborative endeavours can provide clients with important information on either self-defeating behaviours or self-limiting beliefs (Lakoff & Johnson, 2003).

Metaphors as linguistic expressions

So, what would be a working definition of metaphor? It seems useful to set aside the schoolboy semantics of metaphors versus analogies or similes in favour of an understanding which is both succinct and relatable. In the simplest of terms, metaphors are linguistic expressions that describe one thing in terms of another. As such, and for our purposes as coaches, they provide a powerful means by which to conceptualise and articulate complex, often ineffable, psychological experiences (Lakoff & Johnson, 2003), as well as much else of relevance to the process of coaching.

For example, in the context of coaching conversations, metaphors can help clients gain insights into unwanted thought processes, emotional states, and behavioural patterns, offering new angles from which to view their circumstances (Beck et al., 1974; Holmes et al., 2007). After all, distress, confusion, and uncomfortable feelings tend to make it harder to think objectively. A carefully considered metaphor can lessen emotional charge and help with taking stock of a situation. The big 'win' is often a sense of being able to choose how to react and respond, and of having a more reliable strategy for doing so (Stott et al., 2010b).

The constructive quality of metaphors

There is an important point to keep in mind, however. It should be the client who leads on the construction of metaphors. As such, it is wise to pay close attention to client-generated metaphors (which may arise spontaneously).

Such metaphors stand out for the client, so they may well stand out for you as a signal that the client is making sense of a problem or issue. Finally, what strengthens the usefulness of a client-generated metaphor is the imagery associated with it (Stott et al., 2010b), which is likely to be both memorable and wedded to the client's culture, values, or even upbringing.

The constructive quality of metaphors lends itself to a more detached and observational stance, so that the client's insights can be translated into new ways of thinking and behaving. What is exciting about working in this way is its flexibility, in the sense that the coaching conversation can be either personal and exploratory (where you might feel more of a witness than a facilitator) or collaborative and interactive (where your input, at just the right moment, might lend additional meaning to a client-generated metaphor).

Anticipating and testing the serviceability of a metaphor

But how do we as coaches best play a role in the selection of a metaphor which ends up being meaningful to the client? Being too directive or taking the lead is likely to result in a client replacing your suggestion with one of their own (which is as it should be). And yet, you should remain mindful of the need to choose metaphors which encourage high levels of processing and understanding. To do so, it is usually best to leave decisions on *content* in the hands of your client. Your focus might best be placed on anticipating whether the targeted change or process can be articulated within a client-generated metaphor. If confident that this is likely, you might wish to lead on ensuring that core elements of the metaphor strongly map to the specific issues involved in the targeted change or process.

Finally, once there is a set of clear understandings, you can encourage the client to test out the serviceability of their chosen metaphor "out there in the real world". Often, this last step reveals the flaws in what has been co-constructed. As an example, this author recalls a client describing certain life events (such as a relationship which had ended badly, an unwanted career change, and certain milestone birthdays) as painful aspects of her personal history. The client devised a metaphor involving a Russian doll. She considered that each outer layer (i.e., each successive doll) represented various 'personal traumas' accumulated over the years.

Refining the serviceability of a metaphor gone wrong

The client later reported that she found this metaphor unsatisfactory, particularly because the notion of her life entailing "bruises and scars, which had mostly healed over" seemed poorly articulated with the Russian doll metaphor. What resulted was the co-creation of a metaphor involving the concentric rings of a tree trunk, which of course are known to record the history of pest infestations, diseases, destructive events, droughts, floods, and other circumstances in which a tree is unable to photosynthesise optimally. This metaphor, to the client's mind, did a much better job of conveying her story of survival and healing.

As was the case in the previous example, the benefit of working with metaphors is often an ability for the client to temporarily gain distance from avoided feelings (or the situations which give rise to those feelings). Such distancing can prepare the client to address situations of challenge, all from the perspective shift arising from a well-chosen metaphor (Stott et al., 2010b). After all, insight for insight's sake is of little practical use; it is the ability to integrate fresh perspectives into daily living which arguably matters to most coaching clients.

Challenges when working with imagery and metaphors

It is argued that the core principles involved in the use of imagery and metaphors are relatively straightforward. Incorporating them into coaching conversations is often demanding of the coach, but this should never be the case for the client (Stott et al., 2010b). The demands placed on the coach might well be a reason why imagery and metaphors, despite their presence in everyday conversation, might not yet figure in your coaching interventions. It's also understandable for a coach, particularly in the context of an arts-based intervention, to harbour misgivings about "opening up Pandora's box" (itself a potent metaphor) by invoking unwanted distress in a session.

Without a doubt, there are very real differences between the typical coaching conversation and moments of working with imagery. Such moments can feel a lot less structured; they can be subject to unusual twists and turns, and it's not uncommon for a client to suddenly outpace the coach (Stopa, 2021). As such, working with imagery often requires the coach to exhibit tremendous agility, sometimes doing so amid feelings of confusion, trepidation, or of somehow being a 'spectator' to the client's process. That said, the skills you rely on already will serve you well in work with imagery and metaphors. Soon you will move with dexterity between a typical coaching conversation (i.e., one driven largely by words) and this less clearly navigable way of working (Stopa, 2021).

Whilst working with imagery and metaphors presents a likely means of facilitating personal growth, it is not without its challenges. Coaches must also navigate individual differences in terms of the client's ability to generate and engage with mental imagery, as well as general receptiveness to metaphorical thinking (Hackmann et al., 2011b; Hales et al., 2014). Research indicates that a fraction of the population appears to be largely unable to voluntarily create images, and some individuals are known as 'non-mental imagers' (Stopa, 2021, p. 265).

Attending to individual cultures, values, and worldviews

Even when the desired level of engagement is in evidence, work with imagery or metaphors must remain true to the client's culture, values, and way of understanding the world (Stott et al., 2010b). Given that this is the case, it sometimes proves necessary to set aside your own frame of reference as it may differ from the worldview of your client (Stopa, 2021; Passmore, 2022).

When working with imagery and metaphors, it is necessary to remain mindful of various ethical considerations (Holmes et al., 2008; Blackwell, 2019). For example, when working with neurodivergent clients, coaches may need to navigate a set of very specific concerns (American Psychiatric Association, 2013). It is not uncommon for autistic individuals to experience differences in sensory processing and to interpret information in a literal manner (Koegel et al., 2014). This can sometimes lead to misunderstandings or confusion, particularly when metaphors creep into coaching conversations – either unwittingly or by design.

Various other sensitivities may call for adjustment in terms of the type of imagery or metaphor to be used. What is intended to relax or inspire might instead irritate or distress some clients (Robertson & Simmons, 2013). As such, coaches may wish to modify their stock-in-trade interventions, ensuring they involve clients in the selection of imagery or metaphors (Grandin, 2006).

Conclusions and future directions

It is without doubt that future research will continue to provide insight into the mechanisms underlying the use of imagery and metaphors, all whilst identifying best practices for their place in coaching interventions – as well as advancing the onward march of digital technologies.

The strategic use of imagery and metaphors in coaching requires an understanding of human cognition, creativity, and empathy, enabling coaches to co-create interventions, arts-based or otherwise, that resonate with their clients. As we advance our collective understanding of various forms of conceptual framing, the refinement of metaphorical interventions will continue to enrich the coaching community, offering novel pathways to understanding and change. The continued exploration of imagery and metaphors thus offers exciting prospects for enhancing the effectiveness and personalisation of coaching conversations and practices.

Case studies

Sailing through choppy waters (i.e., navigating career transitions)

John, a mid-level manager in a technology firm, faced significant anxiety and uncertainty about a potential career change. Feeling both excited and daunted by the opportunity, he sought coaching to clarify his path forward.

The coach worked with John using the metaphor of *sailing through choppy waters* to frame John's career transition. This co-created imagery helped John visualise his journey as an explorer, acknowledging the uncertainties but also recognising his skills as a navigator and the potential for discovery.

John later reported a noticeable shift in perspective (Lakoff & Johnson, 2003), feeling more equipped to handle the uncertainty of his career change. He developed a strategic plan, identifying resources and support systems akin to 'navigational tools' which guided his transition.

Inner critic as heckler (i.e., overcoming performance anxiety)

Emma, a professional singer, struggled with performance anxiety, often hindered by her so-called inner critic. She sought coaching to find strategies to improve her performance.

The coach worked with Emma to co-create the metaphor of the *inner critic as a heckler* in a theatre, disrupting the performance. Through this imagery, Emma was encouraged to visualise confronting and silencing the heckler, thereby reclaiming her stage.

Emma later reported a decrease in performance anxiety and an increase in confidence (Hackmann et al., 2011b). She adopted techniques to acknowledge and then dismiss her inner critic, allowing her to focus on her performance.

The oak and the reed (i.e., building greater resilience)

Liam, facing recurrent setbacks in his personal and professional life, reported feeling increasingly unconfident and spoke of an unhelpful sense of fragility. He engaged in coaching to build resilience.

Drawing on Aesop's Fable *The Oak and the Reed*, the coach worked with Liam to depict resilience not as unwavering strength but as flexibility in the face of adversity. This metaphor helped Liam understand that resilience could mean bending, but not breaking, under pressure.

Liam embraced the concept of flexibility as strength, applying it to his approach to challenges. Over time, he reported feeling more adaptable and less defeated by setbacks.

Spinning plates (i.e., managing work – life balance)

Sarah, a self-described high-achieving executive, struggled with managing her work – life balance, feeling increasingly overwhelmed by her various responsibilities.

Her work with a coach involved co-creating the metaphor of *spinning plates*. This description of a complex set of competing responsibilities served to help Sarah visualise her daily tasks and priorities. Some plates were made of fine porcelain, representing non-negotiable aspects of her life, whilst others were everyday plastic, signifying areas where she could be more flexible.

Sarah identified her 'porcelain plates' as family time and health, prioritising them accordingly. She learned to 'drop' some of the plastic plates when necessary, alleviating her sense of overwhelm (Bennett-Levy et al., 2004).

The case studies, whilst inspired by theoretical concepts and practical applications from genuine sources, are amalgamated scenarios presented to illustrate the use of imagery and metaphors in coaching interventions. The references provided in each instance support the theoretical foundation of the interventions depicted.

Discussion points

- What did this chapter make you think about regarding your own reactions to the deliberate use of imagery and metaphors in a coaching conversation?
- What are some of your reflections on the dual nature of imagery in terms of its power to evoke either positive or negative emotion in your coaching clients?
- What are your thoughts on cultural and other individual differences in terms of shaping your response to the potential use of imagery and metaphor in either arts-based or other interventions?

Suggested resources

Hackmann, A., Bennett-Levy, J., & Holmes, E. A. (2011a). *Oxford guide to imagery in cognitive therapy*. Oxford University Press.

Stott, R., Mansell, W., Salkovskis, P. M., Lavender, A., & Cartwright-Hatton, S. (2010a). *The oxford guide to metaphors in CBT: Building cognitive bridges: Building cognitive bridges*. Oxford University Press.

References

American Psychiatric Association. (2013). *Diagnostic and statistical manual of mental disorders* (5th ed.).

Baddeley, A. D., & Andrade, J. (2000). Working memory and the vividness of imagery. *Journal of Experimental Psychology: General, 129*(1), 126–145.

Beck, A. T., Weissman, A., Lester, D., & Trexler, L. (1974). The measurement of pessimism: The hopelessness scale. *Journal of Consulting and Clinical Psychology, 42*(6), 861–865.

Bennett-Levy, J., Butler, G., Fennell, M., Hackmann, A., Mueller, M., & Westbrook, D. (2004). *Oxford guide to behavioural experiments in cognitive therapy*. Oxford University Press.

Blackwell, S. E. (2019). Mental imagery: From basic research to clinical practice. *Journal of Psychotherapy Integration, 29*, 235–247.

Brewin, C. R., Gregory, J. D., Lipton, M., & Burgess, N. (2010). Intrusive images in psychological disorders: Characteristics, neural mechanisms, and treatment implications. *Psychological Review, 117*(1), 210–232.

Gilbert, P. (2005). *Compassion: Conceptualisations, research and use in psychotherapy*. Routledge.

Grandin, T. (2006). *Thinking in pictures: My life with autism*. Vintage Books.

Hackmann, A., Bennett-Levy, J., & Holmes, E. A. (2011b). *Oxford guide to imagery in cognitive therapy*. Oxford University Press.

Hales, S. A., Blackwell, S. E., Di Simplicio, M., Iyadurai, L., Young, K., & Holmes, E. A. (2014). Imagery-based cognitive-behavioural assessment. In G. P. Brown & D. A. Clark (Eds.), *Assessment in cognitive therapy*. New York: Guilford Press.

Holmes, E. A., & Mathews, A. (2005). Mental imagery and emotion: A special relationship? *Emotion, 5*(4), 489–497.

Holmes, E.A., Crane, C., Fennell, M.J., & Williams, J.M. (2007). Imagery about suicide in depression – Flash-forwards? *Journal of Behaviour Therapy and Experimental Psychiatry, 38*(4), 423–434.

Holmes, E.A., Mathews, A., Mackintosh, B., & Dalgleish, T. (2008). The causal effect of mental imagery on emotion assessed using picture-word cues. *Emotion, 8*(3), 395–409.

Koegel, L. K., Koegel, R. L., Ashbaugh, K., & Bradshaw, J. (2014). The importance of early identification and intervention for children with or at risk for autism spectrum disorders. *International Journal of Speech-Language Pathology, 16*(1), 50–56.

Kosslyn, S. M., Thompson, W. L., & Ganis, G. (2001). Neural foundations of imagery. *Nature Reviews Neuroscience, 2*(9), 635–642.

Lakoff, G., & Johnson, M. (2003). *Metaphors we live by*. University of Chicago Press.

Norem, J. K. (2001). *The positive power of negative thinking: Using defensive pessimism to harness anxiety and perform at your peak*. Cambridge, MA: Basic Books.

Padesky, C.A., & Holmes, E.A. (2023). Imagery: The language of emotion. In Padesky, C. A., & Kennerley, H. *Dialogues for discovery: Improving psychotherapy's effectiveness*. Oxford, UK: Oxford University Press.

Passmore, J. (2022). The role of metaphor in coaching. *The Coaching Psychologist, 18*(2), 44–46.

Robertson, A. E., & Simmons, D. R. (2013). The sensory experiences of adults with autism spectrum disorder: A qualitative analysis. *Perception, 42*(5), 123–134.

Schacter, D. L., Addis, D. R., & Buckner, R. L. (2007). Remembering the past to imagine the future: The prospective brain. *Nature Reviews: Neuroscience, 8*(9), 657–661.

Stott, R., Mansell, W., Salkovskis, P. M., Lavender, A., & Cartwright-Hatton, S. (2010b). *The oxford guide to metaphors in CBT: Building cognitive bridges*. Oxford University Press.

Stopa, L. (2021). *Imagery in cognitive-behavioural therapy*. New Yof: Guildford Press.

Taylor, S. E., Pham, L. B., Rivkin, I. D., & Armor, D. A. (1998). Harnessing the imagination: Mental simulation, self-regulation, and coping. *American Psychologist, 53*(4), 429–439.

Wells, A. (2000). *Emotional disorders and metacognition: Innovative cognitive therapy*. Wiley.

Chapter 3

Exploring the self through photography

Neil Gibson

Introduction

At the turn of the 20th century, photography was a curiosity, a technique whereby light was permitted through a lens, 'painting' an image on photosensitive paper, and was reserved for those who could afford to dabble in these techniques. Nowadays, photography is one of the most accessible creative tools at our disposal, thanks to the rise in technology and the prevalence of photo-sharing sites across the internet. As a result, we are generally considered to be visually literate in the sense that we have ways of decoding and interpreting images, and this has led to photography being incorporated into therapeutic practices such as exploring mental illness, rehabilitation, assisting recovery, and challenging social issues (Gibson, 2018b; Stevens & Spears, 2009; Glover-Graf & Miller, 2006; Perchick, 1992).

There are generally two schools of using photography in a therapeutic manner: phototherapy and therapeutic photography. Phototherapy refers to the use of photographs in formal counselling and therapy settings, whereas therapeutic photography refers to the use of photography in settings where the intention is to improve a situation, but the involvement of a counsellor or therapist may not be required (Weiser, 1999; Gibson, 2018b).

When considering the use of photography in coaching, it is fair to recognise that this straddles both spheres of phototherapy and therapeutic photography as a supervised helping profession. This chapter will delve into the use of photography to explore the self, using skills for self-discovery, guiding one-to-one exploration, and using these exercises in a group environment.

Theory, basic concepts, and key developments

Bronfenbrenner

It can be helpful to consider the work of Uri Bronfenbrenner (2009) (see Figure 3.1) and his socio-ecological theory when using photographic interventions to explore the self. Bronfenbrenner proposed that we are all influenced by many

DOI: 10.4324/9781003453437-4

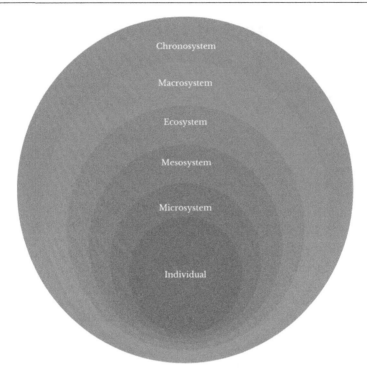

Figure 3.1 Bronfenbrenner's (2009) socio-ecological model.

'layers' of society. At the micro-level, we spend our formative years with family and carers, and as we grow, our micro-system includes partners and close friends; at the other end of the scale, we are impacted by the macro system where societal norms, cultures, legislation, media, beliefs, and attitudes all filter downwards to shape our everyday experiences. In between these layers, Bronfenbrenner explored the meso- and exo-systems where community interactions take place, including school attendance and workplace pressures, which, again, impact on the individual at the centre of the model.

Using this model to consider how to incorporate photography into self-exploration, it could be suggested that at micro-levels, psychological and psychodynamic approaches might aid understanding of the self and behaviours, whilst macro-levels may invite a more sociological understanding of things that impact our well-being and welfare.

If we think about Bronfenbrenner's model and relate it more specifically to photography, we can see that the many uses of exploration through visual means align with the different layers of his model. Using a similar approach, we can layer the explorations to give us the model presented in Figure 3.2. Each level encompasses a range of theoretical approaches which can be used alongside the photograph to enable understanding of the dialogue and the

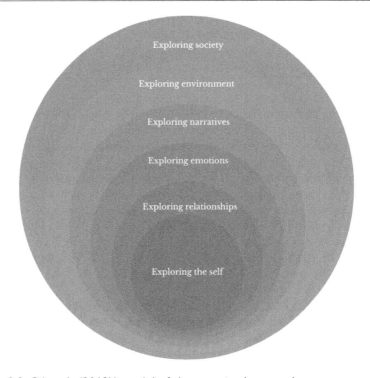

Figure 3.2 Gibson's (2018b) model of therapeutic photography.

impact this might have on behaviour. Looking specifically at the central layer where self-exploration is the focus, psychodynamic and psychological theories can be helpful when the question "Who am I?" is being asked and answered through the production of photographs.

Winnicott

Donald Winnicott (1965, 1971) was a psychoanalyst whose writings provide valuable insight into therapeutic practice. He identified that for any therapeutic relationship to be effective and lead to successful outcomes for a participant, there needs to be a therapeutic alliance so that a safe space can develop. This safe space links into the writings by other theorists on having a milieu where exploration can take place without fear of judgement and where empathy and unconditional positive regard take place (Bowlby, 1988; Rogers, 1951). Introducing photographs to a therapeutic working relationship involves recognising different dynamics within the communication – eye contact is drawn towards the image, thus providing a less intimidating environment than traditional talking therapies where a practitioner engages with a client across a table and holds eye contact throughout the session; a photograph invites the client and the practitioner to lean in and view the image, thus creating a feeling of warmth and interest through the body language, and the sense of control a client has in choosing an image, framing an image, and exploring an image cannot be underestimated – all elements which contribute to the formation of a safe space.

Winnicott also recognised the importance of transitional objects and, more importantly, a transitional space. This links into the safe space and should encourage exploration and re-evaluation through talking about experiences and learning from them. Again, introducing photography into this dynamic can assist this process and provides a way for issues to be externalised and objectified within an image. By doing this, the photograph can also help bypass any potential defence mechanisms – if a client chooses to explore an issue by making an image of it, then it is real for all to see and can literally be held at arm's length, no longer confined to the self. Examples of this might include when someone chooses to share a particular issue they are having, such as problems with alcohol, problems within a relationship, or problems with self-image. Once externalised and objectified, it can be explored, and perspectives can be challenged and re-framed.

The final aspect of Winnicott's work links to his writings about True Self and False Self. He was not the only theorist to recognise that we have different personas for different situations; indeed, Mead (1934) wrote about the 'I' and the 'me', whilst Jung (1983) recognised the mask (or personas) we adopt to fit into different settings. Photographs can help us explore our interactions with different aspects of society and help us visualise how we might need to adapt behaviour, how we change to fit in, and, potentially, when this might cause us problems. This is an area which will be explored further as we look at how to use knowledge of theories when we utilise photography for self-exploration or guided exploration for clients.

Practice

How to 'use' photographs

With therapeutic photography, the photo is not there to be decoded. It is a vessel for communication and a catalyst for exploring. When analysed, the entire process of taking and talking about photographs can be linked to therapeutic practice. To begin with, the idea behind the captured image must be formed – what do you want to show in the image? This process requires creativity and control, and the decision to commit an image to the memory card (or other means of image capture) on your phone or camera is borne. Then the process of searching for the image begins – it might be a very easy and straightforward process, or it might be a bit more complex and encourage you to explore the environment for what you want/need. This stage invites you to slow down, to notice things around you, and to be in the moment – akin to mindfulness. Once found, the process of selection begins, and you actively edit and filter out the images that don't quite hit the mark – again, the element of control is strong at this stage. Then, once an image has been selected, it can be shared with others – the process of putting your creativity on display invites comments and questions; the eye contact is normally on the image; body language is warm and inviting; listeners seek out information to form familiar connections – the process of enhancing self-esteem is dominant. Finally, there is a period of reflection, and once the sharing is complete, you make sense of the process and the feedback received – you have produced something worthy of exploration, and this may well have a positive impact on self-efficacy.

How to initiate self-exploration

Initiating self-exploration is a personal decision and calls for an adjustment around how photographs may typically be used. It is not unusual for images to be taken and then shared on social media sites in the pursuit of 'likes', but photography for self-exploration requires a shift in perception and outcome. The photographs taken are not intended to be widely shared; indeed, it may not be necessary to show the photograph at all. It is used as a catalyst for communication and a vessel to enable someone to talk about the image and open up about specific issues or concerns. Of course, the visual element of the image is also important, and participants should be encouraged to show their photograph/s to others, particularly in group work, as the information contained in the image can enhance understanding and perception, but the intention of the image is not to simply obtain aesthetic approval.

Self-portraits

When we think about self-portraits, it is tempting to assume that the content of an image will be a shot that includes the head and shoulders of the subject, looking directly into the lens. Perhaps this perception of a self-portrait is correct; after all, looking at the self-portraits of many great artists in art galleries certainly conforms to this style, but when it comes to the dynamics of therapeutic photography, we need to consider *control* and *safety*.

The camera can be a powerful tool, and many people may have memories of being photographed, and for some, these memories might not be good (Berman, 1993b). It might be that they were belittled and shamed, teased for how they looked in an image, or it might be that photography was used as a tool to exert power on the family unit by a domineering parent. As photography has become widespread, so has the concept of the 'selfie', and this, too, can be a factor for conjuring up feelings of anxiety when we think about self-portraits. Therefore, it is essential to emphasise the fact that the photographer is in control of the image and what they choose to capture for their *self*-portrait. The exercise should feel safe, so in order to do that, the photographer needs to consider aspects of the self that they wish to capture – put simply, what is positive about them? And how can that be captured in an image? It might be a quality, a piece of jewellery, a tattoo, how they relate to others – there are countless options and equally countless ways the exercise of taking a self-portrait can be executed. By the very nature of capturing a concept of the self, it invites abstract interpretation.

Once we have a self-portrait, we can enjoy the aesthetic of the end result, and we can share it with others. This might invite feedback about the image, which, in turn, may positively impact our self-esteem, but we can also use the image to ask the important question of "Who am I?"

This question will not be definitively answered by one photograph, but it will give an insight into a part of the identity. Firstly, what was communicated in the image? Defining this will give some information from the outset – information we can build on by considering how that was communicated in the image, how the photographer felt about sharing that information, and (if we are sharing images in a group) how that was received by other people in the group. We can then give consideration to theoretical perspectives which give consideration to the self in society and explore how these can be used to further explore the self. A good example is to think about the different systems within Bronfenbrenner's socio-ecological model – we all function within a micro-system which includes immediate family, close friends, and loved ones, so how does the information shared help or hinder these relationships? We can then widen this out to consider relationships in the wider community and across different levels of society and determine if the shared information is something which is prized and celebrated or something that may contribute to feelings of isolation. Taking this to the outer layers of Bronfenbrenner's model, we can consider beliefs, values, and attitudes that dominate at the macro level and consider the shared information in the light of the society we inhabit – from one self-portrait, we can explore on so many different levels to help provide an answer to understanding who we are, and why we are.

How I see myself, how others see me

Winnicott (1965, 1971) was one of many theorists to identify different aspects of identity and how we have a private persona and a public one. In his writings, he termed this the True Self and False Self. Another photographic exercise that can be used to explore this concept is one termed "How I See Myself; How Others See Me" and asks participants to take two photographs, one for each question. The questions are deliberately vague and invite interpretation from each participant, particularly when it comes to "how others see me" – who are the others? Family? Friends? Colleagues? Strangers? The options are numerous, and it is up to each participant to consider which perspective they will approach the exercise from.

Once photographs have been produced, the Winnicottian theory can be considered. The "How I See Myself" image can equate to the True Self, the self in the privacy of personal space where there are no pretences and nobody to communicate with other than the self. The "how others see me" can equate to the False Self, how we adjust to communicate and to be accepted by other people in society. Ideally, there should not be much difference between the two images, but there will always be an appreciation that we have to adjust our selves in different social situations, and this is just part of being human and having many identities. However, if the difference between the True Self and False Self is so great to cause an individual to have feelings of anxiety, then this suggests that a re-evaluation of our social self might be required, and in some cases, this might suggest that further therapeutic work might be required to address these anxious feelings.

Outcomes

It is important to remember that therapeutic photography is not therapeutic by accident; it is therapeutic by intent. Certainly, the act of taking and viewing photographs can be fun and interesting, and it can help initiate and form bonds; these are all therapeutic in their way, but when we use photography in a structured way for ourselves, or with groups, then there are generally three clear intended outcomes. Firstly, there should be a positive impact on our self-efficacy – the ability to be productive and see change from this process. The very act of taking a photograph produces something, and if that something generates interest from others, or if you find something within the image that engages you and interests you, then you have been efficient. Secondly, the experience should have a positive impact on self-esteem, particularly when sharing images within a group environment. Not only do you have immediate feedback from other participants about the information you share, but you also get a privileged insight into the lives of others which you can learn from and benefit from. The final outcome is linked to empowerment and the social learning element of sharing images within a group environment, particularly if photographic exercises are geared towards capturing the skills learned in self-exploration to then explore social and environmental issues that might be impacting on our lives. This draws on the research methodology known as photovoice (Wang, 1999) and ultimately aims to give another form of communication (or voice) to marginalised communities as a way of bringing information together and exploring how challenges might be addressed.

Case study

To illustrate how theoretical perspectives can be applied, two images that were taken by the author will be presented and explored. These two images were taken for an exercise entitled "How I See Myself; How Others See Me" and will be presented in the first person. The first image represents "How I See Myself".

The image (Figure 3.3) was taken on a family holiday, and my son is staring across a Finnish lake. The wonder of the scene is captivating, and this encapsulates my curiosity of the world around me. I am in my middle years and, to look at, am very much an adult, but inside, I still feel like a child. I often feel like I am pretending to be an adult and trying to convince other people that I know what I am doing. I don't necessarily feel like this when engaging with my two children, as I enjoy the playful interactions I have with my boys, but in adult environments, I can feel the young child within me peering at the world through adult eyes and still trying to make sense of the world around me. This is not necessarily a problematic feeling, as I don't believe that human beings should ever stop learning, and I view my critical curiosity as a positive quality of who I am. The image also captures my son, who, biologically speaking, is part of who I am, and I see myself in him. I recognise that there is a high level of dependence in the early years of childhood, but as he is approaching teenage years, more and more, I can see him forming his own identity – I see aspects of myself mirrored back to me, but I am vitally aware that his process of

Figure 3.3 How I see myself.

identity formation needs to be *his* process, not one imposed on him by other family members.

In the image (Figure 3.4) entitled "How Others See Me", I have used another photograph from the same Finnish holiday, and this one shows a family outing to look for cloudberries. The reason I have selected this image is that I believe that a major role that I have within our family unit is that of provider. In choosing this photograph, I thought about who "others" are and selected my family members but could have easily chosen another group of "others" to consider. With two young children, my wife works part time, so my full-time income is the one which pays for all of our living expenses. It gives me a sense of pride to provide for my family and to give us a good quality of life. However, I am also aware that a large part of my identity is tied to my professional self and were that to disappear, I think I would struggle. To that end, I attempt to carve time out with work that allows me to assert other aspects of my identity – through sports, through leisure, through being a husband and father, and through allowing myself time to enjoy new situations and new learnings.

In terms of the Winnicottian True Self and False Self, my identities across different social settings are not that different, and I am fortunate enough in my

Figure 3.4 How others see me – an image of my wife looking for cloudberries in a Finnish forest.

career to be able to bring significant aspects of my True Self into how I present, how I teach, and how I communicate. I do appreciate private time where my True Self can shine through, but none of my False Selves causes me anxiety. When I link this to my images, I come full circle in my exploration of them and recognise that identity is fluid and that dealing with changes that life brings can be coupled with a curiosity for learning and a willingness to adapt.

Discussion points

- Think about the self-exploration and/or exploration with others to explore the self outlined in this chapter. What theoretical perspectives do you use in practice, and where and when could photography fit into these?
- Why does photography assist in the process of exploration and self-disclosure?
- Barthes and Howard (1987) identified that photographs can have two elements: *Studium* and *Punctum*. *Studium* is the element of a photograph that draws us in initially and helps us build a connection with the image – it might be a familiar layout, the light and colours, the presentation – many things can catch our eye and make us engage with the image. *Punctum* is harder to define, as this is something which makes us connect on an emotional level with the image, makes us feel something, and this is often something that no photographer can set out to capture, as it will be a unique connection between the viewer of the image, and the image itself. Think about and discuss the potential therapeutic benefits of photography by looking at some photographs, preferably ones you have created yourself, and ask these two questions:

  1 Why am I drawn to this image?
  2 What does it make me feel?

Suggested resources (reading, videos, etc.)

Berman, L. (1993a). *Beyond the smile: The therapeutic use of the photograph*, Routledge.
Gibson, N. (2018a). *Therapeutic photography: Enhancing self-esteem, self-efficacy and resilience*, Jessica Kingsley Publishers.
Gibson, N. (2023). *Therapeutic photography*. https://therapeutic-photography.ning.com
Loewenthal, D. (2023). *The handbook of phototherapy and therapeutic photography for the professional and activist client*, Routledge.

References

Barthes, R. & Howard, R. (1987). *Camera Lucida: Reflections on photography*. Vintage.
Berman, L. (1993b). *Beyond the smile: The therapeutic use of the photograph*. Routledge.
Bowlby, J. (1988). *A secure base: Clinical applications of attachment theory*. Routledge.

Bronfenbrenner, U. (2009). *The ecology of human development: Experiments by nature and design.* Harvard University Press.

Gibson, N. (2018b). *Therapeutic photography: Enhancing self-esteem, self-efficacy and resilience.* Jessica Kingsley Publishers.

Glover-Graf, N. M. & Miller, E. (2006). The use of phototherapy in group treatment for persons who are chemically dependent, *Rehabilitation Counseling Bulletin*, 49(3), 166–181.

Jung, C. G. (1983). *Memories, dreams, reflections.* Flamingo.

Mead, G. H. (1934). *Mind, self, and society.* University of Chicago Press.

Perchick, M. (1992). Rehabilitation through photography: The power of photography as physical & emotional therapy – Contribution of Josephine U. Herrick's volunteer service photographers organization to teaching photography to wounded World War II servicemen. *PSA Journal*, 58(12), 13–15.

Rogers, C. (1951). *Client centred therapy: It's current practice, implications, and theory.* Houghton Mifflin.

Stevens, R. & Spears, E. H. (2009). Incorporating photography as a therapeutic tool in counseling, *Journal of Creativity in Mental Health*, 4(1), 3–16.

Wang, C. C. (1999). Photovoice: A participatory action research strategy applied to women's health, *Journal of Women's Health*, 8(2), 185–192.

Weiser, J. (1999). *Phototherapy techniques: Exploring the secrets of personal snapshots and family albums.* Photo Therapy Centre Press.

Winnicott, D. W. (1971). *Playing and reality.* Basic Books.

Winnicott, D. W. (1965). *The maturational process and the facilitating environment.* Hogarth Press.

Chapter 4

Photo Coaching®

Patricia Sotomayor

Introduction

Since the origin of photography in 1839, human beings have been interested in portraits. This innovative technique rapidly became a generator of documents that served to witness different ways of life, and from the beginning of the 20th century, it has also been used outside its artistic field with multiple applications, including science and exploration, documenting places and events, a means of communication or a therapeutic tool.

In this chapter, we will focus on the use of portrait photography and body language as a coaching tool. Photo Coaching® is a methodology that originates from my experience as a professional portrait photographer and Master Executive Coach certified by the International Coach Federation (ICF). Throughout years of experience, I have discovered that people obtain additional and valuable information when becoming external observers of themselves.

Theory, basic concepts, and key development

Early portraiture

The first self-portraits of the American Robert Cornelius and the French Hippolyte Bayard appeared in 1839. The photographic technique developed rapidly, and people's interest in collecting portraits of contemporary celebrities or exchanging their own with their bourgeois families rocketed.

These first portrait photographers quickly developed an interest in the personality of their subjects. Around 1860, Gaspar Félix Tournachon (Nadar) in France and Julia Margaret Cameron in the United Kingdom sought in their photographic portraits "to collect the greatness of the inner man, not only that of the exterior" trying to get to know their subjects and capture the "intimate resemblance" (Nadar 1895).

Subsequently, photographers such as the German August Sander or the French Henry Cartier-Bresson, already at the beginning of the 20th century,

DOI: 10.4324/9781003453437-5

concentrated their efforts on capturing objective photographs, admiring the absence of deceit. Thus, Sander would comment that "photography can represent things with great beauty or implacable truth. To see the truth, we must accept it whether it is favourable or not" (Sander 1929) and Cartier-Bresson (1952) would later be recognised for his ability to capture the 'decisive moment', especially in his portraits in which he reproduced significant moments of the person's personality, their expectations and feelings.

Later photographers such as Irving Penn or Diane Arbus were known for their physical and mental portraits in which, in addition to facilitating the recognition of the person, they showed the interior and personality of the subject. Arbus especially wanted to capture what they pretended as individuals and the essence of people. Not only did she capture "what these people were but what they would like to be" (Arbus, 1972).

Photography has also been used outside its artistic field since the beginning of the 20th century. Renowned researchers in clinical psychology have highlighted photography as a therapeutic tool (Willig, 2013). Methodologies such as Photo-Elicitation that use existing photographs to explore moments of transition or change (Del Busso, 2011), the Photo-Production that promotes access to researchers to the inner world of the participants (Frith & Harcourt, 2007; Del Busso, 2011) or the photo voice that uses the photographs to raise the awareness of the participants regarding themselves or towards social action (Hodgetts et al., 2007) are used on numerous occasions in the field of organisational or cultural transformation of companies.

Portraiture as a coaching tool

Observing our own portrait puts us in front of what we usually show the world and what we often broadcast unconsciously. Looking at ourselves from a distance and interpreting what this image is telling us reveals new information about our own reality, allowing us to evaluate it and decide if we want to modify it or not to achieve our purpose.

Barthes (1993) believed that photography captured a moment by offering visual evidence of a person's existence. Viewing our own portraits can evoke thoughts about what we see or what is absent (Berger, 2013), inviting us to ask ourselves questions about what we perceive (Weiser, 1990) or help us explore our own narratives and internal dialogues (Lemon, 2007).

Reflecting on our gestures or posture can bring out deeply rooted beliefs. Observing them and sharing our impressions with a coach makes it easier for us to discover which ideas are still helpful to us and, therefore, we want to keep them or which ones are preventing us from moving forward and, thus, we intend to leave behind to open new options.

Every coaching process starts with exploring the reality of people. We usually use ontological tools such as interviews or initial assessments to do this. This way, people will share how they live in the current moment. Today's dominant style in executive coaching is usually the conversational format between coach and coachee (Flaherty, 2010; Ives, 2008; Ives & Cox, 2012).

The language coachees choose to define what they are experiencing generates their own reality, and therefore, mirroring back how they are framing it is usually a good starting point for them to become aware of the moment they are living and how they feel about it.

In this context, 'our body is also words' (Wolk, 2013, p. 151), and one of the seasoned coach's skills is to mirror the coherence between what the person is saying and how they manifest it through their body or the energy they are using to formulate their ideas, to return it productively during the session.

Registering this 'language' in photographs and showing them back to the persons we are working with allows us to share unbiased proof of how they live and express that reality. This will let them explore whether the meaning of these gestures is consistent with their wording and how they emphasise or diminish their message.

Platon Antoniou, a British photographer born in Greece in 1968, who has portrayed various of the most famous world leaders and public figures, points out that "taking a picture is very technical but 99.9% is spent on the connection that allows me to reach them" (Antoniuou, 2020).

A portrait session at the beginning of a coaching process, both with individuals and teams, will give them tangible evidence of the starting point. This will facilitate the measurement of progress throughout the entire professional coaching relationship.

Prestigious studies carried out by experts show that photography enriches the coaching process. Bringing in creative approaches, metaphors, or visual elements facilitates communication and allows in-depth exploration of concepts (Gash, 2017).

Studies such as the one by Donaldson-Wright and Hefferon (2020) discovered that using photographs in coaching sessions was an instrumental technique for discovering the clients' values. This is aligned with previous studies such as the one from Hayes et al. (2012), which confirmed that using photographs in coaching processes helped clarify the objectives, connecting the person with their values, which motivated individuals towards action.

Seeing oneself from the outside in a photograph as an external observer allows exploration, reflection, and discussion regarding one's identity (Gibson, 2018).

The Photo Coaching® methodology tangibly collects all the above through the evidence of photographs. Observing these snapshots facilitates both in-depth exploration of coachees' beliefs, measuring the gap between where they are and where they want to be, and celebrating achievements at every step of the process.

Challenging people to go deeper and to question what is behind the image allows us to access a more profound layer, protected by what August Sander (a German photographer known mainly for his documentary project *People of the Twentieth Century – A Photographic Portrait of Germany*, 1927) called a *social mask* in his archetypal portraits (Sander 1929).

Human beings rely on gestures to emphasise or specify what they want to say. The same gesture can mean completely different concepts for each person depending on culture (both social and corporate), education, or personality.

Photographs can have multiple meanings and that is where their potential intrigue lies. "Portraits show people in a specific period of life, (…) group people who later disperse, change, follow the course of their independent destinies" (Sontag, 2021).

Many scientific studies have been based on body language research to decipher the meaning of it and give specific definitions to specific gestures. From Flora Davis, an American psychologist specialising in non-verbal language, to Bruno Munari, an Italian artist and designer, human beings have extensively investigated communication through gestures.

Far from offering information about the meaning of these gestures, Photo Coaching® allows people to delve into the meaning of what they are seeing and to explore the coherence with their thoughts and emotions with curiosity.

In a world dominated by images, it has transpired that photographs have become our most direct means of representation of unique human experience. Professional profile portraits reflect who we are, what we value, and what we are capable of. The photographs that join our communications on social media, web pages, or professional summaries add nuances to the written information.

In the digital age, the photographic image has acquired a new meaning in the social and professional field: individual identity and its visibility offer immediate and direct information to those who want to know more about us.

LinkedIn, a digital social network whose aim is to collect professional profiles, celebrated its 20th anniversary in 2023, reaching 875 million members in 200 countries around the world. Ninety one percent of decision-making executives rate LinkedIn as their first choice for professionally relevant content, and LinkedIn posts with images see two times higher comment rates. A profile with a portrait receives 21 times more visits than one without an image and nine times more contact requests (LinkedIn Business Statistics, 2023).

These numbers prove that, as a society, we are transitioning from a text-based communication style to an increasingly visual one.

When we are aware of what our gestures and our portraits convey, we speak more languages and, therefore, we communicate better.

Practice

Putting the Photo Coaching® methodology into practice requires capturing portraits and gestures of the people with whom we will work to view them on a device that allows them to be observed from a certain distance.

The experience varies if the photographs are taken in a photography studio by an expert person, as is the case that I am going to describe in the next section, or if screenshots are taken through a computer screen. The essence, however, is the same, and it is about challenging people with their own portraits.

If capturing portraits in a face-to-face session is not possible, working with the profile photos from social networks or teams' photos on their web pages can also be exciting resources to explore the reality of people and call into questions.

Regardless of whether they are used to being in front of a camera or not, people tend to feel somewhat uneasy about what will happen when they arrive at the session. It is essential to spend time building trust in the process and the necessary rapport to allow those emotions to surface and to be able to normalise them.

We will then spend time exploring the session's purpose and how the photos' results will relate to what people want to work on in the coaching process before moving to the shooting. I use a black or white background in my studio, but any neutral background that enables the focus on the people will do.

Having these portraits taken at the beginning of the coaching process will frame the session into the exploration of the reality that people are living. Thus, by inviting them to stand or sit in front of the camera, the questions can be directed towards the expression of how they are living the current moment, what is important to them, what they would like to achieve, which are the values that move them.

Their answers will go along with gestures that will be captured throughout the session. We may invite them to reflect in silence on what they have just shared and to look at the camera while they remain connected with that thought.

It is essential to spend some time at the beginning of the session normalising the fact that they may feel strange when talking to someone behind a camera, and it will be necessary for the photographer, in this case, the coach, not to lose connection with them during the exercise. Simplifying the photographs as much as possible is essential to do this. Finding fixed lighting and placing the camera or computer parameters with which we feel comfortable will facilitate the focus on the people and not on the machine.

The process of taking photographs usually takes 30 or 40 minutes at most as it is an intense process in which the coach will listen actively while capturing the images, inviting the coachees to reflect on a gesture of what they are saying.

Hands, shoulders, and neck tend to reflect more information than other body parts in individual portraits. The interactions between the subjects or the different positions they can adopt in group portraits can also be interesting information to capture.

At the end of the photo shoot, it is essential to change the scene and spend some time with the coachee talking about the information that has surfaced and what they take away from the experience. This will help us contextualise what will happen in the subsequent viewing of the photographs.

It is advisable to carry out the viewing in a different session. Allowing a couple of days between the photo-shooting and viewing sessions will help people disconnect from the experience and connect with the external observer. Doing it right after the shooting will require a break where you can work on the images you have captured.

The selection of images that we will show will be intentionally related to the goal of the person or their team. Thus, choosing portraits that offer more information or specific gestures that are linked to particular values or emotions is necessary in order to avoid saturating the viewing session with empty content images.

A selection of ten to fifteen photographs is usually enough to share during the viewing. Powerful and open questions will allow the coachee to deepen into their thoughts, constantly inviting the person to observe themselves from the outside and connect with what the portrait transmits to them.

These viewings often reveal information that can be challenging to observe. Clients may feel the same strangeness as when they hear their recorded voice for the first time. Therefore, sustaining this discomfort and working productively on it is essential. Photographs should not be sent in advance in order to help them overcome the natural initial criticism towards a deeper reflection on what they are seeing.

Once the Photo Coaching® process is finished, all the images are digitally sent to the people portrayed. This way, they can return to them throughout the coaching process for additional information or as a simple measure of progress between sessions.

Quite commonly, people observe their portraits, find coherence with their thoughts and emotions, and feel represented by them. They can define a goal in this first viewing session, and they develop an action plan to achieve it. These 'capsule' sessions are very powerful for recording specific moments in people's lives, and some of my clients use them to register essential moments in their careers or milestones achieved so they can return to them later in time.

When a 'gap' is discovered between what they observe and where they want to be or what they want to achieve, this initial Photo Coaching® session may be the beginning of a support process to reinforce what works for them to continue moving forward or work on those skills or abilities they want to improve.

Repeating this photo-shooting at the end of the support process offers the possibility of making a complete viewing set with the original and final images. This opens the door to recognising achievements, reflecting on where they were at the beginning and where they are now, and celebrating success and learning throughout the whole process. The result of these photographs at the end of the process is usually images that show the satisfaction of the work done and the effort invested in achieving it.

Case study

Alex knew about my work through social media, and we had previously met at one of my talks about talent development. She was in a moment of professional transition. She had dedicated her entire career to corporate banking. After struggling with poor quarterly results during the past year, she decided to spend a few months reflecting on her career. At that time, the only option that seemed possible for Alex was to resign from her current position and seek an alternative at another bank.

After an initial conversation, we decided to make the first Photo Coaching® capsule after an initial written evaluation.

While the photo-shooting ran smoothly, and Alex said she enjoyed it and found it interesting, it was during the viewing that the moment of uncertainty that Alex was experiencing emerged. She first recognised the security and confidence in the portraits, as she was used to posing for corporate pictures. However, when I challenged Alex to explore deeper, she chose a couple of gestures that showed her hands and neck, which she identified as difficulties in adapting to the company's changes, lack of focus on her end, and prioritisation issues in time management.

Alex decided to work on these aspects before planning her professional future. We did a Myers-Briggs Type Indicator (MBTI) Step I & II assessment to give Alex more information regarding her personality and preferences. After the initial sessions, Alex could set a concrete goal to work towards and initiate concrete actions that allowed her to measure progress every time we met.

We repeated the Photo Coaching® capsule before the process ended. I showed Alex the initial and final photographs in the viewing session. This allowed Alex to see where they were at the start and all she had achieved since then. Some gestures that captured the final session were like the initial ones, but their meaning was completely different.

At the end of the process, she recognised an increase in her self-confidence; her images transmitted security and strength to her, and she closed the process, wanting to use all the resources she had discovered she had during the coaching process. The options multiplied, allowing Alex to stay in the same company and develop her next steps from the inside.

Alex has come to the studio a couple more times since then. On the first occasion she wanted to renew her corporate portrait as she was promoted to a management position. After that, she came back to commemorate an important personal event, such as her 50th birthday, and what it meant to her to achieve that milestone healthy and happy.

Discussion points

As a starting point you may use your own portraits or the photographs you use to represent yourself in social media. You can also apply this exercise to your clients:

- Which photographs do you use to represent yourself in WhatsApp, LinkedIn, Instagram, etc? Which ones do you send when someone asks you for a photograph to be included in your company's profile or as a speaker at a conference?
- If someone else observes these images, what do you think they are telling them? What do they know about the person they observe from looking at their picture?
- Do these images represent what is important for you now?
- Would you like to keep them or change them in any way?

Suggested resources

Antoniuou, P. (2020). *Abstract, The art of design*. Netflix.
Arbus, D. (1972). *Revelations: Diane Arbus*. SF MOMA Catalogue.
Barthes, R. (1993). *Camera Lucida: Reflections on photography*. Vintage Classics.
Berger, J. (2013). *Understanding a photograph*. Penguin.
Cartier-Bresson, H. (1952). *The decisive moment*. Simon and Schuster.
Nadar, F. (1895–1905). *When I was a photographer – French: Quand j'etais photographe*. Hachette Livre BNF
Sander, A. (1929). *Face of our time – German: Antlitz der Zeit*. Transmare-Verlag, Munich.
Wolk, L. (2013). *Coaching. El Arte de soplar las brasas*. Gran Aldea Editores.

References

Del Busso, L. (2011). Using photographs to explore embodiment or pleasure in every-day life, in Reavey, P. (ed.) *Visual methods in psychology: using and interpreting image in qualitative research*. Psychology Press.
Donaldson-Wright, M. & Hefferon, K. (2020). A new vision!': Exploring coachee experiences of using photography in coaching – An interpretative phenomenological analysis. *International Journal of Evidence-Based Coaching and Mentoring*, 18(2), 166–182.
Flaherty, J. (2010). *Coaching: Evoking excellence in others* (3rd edn.). Butterworth-Heinemann.
Ives, Y. (2008). What is coaching? An exploration of conflicting paradigms. *International Journal of Evidence-Based Coaching & Mentoring*, 6(2), 100–113.
Ives, Y. & Cox, E. (2012). *Goal-focused coaching: Theory and practice*. Routledge.
Frith, H. & Harcourt, D. (2007). Using photographs to capture women's experiences of chemotherapy: Reflecting on the method. *Qualitative Health Research*, 17(10), 1340–1350.
Gash, J. (2017). *Coaching creativity: Transforming your practice*. Routledge.
Gibson, N. (2018). *Therapeutic photography: Enhancing self-esteem, self-efficacy and resilience*. Jessica Kingsley Publishers.
Hayes, S.C., Srosahl, K.D. & Wilson, K.G. (2012). *Acceptance and commitment therapy: The process and practice of mindful change* (2nd edn.). Guildford Press.
Hodgetts, D., Radley, A., Chamberlain, K. & Hodgetts, A. (2007). Health inequalities and homelessness: considering material, spatial and relational dimensions. *Journal of Health Psychology*, 12(5), 709–725.

Lemon, N. (2007). Take a photograph: teacher reflection through narrative. *Reflective Practice*, *8*(2), 177–191.

LinkedIn Business Statistics. (2023). https://blog.hootsuite.com/linkedin-statistics-business

Sontag, S. (2021). On photography. In *Illuminations* (pp. 230–234). Routledge.

Weiser, J. (1990). More than meets the eye: Using ordinary snapshots as tools for therapy, in Laidlaw, T. and Malmo, C. (eds.) *Healing voices: Feminist approaches to therapy with women*. Jossey-Bass.

Willig, C. (2013). *Introducing qualitative research in psychology*. McGraw-Hill education.

Chapter 5

Coaching re-imagined
The four creative inner tools of the coach

Andrew Machon and Adrian Machon

Introduction

In this chapter, we take the time to relax and discuss how to stimulate and facilitate the deep inner work that evokes lasting insight and creative change. We have kept to methodical referencing whilst taking some poetic licence and freedom of expression with this topic to touch into this work's depth and potential. This chapter explores how the coach and coachee can both learn to access their source of creativity and operate more artfully in practice. Though we may automatically seek resources outwardly, this work is novel in spotlighting four essential inner tools – namely, the Spirit Level, the Compass, the Wand, and the Mirror. Their practical value is brought to life primarily through the experience of the coach and their coachees. Commonly, the key reference for coaches wishing to develop their practice is coaching competencies. Such frameworks mainly define the coaching process as seen objectively from the outside perspective. We believe these inner tools add to the value of competencies to reveal how we experience coaching from the inside out uniquely. These innate tools collectively describe a deeper understanding of how we employ 'self as an instrument' and reveal how we can build resourcefulness, foster creative expression, cultivate co-creative relationships, and essentially enable lasting development and growth.

Development and art

We approach this chapter with gratitude, as it gives us time to pause and deeply consider the precious few things we would like to offer regarding our shared experience about coaching with art forms. Above all else, we seek to convey that art and development have a primal and vital co-partnership in facilitating more profound, lasting personal development and change. The key question is, How do we purposefully and most effectively tap this potential as coaches, creating the field and space for creative learning and growth?

To begin, we observe how people often disown their own artistry (their inner artist), feeling that the gift of artistic expression in all its various forms sits with

DOI: 10.4324/9781003453437-6

the gifted, extraordinary few. Like the sun in the solar system providing life energy to all planets, we, too, may easily imagine the generator of creativity *lies outside of ourselves*, something we have forgotten or believe we no longer possess. In truth, we put forward that *we are each a sun*, each naturally able to tap into this innate potential to creatively express, compose, author, and narrate our lives. As Don Miguel Ruiz (Ruiz & Mills, 2001) reminds us, "Every human is an artist. The dream of your life is to make beautiful art" (p. 17).

Mining this creative capacity, then, becomes the pearl of great worth. Here, coaches are invited to continue to find new ways to be open to supporting what amounts to deep inner work. We will illustrate how accessing this through coaching lies not only in evoking the coachee's response but also, in parallel, developing the inner state and capacities of the coach. And how these together give rise to a rich, co-creative partnership and exchange. To further explore how to do this, we will offer you four inner tools that have, in our experience, collectively enabled this creative source to be mined within the coaching space. These are the Spirit Level, the Compass, the Mirror, and the Wand.

Pause point

Take a moment to check where you are with this belief of innate creative potential lying within us:

What does it touch or evoke in you?

We have positioned how coaching involves, at its heart, a co-creative relationship, whereby both coachee and coach can experience a developmental, mutual benefit (Fletcher, 2007). And in this context, we are defining art broadly and simply as that which involves human creative skill and imagination. This includes all its art forms: image, music, movement, performance, and narrative (both verbal and written). Elements taken from these art forms and specifically chosen (or created) by the coachee become transitional objects for them, something familiar that can create ease and mediate learning (Colman, 2015), allowing through their use in the coaching work to tap into creative and emergent thinking. For simplicity, we might name these artistic objects *artefacts*. Therefore, the coach's invitation as an artist is now to nurture a co-creative and skilful use of the imagination with the coachee in service of growth.

However, how do we, as coaches, facilitate the movement from a mind that is outward-facing and often distracted, rational, and caught up in busyness to a mind more able to be oriented inwardly to explore its own deeper and creative nature? Nurturing this inward awareness and attentiveness helps create a doorway and bridge to an untapped potential and our own and the coachee's breadth, depth, and wholeness. So, how do we illuminate this essential bridging quality through the use of art and artistry within development?

Creative coaching practice: The four inner tools

In our work with coachees and groups over many years of conversation and practice, there has emerged a small set of four inner tools whose instrumentation has proven to be of continuous and valuable use in helping us open and operate within the co-creative field, allowing the coach to become 'self as instrument' for those seeking their help. For some who coach, you may instinctually already carry out some of what each of these tools seeks to offer. However, their collective use is explored to emphasise the importance of a preparatory and ongoing conscious inner reorientation and depth of practice. Also, the tools in use speak to the inestimable value of learning how to tap into and mine the source of creativity within each of us, the flow of which allows us to become the inner artist, composer, author, and narrator and to discover and re-shape our lives imaginatively. Without such tools, it is easy for the coaching to lose itself in the often fluid and seductive energy of the creative experience. These tools can collectively help us nurture a turning around in the seat of consciousness described earlier.

In this chapter, we can give you a taster of the tools whilst offering you sources for deeper exploration of their application if you wish (Machon, 2010a, 2022, 2023). We have blended within each tool's purpose and use with feedback from coaches who have worked with these inner instruments for some time. Together, these tools seek to cause and strengthen the inner reorientation of attention and focus in order to deepen the co-creative work and enrich the coaching experience and its outputs.

Pause point

Before reading on, in the exploration of 'self as an instrument' and how we enable the development of others, what 'tools' are you employing when you are operating at your best as a coach?

The Spirit Level

The Spirit Level is the first of the inner tools becoming useful in consciously preparing for co-creative work and the one we most commonly overlook. In life, the Spirit Level in design work and carpentry serves to ensure when something is in alignment, made level, centred, and brought into balance. For the coach and coachee, the inner Spirit Level reminds them to take time to centre and balance within themselves before and at checkpoints during the co-creative coaching conversations.

This tool seeks to address a mental/emotional state of being 'out of balance', typified in either the coach or coachee as habitual and conditioned thinking and fast-paced reactivity such as snap or critical judgements, creating prejudices and narrowed perceptions. When the mind is 'out of balance', what is being offered is a restricted mental/emotional bandwidth of awareness and perception, one that is likely more blinkered to the flow of the creative work and its full potential. This tends to inhibit the spaciousness and open-minded receptiveness needed to access the inner artist in both the coach and coachee.

In essence, the inner Spirit Level serves to set an intention to shift consciously and skilfully towards being more fully present and available. This conscious inner reorientation evokes within the coach a quality of presence and becoming an observer and witness. This, in turn, cultivates a more fluid inner spaciousness, creating a neutral, unconditional, and receptive space in which the coachee can explore and creatively discover. Such a tool nurtures (both for the coach and coachee) a centre of awareness that is less likely to default to habitual and reactive self-referencing and more in service of imaginative and creative discovery. This mindfulness assists the coach in connecting, listening, questioning, noticing, hearing, holding, and offering back (Passmore & Marianetti, 2007; Kabat-Zinn, 2013).

A vital sign of effective use of the inner Spirit Level is, within the coach, the adoption of a willingness 'not to know', enabling the coachee a gradual 'coming into knowing'.

This first tool also prepares the ground for the other inner tools to come into use and gradually gifted between coach and coachee.

Pause point

Do you activate and use the inner Spirit Level when you coach? If so, how do you do it?

What is it offering you?

Quotes from coaches

"The Spirit Level acts as a reminder for me to check in and balance myself prior to coaching – physically, emotionally, spiritually, mentally. I can then receive whatever my coachee is bringing in a more unfiltered way and engage with them just as they are".

"The Spirit level allows me to take a moment to breathe and re-set. "It's a great form of self-management".

"The Spirit level, for me, is probably the most important coaching tool… learning how to remain calm and steady as a coach. And then enabling my coachee to do the same for themselves, role modelling and enabling understanding of how this can be done. It is such a profound and transformational tool…a level spirit represents the foundations of coaching mastery".

The Compass

The Compass is the second inner tool. In essence, this is a tool for activating or motivating the inner artist and guide within both the coach and the coachee. Walkers will often remind themselves never to set off without a compass if they are to avoid getting lost. The same appears true in coaching, reminding both the coach and coachee that they possess an innate guide and source of insight and directionality. An inner reference and source of motivation and creativity to which they can return to reset their vital coordinates and to remember what is important that will inform their choices and energise their next steps in the creative work.

The Compass is a constant reminder of their innate resourcefulness, where potential lies, and where their longing and inspiration are to be discovered. When the inner Compass is activated, the coach and coachee will learn to become consciously aligned with their source and potential, and experience an emergent awareness of their creative nature, which in our experience can include imaginative play, joy, spontaneity, realisation, and choice of direction that they are willing to make and take.

Here, the default mind that the tool is working against is the mind that tends towards busyness and distraction, and a reaching outside of themselves and to others for answers and solutions. What is meaningful, precious, emergent, and coming to the surface can be easily overlooked and lost. Yet, this may be immensely evocative material that will in time inform their beliefs and perception of themselves, their ongoing journey, and even how they see the world.

The inner Spirit Level and Compass work hand in hand. They permit the coach to work more deeply, to consider the coachee's emotions, aspirations, and intentions and what is subtly seeking to come into form and find creative expression. In time, they permit the coachee to embrace and be open to the inner work rather than distrust or fear it. It brings about a gradual inward settling or 'seatedness', which will deepen their experience of themselves and build confidence.

One vital sign of the inner Compass in action is an awareness of inner guidance, will and agency, a clear sense of intentionality amid the creative dance. This sense of being settled and seated within builds self-trust and reliance.

Pause point

Do you use the inner Compass when you coach? If so, how do you use it? What is it offering you?

Quotes from coaches

"The notion of the Compass reminds me to take a step back and keep perspective of the overall situation – the coachee/their goals/myself – and to think of where we're going. It also enables me to ask powerful questions (particularly if a coachee is getting lost in the details) about where they want to be heading and what's important. This often shifts the coachee's thinking to a deeper level".

"The Compass is a constant reminder for me of the unwavering faith in our coachees, the direction in which they travel is always their choice and we support them, even when the coachees is in their darkest moments and feel they don't know the way. We stay, listen and enable".

The Mirror

The Mirror is the third inner tool, reminding the coach of the vitalness of reflection during coaching and noticing the co-creative dynamic. When the coach is present and able to reflect what they see and hear, the coachee in turn feels more fully seen and heard. This builds trust and confidence in the coaching relationship (Lliffe-Wood, 2014), permitting deeper self-exploration, whilst allowing the natural flow of the coaching work. The Mirror evokes vital truth telling. We might recall the mirror of the Wicked Queen in the fairy tale of *Snow White* (Zipes, 2015) told the truth about who was fairest.

The essential service this tool offers them is in tapping into the emergent work, what is surfacing, and what is calling to be recognised and known. All forms of artwork are evocative (Stroud, 2007); they arouse and touch something deeply within us, marking a resonance, something distantly recognised and surfacing, now coming into being. The verb "to evoke" is derived from the French verb 'vocare', which literally means "to call to" (Dictionary.com, 2023). In the co-creative coaching conversation, both the coach and the coachee are invited to draw into form and capture the meaning of what is both illusive and yet seeking expression.

The default mind. This tool is working against is that of both the coach and the coachee's overthinking and becoming caught up in one's own thoughts and agenda. The intent is for receptivity, reflection, and responsiveness, not rumination or reaction.

The Mirror often evokes in the coach the gift of the beautiful question, not pulled from memory and habitual use but from the fertile soil of the present moment through attentive listening.

One vital sign of success in applying this tool is in the capacity not only to hear what is being spoken but also to deeply listen and intuit. To recognise and reflect on what is present and coming into being in the shared co-creative experience. This involves sensitivity, honesty, and subtlety to all detail and nuance. In doing this well, the coach models a quality of detached involvement.

This skilful capturing and holding of what is being reflected and evoked is precious and the result of it may unfold and continue to unfold long after these few moments of co-creative coaching together. Jung (2014) affirms "Only in our creative acts do we step forth into the light of consciousness and see ourselves as whole and complete" (p. 737)

Pause point

If and how you use the inner Mirror when you coach, what is it offering you?

Quotes from coaches

"The Mirror is very powerful. Being able to offer what I see/experience in an unattached way is a way to be of service, it enables the coachee to understand exactly how they are showing up in that moment, not how they would like to be, but how I am truly and honestly receiving them, and it's rare that people are offered a true/authentic mirror in organisational life".

"The Mirror is perhaps the most powerful coaching tool of them all –It is hard to look in the mirror for long, one needs to be held and supported to do so, but the rewards are astonishing".

"Through the Mirror, I am a truth seeker and a truth speaker".

The Wand

The Wand is the fourth and final of the tools. Its use necessitates the artistry of the coach, inviting the skilled use of their imagination. The inner Wand works its magic in being a vital transporter. This permits the coachee to 'step into' the experience of their desired future from what is being evoked whilst distracting them away from the trappings of rationalised shortcuts and fixes, overthinking, and rumination. When using the Wand well, rationality and the need to work things out is superseded by imaginative creativity freely flowing in the creative experience. This can often be an incredibly active part of the co-creative process. The inner Wand evokes motion, movement, sense-making, and gentle ownership of what is emerging and coming into being, playing it forward into a new composition, narrative, and creation.

The default mind the inner Wand plays against is the coachee's forgetfulness, distraction, and lack of agency to anchor and secure the work.

A vital sign of success with this inner tool for the coach and coachee is the capacity to realise their desired future experientially. This involves a 'leap of faith', realising new experiences and psychological ground fostering learning, insight, and meaning-making.

Pause point

If so, how do you use the inner wand when you coach?
What is this offering you?

Quotes from coaches

"The Wand enables me to ask questions which can shift a coachee out of a mental cul-de-sac or rut. It triggers their imagination to move from problem to possibility and brings hope to a conversation. To ask a 'wand' question can be powerful, such as: 'What would you do if there were no negative consequences?' or 'If money was unlimited, how would you move forward?' This can significantly open up a coachee's imagination and creativity, enabling them to move forward."

"The Wand is the most wonderful and joyful coaching tool – the one that enables unfettered dreaming of things we might never have imagined without it. It's amazing how this can unlock and unleash whole new possibilities. You could call it the lovely coaching question, 'What if' on steroids! And as its name suggests, it is magical!"

A metaphor to 'hold' this co-creative work

As you operate with these tools in the co-creative space, we have found certain metaphors that are able to capture, express, and animate the intimate nature of this co-creative experience. For example, we have used a powerful and inspirational metaphor of a flowing river. Thihk Nhat Hanh (2002) wrote this phrase in his personal calligraphy work, "Go as a river". Consider, for a moment, how does a river go? What might this mean for us in re-imagining coaching when working artistically? As a metaphor, it may offer an inner pictorial experience of being present in the flow together, evoking a sense of surrender and letting go whilst remaining present and being deeply touched by all movement and flow. Such metaphors have a way of holding subtlety and depth and will often continue to unfold in their meaning as we engage with them. They can also speak to where words cannot easily go.

Pause point

Imagine you are coaching at your best and experiencing what it means to 'go as a river'.
What does this evoke for you?

Are there other metaphors that encompass how you coach creatively when at your best?

One of the author's own pieces of creative writing is entitled: "To the River". It is the story of a pilgrim who searches to find his way from a place of feeling lost and in the wilderness. He comes to relate with both a beautiful river weaving through the landscape, and later, he discovers a river within him, his source and flow of creativity. Here is an excerpt:

> There is a world beneath and beyond, and we are blindness itself, lost amongst the surface coverings, turning pagan under the long shadow of disbelief. There is a river within out from the source, unconditioned and always in flow. It is our lineage, our root, our ground of being. It is our wealth, our untold story. And in that moment, there is something loosened from within him. The experience is in one way subtle, in another way eternally precise; it is the melting of his own inner ice.
>
> (Machon, 2010b, p. 120)

Discussion and conclusion

In giving our attention more fully to the creative, we are uncovering the essential value of how the re-imagining of coaching might serve the profession. Commonly, the primary references for the development of 'would-be' coaches are competency frameworks. Such frameworks enhance the professional credibility of coaching by providing an objective view of coaching content, structure, process, and standard. They essentially seek to define and describe what we do when we coach. In the re-imagining of coaching, we strive to include a more qualitative and subjective view, in essence, a chance to look at coaching from the inside out and "how we are in what we do" to be considered and explored (and valued) more fully. We believe that marrying competency frameworks with creative explorations into the nature of coaching offers the coach a more wholesome vision and guidance of what it means to coach at our best, both with our own uniqueness and expressive freedom! Indeed, we support how re-imagining the 'self as an instrument' has revealed essential inner tools that can combine to enable the vital developmental bridge between the rational and the imaginative. We hope that the re-imagination of coaching will continue along these lines in the spirit of deepening its lasting impact and service. We give the final word to one user of the inner tools who shared with us,

> As a whole, the tools are now "in my bones". They are part of the core of who I am as a coach and human being. I no longer call on them; they are the essence of what I do. They emerge, and I use them effortlessly. My coachee experience is more profound, and undoubtedly, I can operate with more creativity, which didn't seem to come naturally to me. Everybody benefits, my clients, my family, and my friends. Thank you for such beautiful gifts.

Discussion points

Here, we leave you with three questions to help deepen your reflection:

- How would you imagine these four inner tools will serve you?
- How will they deepen your capacity to work creatively?
- How will these tools foster your creative freedom when coaching others?

References

Colman, A. M. (2015). *A dictionary of psychology*. Oxford quick reference.

Dictionary.com. (2023). *Dictionary.com*. https://www.dictionary.com/browse/evoke

Fletcher, S. (2007). Educational research mentoring and coaching as co-creative synergy. *International Journal of Evidence-Based Coaching and Mentoring*, 5(2) 1–11.

Jung, C. G. (2014). *The structure and dynamics of the psyche*. Routledge.

Kabat-Zinn, J. (2013). *Full catastrophe living, revised edition: How to cope with stress, pain and illness using mindfulness meditation*. Hachette.

Lliffe-Wood, M. (2014). *Coaching presence – Building consciousness and awareness in coaching interventions*. Kogan Page.

Machon, A. (2010a). *Out of the wilderness – A journey to our deeper self*. Kindle Direct Publishing.

Machon, A. (2010b). *The coaching secret: How to be an exceptional coach*. Pearson Education.

Machon, A. (2022). The relational context of change. In P. Worth (Ed.), *Positive psychology across the lifespan – An existential perspective*. Routledge.

Machon, A. (2023). *The essential instruments*. https://youtu.be/N1NFuBibuuo?si=QzEr6BZm5jSLLAu3

Passmore, J. & Marianetti, O. (2007). The role of mindfulness in coaching. *The Coaching Psychologist*, 3(3), 131–137.

Ruiz, D. M., & Mills, J. (2001). *The circle of fire*. Amber Allen.

Stroud, S. R. (2007). Dewey on art as evocative communication. *Education and Culture*, 23(2), 6–26.

Hanh, T. N. (2002). *Teachings on love*. Parallax Press.

Zipes, J. (Ed.). (2015). *The Oxford companion to fairy tales*. Oxford Companions.

Chapter 6

Illustrated coaching
Development through the co-creation of visual inscapes

Meirion Jones and Andrew Machon

Introduction – contextual background

Illustrated Coaching is a coaching method that captures the themes of a coaching conversation – often expressed using metaphors, analogies, symbols, and motifs – in the form of one, or a succession, of vivid and powerful illustrations. Unlike most arts-based coaching where the coachee or subject produces the imagery, in Illustrated Coaching, it is the coach who first creates the images, working with the coachee in a process of close and often intimate co-creativity. Relieved of any pressure arising from doubts about their drawing ability, the coachee is freed to fully explore and expand upon whatever initial metaphors and images come to mind.

As the coaching process continues through a series of conversations stimulated by the work-in-progress illustration, the visual inner psychological landscape – what we term the 'inscape', representing the coachee's key themes, interests, aspirations, and concerns – is literally drawn out and comes into ever sharper focus. Commonly, the visual symbolism of the picture becomes progressively richer and more complex, more personal, and, in our experience, more revelatory.

With the coach and coachee working co-creatively, these illustrations can trigger insightful responses and realisations, leading to expanded self-awareness and access to new psychological resources.

Extensive practical experience of applying this method over the past five years – first with a cohort of curious and open-minded coaches as test subjects and then expanding the work to encompass business clients (often senior leaders working in large and complex organisations) – support how this approach effectively by-passes traditional, chiefly verbal and textual, modes of interaction. Instead, these illustrations can stimulate new and different ways of conceptualising, working with, and understanding whatever themes and challenges the coachee is holding. This co-creative illustrative approach leads to the following:

- New expanded self-awareness, together with richer learning and meaning-making

DOI: 10.4324/9781003453437-7

- Creation of new perceptual lenses through which the clients can review and re-vision their opportunities
- Teaching a more creative approach to self-development

Theory, basic concepts, and key developments

So much of what we believe and how we behave is automatic and unquestioned, unspooling like the music in a pianola. To what extent does the unconscious govern our reactions and behaviours? Jung (2014) stated that if our inner situations remain unconscious, we experience them outwardly as fate, projecting out the division and conflict that we cannot yet acknowledge and own within. Illustrated Coaching provides the client with the chance to take control and own their own dilemmas and inner conflicts, to explore and make more conscious what they may hide. This helps the client to interrogate their reality and increase their self-awareness, enabling them to make purposeful decisions about their lives. In the words of US coach Goldsmith (2016), "Awareness is a difference maker…providing us with a little breathing space… to consider our options and make a better behavioural choice" (p. 230). Illustrated Coaching is a powerful means of helping to make that difference. Coaching creates the psychological space for the client to come to know themselves more fully, and Illustrated Coaching facilitates the often-transformative developmental opportunity to bring into form what sits on the edge of our consciousness, awaiting remembrance.

A critical aspect of the coaching relationship is the chance for our clients to tell their stories and to feel truly seen and heard. We are all storytellers, and the stories we tell about ourselves when witnessed help us to discover and understand who we really are. Through our stories, we reveal our identity, build maturity, and enhance meaning-making through adversity and well-being, together with higher levels of mental health (McAdams & McLean, 2013). Initially, our stories are often rudimentary and imperfectly understood. They are commonly summarised via a mental shorthand, employing simple visual metaphors (such as "finding the path", "in over my head", "mountain to climb", and "reaching for the stars"), which we can use unquestioningly to furnish a vague sense of purpose and meaning. Illustrated Coaching reveals the meaning beneath these metaphors, giving them form and immersing the coachee in their significance. In doing so, it helps the coachee to recognise themselves more fully, to understand the drives or beliefs that motivate or hinder them, and offers a vital chance to confront the challenges, doubts, or fears they experience and grasp their significance.

Drawing out these stories and metaphors and giving them form may offer the coachee fresh insights and new awareness. Moreover, since we live in a primarily verbal and textual world, the alternative, additional non-verbal route offered by Illustrated Coaching can lead to dramatic and disruptive reframing, which, in our experience is often a precursor to significant change.

This contrast and coherence between the verbal and the visual are critical to consider. Coaching is a wonderful tool for personal growth. It can unlock new resources of self-confidence and personal agency and enhance the creativity and decision-making of the coachee. A coaching session is, in essence, a conversation: language and text are its most common tools. Given that the lion's share of the brain's function is devoted to processing non-verbal imagery (Massachusetts Institute of Technology, 1999), the pictures we see and create through our imagination and the use of visualisation techniques in coaching is now emerging as an invaluable addition to the coaching toolbox. We support the view of Kremer, Moran, and Kearney (2019), who illustrate how mental imagery in coaching can offer insight into problems and shape personality.

Thinking pictorially inevitably creatively disrupts in that it steals us away from our preoccupation with rationality and problem-solving and opens our minds to more reflective and creative thinking. This enhances brain neuroplasticity, whereby the brain can continually adapt and change seemingly throughout life in response to learning (Johnson & Xue, 2018) which in turn informs and creates different, potentially more powerful, developmental choices.

Of course, visualisation has long been used as a therapeutic tool. As the psychotherapist Valerie Thomas (2016) says, exploring a client's mental images provides "deep level schemas, or 'experiential gestalts' that restructure the individual's perception of self and the self-concerning the environment" (p. 82). Sometimes, a visualisation activity can be as simple as inviting a coachee to describe their challenges by sketching simple images such as stick drawings, basic shapes, symbols, and even colours. However, when an individual learns how to perceive and create images in their head that portray their world, they discover a secret of how to change themselves. Lakoff and Johnson (1980) also support how human thought processes are largely metaphorical, and exploring the meaning underpinning visual metaphor can significantly expand the opportunities for self-reflection and build new awareness.

Illustrated Coaching weaves these principles together, with the one critical difference being that of a skilful coach/illustrator facilitating the realisation of the imagery. In doing so, the act of drawing becomes an exploratory, emergent, and organic process. Presented with successive iterative versions of their metaphorical imagery, the coachee is developmentally led towards self-actualisation and the realisation of their fuller potential (Rogers, 1951).

Images and ideas that may, at the start of the process, have seemed trite or simplistic or obscure and lacking meaning start to find their place and make sense. New variations may be created with additional imagery incorporated into the picture. Meaning-making evolves out of the process of creating the drawing together with the opportunity to return to, revisit, and contemplate the drawing over time.

Illustrated Coaching directly taps into our instinctive use of imagery, metaphors, and storytelling. Visualisation, in this way, can free the learner to explore these themes spontaneously and with less inhibition. An individual can reflect more deeply and holistically on the significance of the images and any symbolism or meaning that's personal to them and set themselves more inspiring and stretching goals.

Practice

The effectiveness of Illustrated Coaching depends in no small part on the illustrative skill of the coach to capture the coachee's imagery authentically. As a painter, illustrator, and executive coach, Meirion Jones has long been intrigued about how these modes may complement each other. Working with coachees for whom this approach offers an intriguing alternative to more conventional coaching, Meirion captures the discussion themes in the form of digital illustrations. Rather than asking the coachee typical coaching questions, he invites them to describe what they see when they reflect on themes that concern and or inspire them. The very act of describing the images that reveal themselves encourages the coachee to push further into their visual inscapes and, in the process, tap into non-verbal meaning and deeper understanding.

This approach is valuable when the coachee has difficulty expressing themselves in spoken language, for example, when the themes are complex and bound up in values and deep-rooted behaviour patterns and beliefs. The more profound questions of identity and purpose lend themselves particularly well to this approach.

Equally, the approach can be highly effective when the coachee is extremely articulate and superficially self-aware. The linguistic facility of some coachees can be so great that an unconscious rationalising dexterity may stifle deeper self-reflection. In these cases, the disruption effected by abandoning the reasoning verbal mode in favour of a non-rational illustrative approach using imagery and metaphor can yield major breakthroughs.

Sometimes, the technique can be helpful to developmentally disrupt a coachee's habitual beliefs and attitudes, encouraging them to employ a different language and new perspective to explore their challenges and responses to them.

The process is underpinned by exploiting the extraordinary digital painting resources now available – working with an iPad or similar and using dedicated software to draw and paint during the coaching session. Visual motifs and metaphors are captured in the moment as they arise during the conversation. Following the initial coaching session, the coach then begins incorporating them, consolidating them into a thematic whole, which is shared with the coachee in the subsequent sessions. Presented with a visual realisation of what has been up until then, abstract, unrealised, and, often, unacknowledged mental imagery, the coachee's thought process becomes richer, more exploratory, more reflective, and ultimately, in our experience, more revelatory.

From a logistical standpoint, using digital painting tools provides a speed of response and flexibility that working in conventional media would not permit. Digital working also allows for fast and substantial revisions, adding and removing design components and, occasionally, even starting afresh. This flexibility has a freeing effect on the coachee, allowing them to explore their visual inscapes unencumbered by whatever limiting beliefs they may harbour about their drawing ability. It also allows the design process to continue co-actively on any of the remote conferencing tools.

Case study

One recent client, a senior partner of a leading professional services firm, faced an important career transition after almost three successful decades at the top of his profession. Setting out on a new career phase, he described a bewildering sense of uncertainty and drift, feeling overwhelmed by the importance of the decisions facing him and ill-equipped to make them.

In the preliminary Illustrated Coaching session, he described seeing images of branching paths and his doubts over which path to choose. In particular, the coachee spoke of his need for a "dashboard compass to show where he needed to go".

In the second session, he was presented with an initial sketch in response to the imagery he described (Figure 6.1), notably the branching pathways, the dashboard compass, and the sense of uncertainty represented by the flailing

Figure 6.1 Initial sketch.

Figure 6.2 The sage in deep reflection.

figure. Rather than the compass sitting on a car's dashboard, the coachee was keen that the compass was held to illustrate the physical embodiment of his need for direction.

In conversation, the coachee saw the numerous pathways as an opportunity to practice equanimity and acceptance. He continued to explore the concept of embodying the compass. In the resulting second sketch (Figure 6.2), he now saw himself as seated within the compass, his figure assuming the dress of a sage or mystic in deep reflection.

The coachee now realised that the uncertainty represented by the multiple pathways was an opportunity for purposeful reflection rather than an obstacle to be overcome. The recursive process of self-reflection was captured in a sketch of the compass figure examining multiple receding versions of himself (Figure 6.3). The figure turned away from the viewer, facing the future, while the branching pathways resolved into a mandala representing his journey inwards.

The final digitally painted version (Figure 6.4) consolidated these themes. The coachee's fascination with history was reflected in the palette, dominated by the umber hues of 17th and 18th-century painting, by the astrolabe (a medieval 'compass'), and by the manuscript treatment of the mandala sitting before

Figure 6.3 The mandala of his journey inwards.

Figure 6.4 Final consolidated version.

him like a recently unearthed treasure map. The blue of the robe represented balance and transcendence.

The final picture was 'a light year' away from his initial dashboard compass idea, but the process of creating the image, of growing, refining, adding, and blending its different elements together – and, most importantly, the revealing of his inner purpose – allowed him to realise and achieve a place of calm in which he was able to focus confidently on the next stage of his life. In his own words,

> The illustration stimulated immersive thought, and its power as a catalyst for change cannot be overstated. Sharing my thoughts and seeing them interpreted into the illustration through our follow-on discussions enhanced the coaching experience immensely. The quotient of deeper thinking was tremendous and powerful, leading to incisive two-way conversations and, for me, a breakthrough at an accelerated pace.

Drawing out: Exploration, reflection, and application

In developing and applying the principles of Illustrated Coaching, one abiding question is, How does the involvement of the coach/illustrator affect the metaphorical visual language arising from the coachee's process? After all, if the coach draws the imagery, its origins will unavoidably emerge partly from the coach's own visual inscape, their own inventory of metaphors and motifs. Even the drawing style expresses the coach's sensibilities, preferences, and skills.

In current coaching models, the coach maintains a position of detached involvement, a deliberate closeness, and a conscious distancing that enables the coachee to explore and reflect on their own themes free of any influence from their coach. To achieve this, the coach practices 'multi-lensed', self-vigilance to guard against the possibility of anticipating, interpreting, and directing according to the coach's own experiences, sensibilities and beliefs. In the parlance of co-active coaching, "clients have all the answers, and coaches are unattached" (Kimsey-House et al., 2011). This principle is perhaps most clearly realised in the clean language techniques pioneered by Grove and Panzer (1991) and developed by others, including Lawley and Tompkins (2000), in which the coach uses language expressly structured to minimise the possibility of framing the coachee's response.

In Illustrated Coaching, by contrast, the coach is a necessary, deliberate, and active participant in the process. No matter how much the selection of the imagery serves the coachee's descriptions and symbology, is there also the risk that the coach may misinterpret or (mis)direct the coachee's own nascent ideation process? Might this invalidate the process altogether?

We believe not. The power ever resides with the coachee to describe and inform their image. They invite change, alteration, addition, and deletion. If something does not fit or feel right, the coachee in our experience, will exercise that power. This may leave the coach to consider the extent to which they have been able to work with detached involvement in the service of the coachee and whether they may have imposed something of their own. This can be valuable learning for the coach to take to and explore in their coaching supervision. Such 'impositions' may then provide opportunities for the coach to explore their own process concerning the coachee and continue their own developmental journey and learning in parallel.

In the image development process, the coach illustrator may sometimes have a strong intuition about depicting something in a particular way or adding something more to the image beyond the realms of the current factual discussion. Such interventions demand the coach to reflect deeply, checking the integrity of the inclusion, ensuring that this is added in service of the coachee and not over-influenced by the coach's needs and process. Of course, the final verdict comes from the coachee seeing and accepting the image. However, this allows the coach to creatively visualise, inform and share their intuition with the coachee, quite literally.

What is vital to realise is that although the coach is in control of producing the drawing, every aspect of the image is birthed through relationships. In truth, the drawing, irrespective of the hand, is co-created and always open to modification and change by the coachee.

A common reservation from would-be Illustrated Coaching clients is that they are "not visual" and would, therefore, not benefit from the practice. As noted earlier, the brain's largest proportion of sensory processing is devoted to visual input. Although we may have developed other modal biases or habitually use other modes of meaning-making (text, numbers, sounds, smells), we all appear to possess rich visual inscapes. For some, these are simply under-explored.

In the early development phase of the Illustrated Coaching process, we assumed that it would appeal particularly to 'creative' types with well-developed visual orientation: those working in fields such as advertising and media, gaming, art, and design. While there has been strong interest in this sector, it has struck a chord equally with those from more text-based professions – professional services such as law and accounting, banking, IT, and traditional manufacturing and engineering. This points to a potential for visual expression that might be given less opportunity in these fields. It confirms that we may all possess rich visual inscapes. And it suggests that for some, these are an untapped treasure trove of resources for personal growth.

As we have worked with the Illustrated Coaching approach with clients, we have noticed that it can contagiously inspire clients to take charge and creatively work with their own imagery. Following an Illustrated Coaching journey, several clients have chosen their own medium and begun to draw themselves out. One example was a coachee who, after two rounds of Illustrated Coaching spanning a period of over a year, decided to work towards his own self-portrait. The client chose his own media and worked intently on producing a self-image which notably encompassed their spiritual journey and questions of faith. This topic was deeply personal and meaningful. Ultimately, the final composition was brought back into the coaching relationship for the coachee's journey and composition to be both witnessed and learning and meaning more fully mined.

There are some clients where a single drawing can encapsulate a key dilemma or the emergence of an essential aspect of themselves, a part of themselves which may have previously been hidden. However, in some instances, as in the study case, an initial metaphorical theme can expand to encompass multiple illustrations as the coachee ventures deeper into their inscape. One such sequence used the motif of a tower with several levels, both above and below ground, and stairways leading to chambers either already familiar or that still need to be entirely conceived. Using the Illustrated Coaching process, the coachee took what they described as their "spiritual journey", exploring the different levels of the tower. The coachee delved into the base of the tower, the resulting part of the illustration resembling an oppressive dungeon discovered to be the home of a rejected aspect of themselves. The coachee also described climbing to the top and experiencing a sense of release and potential transcendence.

In this example, one drawing comprised of differing illustrated levels remarkably encapsulated the entire psyche of the client and was able to represent their whole journey, creatively bringing together their history, present key developmental possibilities, and future aspirations.

One final consideration is the drawing skill of the coach. Meirion trained as an illustrator and has, over time, developed a facility to draw quickly, use a range of media and realise imagery that matches and potentiates his coachees' imaginations. If a coach is interested in developing their own Illustrated Coaching practice but feels they lack the drawing skill or experience, is it possible to practice in this way? As noted earlier, the co-creative approach is the critical element in this process. Some Illustrated Coaching clients have the most significant value from simply discussing and playing with images in their 'mind's eye' rather than proceeding to a physical capture. Others, as noted, have gone on to create their own pictures independent of the coach. It is noteworthy how coachees commonly report how a completed illustration is like a talisman, a vital developmental reminder that can continually foster ongoing developmental reflection and learning.

Illustrated Coaching embodies the art forms of image creation and storytelling. As it is concerned with realising the transformative power of 'non-rational meaning', we see the potential for employing other art forms important to enabling development for the same purpose either separately or together with the Illustrated Coaching approach, including poetry, music, sculpture, movement and dance, drama, and improvisation. The seed is the act of intense co-creativity, and we believe it can find its fruition through any of these art forms, allowing the coachee gradually to take charge of their original artistic expression and motivation.

Discussion points

In terms of practical application, consider these questions to guide your own reflection and exploration. Most of these were raised by coaching colleagues who participated in earlier exploratory Illustrated Coaching engagements:

- How do images and metaphors inform your life and work?
- How might Illustrated Coaching naturally contribute to your development?
- For those drawn to the application of Illustrated Coaching, what concrete steps can be taken to integrate this into your coaching practice seamlessly?
- What systematic process can be employed to identify coaching clients for whom the Illustrated Coaching approach would be particularly beneficial?
- In navigating the non-verbal terrain, what practical measures can coaches adopt to minimise the risks associated with parallel process and projection?

Suggested resources

Jones, M. (2022a). *Illustrated coaching*. Retrieved from https://www.illustratedcoaching. com

Jones, M. (2022b). *Words or pictures: what does Britain do better?* Retrieved from https:// www.linkedin.com/pulse/words-pictures-what-does-britain-do-better-meirion-jones

References

Goldsmith, M. (2016). *Triggers*. Profile Books.

Grove, D.J., & Panzer, B.I. (1991). *Resolving traumatic memories: Metaphors and symbols in psychotherapy*. Irvington Publishers Inc.

Jung, C. H. (2014). *Collected Works of CG Jung, Volume 19, Part II: Researches Into the Phenomenology of the Self*. Princeton University Press.

Johnson, A. K., & Xue, B. (2018). Central nervous system neuroplasticity and the sensitization of hypertension. *Nature Reviews Nephrology* 14, 750–766. doi:10.1038/s41581-018-0068-5

Kimsey-House, H., Kimsey-House, K., Sandahl, P., & Whitworth, L., (2011). *Co-active coaching*. Nicholas Brealey Publishing.

Kremer, J., Moran, A.P. & Kearney, C. J. (2019). *Pure sport: Practical sport psychology*. Routledge.

Lakoff, G., & Johnson, M. (1980). *Metaphors we live by*. University of Chicago Press.

Lawley, J., & Tompkins, P. (2000). *Metaphors in mind. Transformation through symbolic modelling*. The Developing Company Press.

McAdams, D.P., & McLean, K.C. (2013). Narrative Identity. *Current Directions in Psychological Science*, 22(3), 233–238. https://doi.org/10.1177/0963721413475622

Massachusetts Institute of Technology. (1999). Brain Processing of Visual Information. *MIT News*. https://news.mit.edu/1996/visualprocessing

Rogers, C. (1951). *On becoming a person. A therapist's view of psychotherapy*. Houghton Mifflin.

Thomas, V. (2016). *Using mental imagery in counselling and psychotherapy: A guide to more inclusive theory and practice*. Routledge.

Chapter 7

The experience of listening to music in coaching

Andrea Giraldez-Hayes

Introduction

Within the coaching realm, using music as a tool for personal advancement has garnered less attention than other art forms. Having been a professional musician myself for many years, and even though I turned my career into psychology, coaching, and psychotherapy, I've always been interested in the impact of music on our emotions, thoughts, and behaviours. Therefore, when the opportunity came, I thoroughly considered how sound and music could help my coaching and supervision clients.

This chapter delves into the significance of music within the coaching context, focusing on its relevance for clients and coaches and drawing on years of research on music therapy and the use of music in psychotherapy, as well as the exploration of the experience of music listening in fields such as psychology, anthropology, neuroscience, sociology or education. The chapter addresses coaches who have previously hesitated to incorporate coach or client-selected music into their sessions and aims to underscore the need for further research into the role of music in coaching.

Music: A universal feature of human experience

From the earliest days of human history, music has been a unifying force, bringing people together to express themselves through sound and dance, to find solace or excitement. For most human beings, music permeates their existence, shaping emotions, thoughts, and behaviours in everyday life. This shared affection for music, termed *musicophilia* (Sacks, 2018), forms a universal connection among all individuals. *Musicophilia*, as described by Sacks, represents the inherent inclination to create and enjoy music across diverse cultures and within each person, except for those afflicted with conditions like amusia or the rare cases of individuals who, while not experiencing any auditory impairment, do not derive pleasure from music, being notable figures Charles Darwin or Sigmund Freud.

DOI: 10.4324/9781003453437-8

We can assert that music is a universal feature of human experience, but despite popular belief, it is not a universal language. Therefore, it is essential to note that some musical forms can be unfamiliar or not even recognisable as music to individuals from different cultures. For example, gamelan music can make sense to Indonesian people, and although people from other cultures may enjoy it, it can make no sense to most. Nevertheless, despite its cultural features, all music can evoke or influence listeners' emotions and convey narratives regardless of the spoken language (Hunter & Schellenberg, 2010; Juslin & Sloboda, 2011).

Music, emotions, and memories

Music plays a significant role in people's daily lives. Whether actively selected for activities like walking or cooking or encountered passively through various media channels like radio, TV, or background ambience in public spaces, its impact can be profound. Many of us have experienced the immediate mood uplift upon hearing a favourite song, been moved to dance, relax, contemplate, shed tears by a particular piece of music, or travelled back to the past when listening to a piece of music related to a past experience, feeling as if we were there. As a matter of fact, many of us harbour memories connected to certain songs, whether tied to particular events, periods or times, individuals, or locations, and these memories often significantly influence our emotional response to a song (Belfi et al., 2016).

We have already pointed out that music is not a universal language; however, the emotional factor is transcultural. Music could not penetrate the hearts of so many people in different cultures unless a basic human disposition transcends cultural boundaries. Psychologists have made several attempts to measure and develop strategies to understand how music generates emotions (Zentner et al., 2008; Mohn, Argstatter & Wilker, 2011). As a result of these attempts, we know emotions are susceptible to being significantly affected by music. Music can also affect mood and behaviour due to its influence on emotions. North and Hargreaves (2008) suggest that when an individual selects a piece of music, it tends to cover specific needs, in general, of an emotional nature, in such a way that if the individual wants to elevate their mood, they will select music that causes serenity, security or joy. If they try to empower themselves physically, they will choose music that motivates and maximises the execution of movements. On the other hand, a recent study (Yoon et al., 2020) suggests that depressed people tend to choose sad music, not actively trying to maintain their negative emotions but rather to find solace and even upliftment.

From a social perspective, music also has a fundamental role. The effects of music, especially when it is chosen, in addition to producing mood changes, generate social ties. These links often have a neurobiological correspondence to love and brotherhood, common feelings among human beings (Panksepp & Bernatzky, 2002).

Research has also shown the profound relationship between music and memory, elucidating how listening to music can evoke vivid recollections. A seminal study by Janata et al. (2007) explored the neural mechanisms underlying music-evoked autobiographical memories (MEAMs). The findings revealed that short musical fragments of popular music are potent triggers for recalling autobiographical memories, ranging from broad recollections of life stages to precise memories of particular events. This and other studies (e.g., Pickering, 2018) underscore how music listening is a potent catalyst for memory retrieval, offering insights into the intricate interplay between music, emotion, and autobiographical memory.

In conclusion, music's significance in daily life undeniably impacts mood, behaviour, and social connections. While not a universal language, its emotional resonance transcends cultural boundaries. Moreover, the profound relationship between music and memory is evident, with studies revealing its ability to evoke vivid recollections. Ultimately, the power of music lies in its multifaceted role in human experience and, as such, has been used in interventions such as therapy and coaching.

Listening to music in therapy and coaching

The use of music, and more specifically, music listening in coaching, is still an unexplored territory. Besides a handful number of research studies (Turner, 2020; McManus & Giraldez Hayes, 2021; Klyk et al., 2022; Wilcox & Nethercott, 2024) and some practical experiences shared by coaches in webinars, short articles, and conferences, our primary source of knowledge remains limited to a considerable body of research produced in the realm of music therapy, where the therapeutic value of sound and music has long been recognised for its ability to address a wide range of emotional and psychological states. Music therapy sessions can involve various activities, including playing instruments, singing, listening, or creating music.

This chapter focuses on music listening in coaching, a technique that aims to create rapport; facilitate visualisations; help the client explore emotions; develop insights; have somatic experiences; activate memories, creative thinking, processing, and problem-solving; or raise self-awareness and awareness of others to enhance their life experience, performance, self-directed learning, and personal growth (Grant, 2001).

My insights and experiences are based on music therapy (Wheeler, 2015; Edwards, 2016; Molino, 2023), Guided Imagery and Music – the Bonny Method (Hall et al., 2006; Ventre & McKinney 2015) and music listening in psychotherapy (Butterton, 2016) as three related but different methodologies that have in common the shared experience of listening to music with another human being and, eventually, helping the client become conscious of the use and impact of music on their everyday lives. Two approaches have been used when listening to music in therapy and coaching: in the first one, the therapist selects the music, and in the second one, the client chooses it. Of course, a combination of both is also a possibility.

Music listening in coaching: From theory to practice

Before delving into the practicalities of using music listening in coaching, it is crucial to clarify that, as an academic and practitioner, my practice is evidence-based and informed by my broader professional identity as a musician, community arts practitioner, psychologist, coach, psychotherapist, and supervisor. As a coaching psychologist, I am responsible for structuring each session and ensuring the safe introduction of any elements brought into our work to deepen or enhance the client's ability to reflect, learn, and grow. However, using music during the coaching psychology and supervision sessions is not an imposition but an invitation informed by ethical considerations. Ultimately, the client is entitled to accept (or not) the invitation to use music in our sessions and to co-create the interventions if needed. Before incorporating music into coaching sessions, coaches should obtain informed consent from clients and ensure they feel comfortable with the proposed interventions. Sensitivity should be exercised when exploring potentially triggering material, and clients should always have the option to opt out of music-based activities. As coaches, we must adhere to ethical guidelines when using music, respecting client autonomy, confidentiality, and boundaries. Any personal information shared in relation to music should be treated with the same confidentiality as other aspects of the coaching relationship. Additionally, coaches should be mindful of the potential for music to evoke intense emotions or memories and be prepared to provide appropriate support and follow-up as needed. A background in psychology, mental health, and/or counselling, specific training to manage challenging situations, and working with a supervisor are highly recommended.

What follows is a concise compilation of techniques I have used during coaching and supervision sessions with clients, which have positively impacted their engagement and understanding of themselves, their aspirations, and their challenges. This compilation is not exhaustive nor dictates how music should be used. Instead, these strategies serve as a foundation open to interpretation and innovation by the coach, tailored to the client's unique circumstances and environment.

Grounding music listening at the beginning of a coaching or a supervision session

Beginning a coaching or supervision session with a moment of centring and grounding can help bring both the coach/supervisor and the client into a present and attentive state of mind, fostering positive energy before engaging with the session's content. Some coaches use relaxation, breathing, or mindfulness techniques, and music can be used for the same purpose.

In preparation for the intervention, the coach can invite the client to close their eyes if that feels comfortable, take a deep breath, and gently release, letting go of any tension, thoughts, and worries and allowing themselves to be fully present at this moment. When the music starts playing, the coach will remain silent. Once the music has ceased, the coach will invite the client to bring their awareness back to the present moment slowly.

Following the relaxation exercise, the coach will lead a conversation (verbal processing) to delve into and comprehend the client's experience. Since it is impossible to discern precisely what the individual is thinking or feeling during relaxation, verbal processing is crucial. The coach can prompt a conversation, such as, "Now, let's take some time to comment on how that experience was for you. … How did the relaxation feel?" It's essential to create space for positive and negative responses. Some clients, particularly those new to relaxation, may feel uncomfortable initially. Negative feedback may arise if the client has been distracted by intrusive thoughts or mentally compiling to-do lists. In each scenario, the coach should listen attentively and reinforce the notion that consistent practice is critical for relaxation to become truly beneficial.

When selecting music for relaxation, it is essential to consider the numerous available options. The most impactful choice is music that aligns with the client's preferences in terms of genre and style. Although the coach can choose the music, considering other factors such as the client's age, energy level, and mood, research suggests combining music and relaxation is most effective when the individual chooses the music (Saperston, 1999). Therefore, another option is to discuss the client's preference before or during the first session, ask them to suggest one or more pieces of music, and play them at the beginning of each session.

Brief centring exercises used during the session can also be beneficial. These moments can precede discussions on challenging topics, serve as interludes between subjects, or disrupt unproductive thought patterns when the client expresses fear or anxiety.

What if you change the soundtrack?

What is the soundtrack of your life? How can a piece of music change your emotional state? Have you ever considered how the same scene in a movie could have a different meaning depending on the accompanying music?

As coaches, we ask meaningful questions and use metaphors (Sullivan, 2008; Thompson, 2021) with our clients, but we can also use soundtracks, a valuable resource for exploring emotions, meaning-making, and perspective.

We could use this exercise during a coaching session when a client brings up an issue that bothered them (adapted from Ready & Burton, 2015). For example, it can be used after the client describes a challenging situation they experienced at work, and they cannot take it off their mind.

We can ask the client to imagine the problem situation in which they felt disappointed and uncomfortable as a movie scene and "watch" it in their mind. Once the scene has finished, we ask the client to rate it using a worry scale of 1 to 10 and note the score.

Then, we can ask the client to choose three pieces of music of different styles. For example, one that matches the emotion they have experienced while living the described situation and contemplating the movie, another that is neutral, and one that does not match the emotions. They could choose, for example, *Deformative* (Black Eyes), *Gymnopédie 1* (Eric Satie), and a light and cheerful piece, such as circus or cartoon music (some clients may prefer dancing music, while others may choose opera excerpts such as the finale of *William Tell Overture*, used in *The Lone Ranger* movie). If the client does not want or does not know what music to select, the coach can suggest three options.

Once the music is selected, we play the first piece loudly while the client "watches" the movie scene in their mind. Once the scene with its accompanying soundtrack has finished, we ask the client to rate their thoughts using the same 1 to 10 scale and note how they now see and feel about the issue. We repeat the same exercise with the other two music excerpts. Finally, we ask the client to rewind the movie and project it again without music, noticing how they feel. Have the emotions changed?

In many cases, the challenging event becomes ridiculous or funny. In others, the effect of negative emotions is diminished or at least neutralised. If the resulting emotions are still unsatisfactory, we can try other musical excerpts combined with the same scene until the client finds the one that gives the best result.

As suggested in this chapter, listening to music can regulate our emotional state (Thoma et al., 2012; Moore, 2013) and help shift moods and energy levels (DeNora, 1999). Different types of music can energise us, calm us down, boost our mood, or help us process difficult emotions.

Using self-selected music

In many music therapy and coaching activities, the professional selects the music. However, some experiences intentionally allow the client to choose their own music. That is the case, for example, of Butterton's (2016) in psychotherapy or Wilcox and Nethercott's (2024) in coaching.

The coach can use different options, including the use of playlists, to help the client engage with self-selected music. For example, the coach can suggest the client complete *The River of Life* exercise (Mercer, 2008; Prasko et al., 2024; see the On Being Project, 2018, for a detailed step-by-step description), a tool designed to help them reflect on their lived experience. Although coaches usually assume that coaching is present and future-oriented (Grant, 2001), different authors, including Giraldez Hayes (2021) and Biswas-Diener (2023), have challenged this idea, not to deny that coaching is present and future-oriented but to recognise the client is the result of their pasts experiences and can learn from them. Even answering simple questions such as, "Tell me about yourself", or "What are you most proud about in your life?" will take the client to review their past experiences, and *The River of Life* is a helpful tool to engage in reflection.

The exercise is structured into five steps:

1 **Reflect**. An invitation for the client to reflect on the course of their lives using the river as a metaphor.
2 **Frame**. Label the approximate dates and identify key events.
3 **Guide**. Consider the people who have accompanied the client through their journey.
4 **Contextualise**. Identify life events in the environment, such as times of significant happiness or suffering, and what is happening in the world.
5 **Evaluate**. The client will note what values, commitments, causes, or principles were most important to them at a given point in their lives and towards what goals, if any, their primary energies were directed, or, metaphorically speaking, what purposes and ends helped to shape the flow of life waters at a given time in their experience.

The River of Life can be complemented by inviting the client to create a playlist that can be used to explore the client's relationship with music throughout their life. It involves adding significant musical experiences, memories, and songs to the timeline or graph created for the exercise. The process of creating this playlist serves several purposes in coaching, including a **life review** that allows the client to reflect on their life journey through the lens of music, recalling meaningful events, people, and contexts associated with specific songs, genres, or musical experiences. This can promote self-awareness, reminiscence, and emotional processing; **identity exploration**, helping the client to explore how their musical preferences, experiences, and associations have influenced their sense of self and identity over time; **emotional expression**, by revisiting significant musical memories, clients can access and process associated emotions, both positive and negative, in a safe coaching environment; and **rapport building** as the process of creating a music history encourages open communication and rapport between the coach and the client.

The information gathered from the playlist can inform the development of individualised music interventions in coaching and help the coach understand the client's musical preferences, abilities, and associations, allowing for more personalised and meaningful coaching experiences.

Another option is inviting the client to create personalised music playlists that can be a practical resource to help them achieve specific goals, including emotion regulation, stress management, increasing motivation, or improving focus. The coach can help the client set specific goals or desired outcomes related to using the playlists, develop a system to track progress, and evaluate the effectiveness of the intervention. The music playlists can also be integrated with other coaching techniques or interventions, such as lyric analysis, uplifting, or music-assisted relaxation. Creating personalised music playlists should be a collaborative process between the coach and the client. Respecting the client's preferences, cultural background, and individual experiences with music is essential. The client and the coach will regularly review and update the playlists as needed to ensure they remain relevant and effective in supporting the client's goals.

Some of the pieces included in the playlists can also be used during the coaching sessions. For example, the client can choose a song or instrumental piece related to the topic they want to discuss during the session. The coach and client will listen to the piece at the beginning of the session, and the coach will ask questions such as why they chose that specific music, how it connects to the topic, and how it makes them feel. The music and the thoughts and emotions it triggers can also be part of the conversation during the session, with reference to their rhythm, style, texture, melody, harmony, etc., and the relationship between these elements and what is being discussed during the session.

Client playlists can serve as valuable resources in coaching. By exploring the music that holds significance to the client—whether through memories, emotions, or life events – coaches can gain deeper insights into their clients' experiences, values, and preferences. This exploration provides a foundation for effectively incorporating music into coaching sessions, tailoring interventions to resonate with the client's journey.

Music as metaphor: Lead like a great conductor

The works of orchestra conductors such as Itay Talgam or Charles Hazlewood go beyond music listening and can allow the use of the orchestra as a metaphor when working with leaders in coaching. The coach can invite the client to watch the videos before engaging in discussions about leadership styles, empowering team members, and working in partnership. With one of my clients, I found it helpful to watch during the session the fragments in Talgam's video, *Lead Like the Great Conductor* (see "Suggested Resources" at the end of this chapter), in which he shows and analyses different orchestra conductor styles. That was an opportunity to reflect on who the client was as a leader and what kind of leader he wanted to become. We also discussed the roles of different team members (for example, the client noticed string players play most of the time, while percussionists may have short but essential interventions, the pace of different musical pieces compared to the pace at work, or how the leader needs to communicate and motivate the team towards achieving their vision and bring all together to focus towards one direction and a shared goal).

Case study

Katherine was a trainee executive coach who practised for over six months. While she had excellent training, she sometimes struggled to find a balance between following a structured coaching process and being flexible enough to adapt to each unique client's circumstances.

Katherine came to Sarah, an expert coaching psychologist supervisor, looking for guidance on developing greater fluidity and responsiveness in her coaching approach without veering too far from proven methodologies.

In their first supervision session, Sarah noticed that Katherine was logical and analytical when describing her coaching style and techniques. He sensed she could benefit from exploring concepts like presence, intuition, spontaneity, and trust from a different angle.

Sarah was aware of the literature and discussions about improvisation in coaching and its parallels with jazz (Read, 2013; Read, 2014). Therefore, for their following session, Sarah invited Katherine to meet her in a lounge where live jazz musicians performed. As the quartet played, Sarah asked Katherine to be present with the music – noticing how it continually reformed and adapted at the moment through the musicians' improvisation while still adhering to a foundational structure.

Sarah then brought in the analogy of how masterful jazz musicians needed to deeply know and internalise music theory, harmony, rhythm, and shared concepts – the "rules" of music. However, true creative mastery was how they spontaneously co-created, riffed off one another, and took turns at the forefront while keeping the overall groove cohesive.

Sarah asked Katherine to reflect on how the experience of immersive jazz listening might translate to the mindset needed for expert coaching. Like musicians, coaches must intimately know the core theories, frameworks, and skills that provide the basis for their craft. Yet, they must also release a strict attachment to "the rules" to be fully present, spontaneous, and tuned to each unique client session's live, unfolding experience.

Over the following weeks, Sarah invited Katherine to engage in some jazz listening exercises – noticing how improvised elements wove together and making shifts felt coherent rather than disjointed. Sarah also shared insights about how the most skilled musicians did not showboat or play in a vacuum but contributed to the united, ever-evolving sound.

Sarah also selected a series of jazz duets, such as the ones played by singers Ella Fitzgerald and Duke Ellington during the 1940s, to bring examples of two people playing instead of a whole band. As Turner (2023) has noticed, jazz duets help illustrate clearly listening and working around each other more intuitively.

For one practice experience, Sarah invited Katherine to journal after each jazz piece, exploring how the emergent group dynamic modelled the needed attunement between coach and client to create authentic forward momentum.

Gradually, the immersive jazz experiences allowed Katherine to viscerally experience and embody how to fuse core methodologies and philosophies with an improvisational mindset of following the client's lead moment by moment. Like the most gifted jazz artists, she gained trust in spontaneously co-creating the journey while providing a grounded, cohesive direction when needed.

In subsequent coaching sessions, Katherine was able to apply these insights – honouring clients by meeting them wherever they were while still providing the needed underlying expertise, structure, and foundational "coaching – music theory" to facilitate transformative growth.

Through the powerful metaphor of jazz improvisation and deep listening, Sarah helped her coach supervisee evolve her coaching mastery to a new level of attunement, responsiveness, and present-focused partnership with her clients.

Conclusion

The integration of music into coaching offers a rich and versatile approach to supporting clients in their personal growth and transformation. Music listening can help clients access new dimensions of self-awareness, creativity, and emotional expression. Coaches can facilitate profound insights and lasting change in their clients' lives by harnessing the power of music alongside techniques from music therapy and music listening in psychotherapy techniques. As coaching continues to evolve, the role of music as a coaching tool is poised to become increasingly recognised and valued in the pursuit of holistic well-being and personal development.

Discussion points

- Should music be considered an essential tool in a coach's repertoire, or is it a supplementary approach that may only be applicable or impactful for some clients?
- Given music's subjective nature and its potential to elicit strong emotional responses, how can coaches ensure that the use of music in sessions is appropriate, ethical, and aligns with the client's cultural, personal, and therapeutic needs?
- While the chapter draws upon research from fields like music therapy and psychology, there is limited empirical evidence specifically examining the efficacy of using music in coaching. Should coaches exercise caution in adopting music-based interventions until more rigorous research is conducted in the coaching context?

Suggested resources

Itay Talgam. *Leading as the great conductors*. https://www.ted.com/talks/itay_talgam_
lead_like_the_great_conductors?language=en
Charles Hazlewood. *Trusting the ensemble*. https://www.ted.com/talks/charles_
hazlewood_trusting_the_ensemble?language=en

References

Belfi, A. M., Karlan, B., & Tranel, D. (2016). Music evokes vivid autobiographical
memories. *Memory*, *24*(7), 979–989.
Biswas-Diener, R. (2023). *Positive provocation: 25 questions to elevate your coaching
practice*. Berret Koehler.
Butterton, M. (2016). *Listening to music in psychotherapy*. CRC Press
DeNora, T. (1999). Music as a technology of the self. *Poetics*, *27*(1), 31–56.
Edwards, J. (Ed.). (2016). *The Oxford handbook of music therapy*. Oxford University
Press.
Giraldez Hayes, A. (2021). Different domains or grey areas? Setting boundaries between
coaching and therapy: A thematic analysis. *The Coaching Psychologist*, *17*(2),
18–29.
Grant, A. M. (2001). *Towards a psychology of coaching*. Unpublished manuscript,
Sydney. Available in https://www.researchgate.net/profile/Anthony-Grant-4/publication/
228598134_Towards_a_psychology_of_coaching/links/54c81fa70cf238bb7d0d9949/
Towards-a-psychology-of-coaching.pdf
Hall, E., Hall, C., Stradling, P., & Young, D. (2006). *Guided imagery: Creative interven-
tions in counselling & psychotherapy*. Sage.
Hunter, P. G., & Schellenberg, E. G. (2010). Music and Emotion. In: M. Riess Jones, R.
Fay & A. Popper (eds.), *Music perception. Springer handbook of auditory research* (pp.
129–146). Springer. https://doi.org/10.1007/978-1-4419-6114-3_5
Klyk, K. L., Palmer, S., & Zimmermann, T. (2022). Dancing and coaching psychology:
The impact of rhythmic movement or music on the effectiveness of a single peer
coaching session. *International Journal of Coaching Psychology*, *3*(2), 1–12.
Janata, P., Tomic, S. T., & Rakowski, S. K. (2007). Characterisation of music-evoked
autobiographical memories. *Memory*, *15*(8), 845–860.
Juslin, P. N., & Sloboda, J. (2011). *Handbook of music and emotion: Theory, research,
applications*. Oxford University Press.
McManus, B. C., & Giraldez Hayes, A. (2021). Exploring the experience of using music
and creative mark-making as a reflective tool during coaching supervision: An
Interpretative Phenomenological Analysis. *Philosophy of Coaching: An International
Journal*, *6*(2), 22–46.
Mercer, J. (2008). *GirlTalk/GodTalk: Why faith matters to teenage girls—And their par-
ents*. John Wiley & Sons.
Mohn, C., Argstatter, H., & Wilker, F. W. (2011). Perception of six basic emotions in
music. *Psychology of Music*, *39*(4), 503–517.
Molino, A. (2023). *Music therapy: A look into the world of healing sound*. Dorrance
Publishing.
Moore, K. S. (2013). A systematic review on the neural effects of music on emotion
regulation: Implications for music therapy practice. *Journal of Music Therapy*, *50*(3),
198–242.

North, A. & Hargreaves, D. (2008). *The social and applied psychology of music*. Oxford University Press.

Panksepp, J., & Bernatzky, G. (2002). Emotional sounds and the brain: The neuro-affective foundations of musical appreciation. *Behavioural processes, 60*(2), 133–155.

Pickering, M. (2018). Popular music and the memory spectrum. In S. Backer et al. (eds.), *The Routledge companion to popular music history and heritage* (pp. 191–198). Routledge.

Prasko, J., Ociskova, M., Burkauskas, J., Vanek, J., Krone, I., Gecaite-Stonciene, J., ... & Juskiene, A. (2024). The river of life method in a schema therapy groups. *Neuroendocrinology Letters, 45*(1).

Read, M. J. (2013). The importance of improvisation in coaching. *Coaching: An International Journal of Theory, Research and Practice, 6*(1), 47–56.

Read, M. J. (2014). What coaches can learn from the history of jazz-based improvisation: A conceptual analysis. *International Journal of Evidence-Based Coaching and Mentoring, 12*(2), 10–23.

Ready, R., & Burton, K. (2015). *Neuro-linguistic programming for dummies*. John Wiley & Sons.

Sacks, O. (2018). *Musicophilia: Tales of music and the brain*. Picador.

Saperston, B. (1999). Music-based individualised relaxation training in medical settings. In *Music therapy and medicine. Silver Spring: American music therapy association* (pp. 41–52).

Sullivan, W. (2008). *Clean language: Revealing metaphors and opening minds*. Crown House Publishing.

The On Being Project. (2018). *The river of life*. Retrieved from https://onbeing.org/wp-content/uploads/2019/05/on-being-river-of-life-exercise.pdf

Thoma, M. V., Ryf, S., Mohiyeddini, C., Ehlert, U., & Nater, U. M. (2012). Emotion regulation through listening to music in everyday situations. *Cognition & Emotion, 26*(3), 550–560.

Thompson, R. (2021). Coaching and mentoring with metaphor. *International Journal of Evidence-Based Coaching and Mentoring, S15*, 212–228.

Turner, A. F. (2020). Coaching and 'all that jazz'. *Coaching Psychologist, 16*(1).

Turner, A. (2023). *The theory and practice of creative coaching: Analysis and methods*. Anthem Press.

Ventre, M., & McKinney, C. H. (2015). The Bonny method of guided imagery and music. In B. L. Wheeler (ed.), *Music therapy handbook* (pp. 96–105). Guildford Publication.

Wheeler, B. L. (Ed.). (2015). *Music therapy handbook*. Guilford Publications.

Wilcox, D. & Nethercott, K. (2024). Coachees' experiences of integrating a self-selected soundtrack into a one-off coaching session. *International Journal of Evidence-Based Coaching and Mentoring, 22*(1), pp. 51–67. 10.24384/bwa7-sn95

Yoon, S., et al. (2020). Why do depressed people prefer sad music? *Emotion, 20*(4), 613–624. https://doi.org/10.1037/emo0000573

Zentner, M., Grandjean, D., & Scherer, K. R. (2008). Emotions evoked by the sound of music: Characterisation, classification, and measurement. *Emotion, 8*(4), 494.

Chapter 8

Coaching in art galleries and public buildings

Strategies for enhancing reflection

Beth McManus

Introduction

When I first trained as a coach, my vision of the perfect physical coaching space was akin to most TV and film depictions of the therapy room: calm, neutral, comfortable chairs or sofas facing each other, some plants, perhaps a deliberately ambiguous framed print or two. Undoubtedly, my mind's eye created a quiet, uninterrupted, and confidential space, and definitely not the complex, fluid, and shared environment of a public building.

Taking coaching outside of the 'inoffensive room' I described is certainly not a novel idea, with many coaches working virtually from the backdrops of their home environment and a rise in coaching outdoors. You may have used art galleries or other public buildings for your own reflective practice or indeed migrated your coaching and supervision with clients into such spaces. The title of this chapter alone might inspire the opportunity to replace popular tools, such as digital photographs and coaching cards, with framed paintings or other artefacts: these spaces can certainly contain rich and varied inspiration for dialogue.

But what if we considered the richness that the *space itself* has to offer to the coaching process rather than limiting its provision to its contents? This chapter encourages you to go beyond the more transactional use of creative artefacts as 'prompts' and use creativity as a *lens* or perspective through which to view the entire session. What if the space could become the coach?

Theory, basic concepts, and key developments

My initial research into the relationship between creativity and reflective practice (McManus & Giraldez-Hayes, 2021) was inspired by artist Naomi Kendrick's "Mindful Marks" session at *The Mindful Living Show* in 2018, where attendees were invited to put on headphones and make marks to music on giant rolls of paper. Whilst I didn't encounter this idea in a gallery setting, these sessions usually took place at Manchester Art Gallery as part of their *Mindful Museum* programme (Manchester Art Gallery, 2021). Through this

DOI: 10.4324/9781003453437-9

practice, I developed an interest in using creativity and creative spaces as an interlude, a pause for the client to indulge in internal reflection before returning to dialogue with their coach or supervisor.

Creativity is well-documented as a portal to surfacing our unconscious (e.g., Ritter et al., 2012), and an adaptation of Fuster's (2013) work, seeing creativity as a *memory of the future*, is central to much of my current thinking. The notion of pausing in a coaching or supervision session (and specifically in a gallery space) to support clients in mindful reflection is an evolution of the work of Kendrick and others using creative, public spaces for well-being and mindfulness outcomes.

Magsamen and Ross's (2023) book *Your Brain on Art* builds on the growing neuroscience of the role of arts for well-being and further positions humans as both *makers* and *beholders* of art. In a gallery setting, it would be easy to conclude that visitors are simply looking, but most of what we 'see' when we look at art is guided by our idiosyncratic experiences: our memories, reasoning, and emotions (Fineberg & Milliken, 2015). We are meaning-making as we observe and interpret each artefact, noticing where our attention is drawn and dismissing objects and spaces where it is not. We pass subconscious judgements on the curation and design of each space, each artist, and other people in the room. As a positive psychology coach and supervisor, well-being is a key facet of my practice, both as a lens through which I view the context presented to me and as an outcome for those I'm working with. As an artist, I am curious about the multiple roles the observer plays in engaging with my work or choosing not to. Both themes extend into the potential of public buildings as both environments for coaching and as substitute coaches.

Much of the emergent literature in arts-based learning speaks of bringing 'arts' into traditional educational (e.g., Vicars & Senior, 2013) or organisational settings (e.g., Meltzer & Schwencke, 2020), but what about bringing the practice, in this case coaching, to the arts space? There is limited literature about coaching in public buildings, with the main focus on coaching employees *of* such institutions (e.g., Metz, 2010). Anecdotally, several coaches have mentioned their use of art galleries as reflective spaces in their own development; however, the literature specifically on coaching or coach development in these environments is scant. One pioneering researcher I would like to acknowledge on this topic is Lorna Mills, whose research on mortality awareness in museums (Mills & Lomas, 2021) validated my initial thinking on these spaces as coaching environments and inspired me to keep going with my own experimentations in public buildings.

There are documented links between museums and art galleries and public health interventions (Camic & Chatterjee, 2013), well-being outcomes (Binnie, 2013; Chatterjee & Camic, 2015; Fears, 2011; Thomson & Chatterjee, 2015), and human flourishing (Cotter & Pawelski, 2021), with further literature linking art more broadly to positive outcomes (Lomas, 2016; see also Shim et al., 2021). There are also innovative learning practices originating in cultural spaces displaying wider learning benefits, such as *slow looking* (Tishman, 2017) and the broader 'Museum Learning' movement (Group for Education in Museums, 2023; see also Anderson, 1999; Museums Association, 2020). Museums have a long history as learning spaces beyond their contents: for example, as places for corporate training (Causey, 2011) and education (Andre et al., 2017), where links to well-being outcomes are, again, strong (Blake, 2022) but not (yet) as coaching spaces. It is my hope that this chapter invites others to consider the potential that art galleries and public buildings represent in the same way that nature has been adopted as an atypical coaching environment and, indeed, for the research on the use of these creative spaces to build in the way it has alongside the surge in coaching practice taking place outdoors (Burns & Passmore, 2022; see also Ivaldi, 2023; Turner, 2022).

Whilst there is research that speaks to the *theoretical* coaching space (e.g., Louis & Fatien Diochon, 2018), there is little that speaks to the *physical* environment for coaching indoors. The Global Code of Ethics for Coaches, Mentors, and Supervisors (2021) mentions the 'setting' of where coaching takes place, suggesting it must offer "optimal conditions for learning and reflection" (p. 4). It does not, however, specify that this setting must be private or neutral. Ioannides (2016) suggests the potential use of museums as therapeutic environments, drawing on a report by Dodd and Jones (2014) that suggested individuals engaging with a museum environment could enhance biological, social, *and* psychological aspects of the self. For me, this provides the perfect backdrop for deeply reflective work to take place.

Practice

It feels important, before divulging my process, to explain that my identity as a coach, my coaching practice, and ongoing research in the field are all firmly rooted in my broader professional identity as a psychologist. I adopt a scientist-practitioner perspective on my coaching practice, viewing coaching as bringing scientific inquiry into work with nonclinical populations in the pursuit of enhanced well-being and performance (Passmore & Lai, 2020). Psychological practice underpins my view of working with creative processes and informs the framework from which I build my experimental practice – some of which is documented in this chapter.

As part of my personal philosophy of coaching and supervision, it is my belief that whilst the client retains ownership of, and agency within, their session, I *always* retain accountability for the structure of each session and for the safe introduction of anything brought inside the container of our work in service of deepening or enhancing the client's ability to reflect, be that a tool, invitation, or question. In line with van Nieuwerburgh (2016), I believe my role includes supporting the creation of a safe and reflective space where the client must take responsibility to make courageous choices; this last point becomes particularly salient when working in an unpredictable and shared environment.

It is therefore my view that working with creativity and arts-based methodologies in coaching and supervision requires a thorough exploration of any proposed practice through the dual lens of ethical practice and client safety before client work can commence. Live observations and necessary adjustments also need to be made throughout any coaching or supervision sessions due to the complex nature of the environment. I would encourage you to formulate a unique version of working in galleries in alignment with your experience, practice, and philosophy of coaching. The Global Code of Ethics, to which I adhere, states that each member must "operate within the limit of their professional competence" (p. 9). I would further advocate that, where possible, coaches seek to explore any new methodologies or ways of working in their own practice – e.g., in self-reflection or their own supervision – before taking them into client work. In working in public spaces and buildings, there is ample opportunity for the practitioner to use their intended space for personal reflective practice, exploring the concept alone to find its edges and its potential.

The following outline and case study are the result of several pilot coaching sessions which took place between 2022 and 2023. I owe a debt of gratitude to each of the clients who volunteered to take part in this experimental work and who have inspired my ongoing thinking in this area. In line with my personal values, whilst entry to these spaces was free, I always made a donation to the gallery for each session and invited my clients to do the same if they could and felt it would be appropriate. I am also a *friend* of both Manchester Art Gallery and The Whitworth: it may be worth exploring similar membership schemes at your local institutions and considering a donation as a thank you to the space.

The process outlined here is a mirror of my earlier research (McManus & Giraldez-Hayes, 2021) using time alone in the art gallery in place of a music and mark-making exercise in an online session. The basic format of the sessions I have been experimenting with is as follows: The coach and client meet outside the front of the gallery and enter the building together. The work takes place in three parts:

- The first space is identified, usually somewhere with seating, and the coach spends some time contracting the session before exploring the client's topic for around 15–20 minutes. The aim of this section is to get the client to a single question or sentence that they would like to think about for the next part of their session.
- The coach then invites the client to spend a further 15–20 minutes in part of the gallery, with clear positioning of the decision to stay in this space, to wander elsewhere, to sit, stand, talk, remain in silence, etc., all remaining with the client. The coach should ideally leave the space and, if possible, the building. I have found the gift shop or café as welcome alternatives to mitigate Manchester's rain.

- Finally, the coach returns to an agreed meeting point where the client decides where they would like the remainder of the session to take place. This could be in the room they have just used, looking at a certain artefact, walking around the gallery as a whole, returning to the first space, finding a new space, or a combination.

Unlike some of the other arts-based methodologies outlined in this book, working in a gallery or museum space requires you to meet the client at the building, and so there is a requirement that the use of creativity, and the space, is an upfront part of your contracting. The transient nature of the space, and of exhibitions, means you could work in a gallery one day and return the next to a completely different or potentially closed-off space. It is always worth planning time to scope the gallery in advance of a client session to understand the available spaces.

When I meet new clients, I often use the metaphor of a 'ball of wool' to explain my role as coach: the wool represents the client's 'stuff' and, particularly, their tangled-up bits of stuckness. I explain that I am never going to take the wool from the client, or do any untangling, but I am simply *holding one end* of the wool to enable them to use both hands to untangle their thinking. Exploring working with the gallery space as coach for part of the session is an extension of this metaphor, where I 'pin' the end of the wool to a wall in the gallery, using the space as temporary coach during a short interlude in our shared dialogue.

Clients will likely want to walk you through their experience when you reconvene: in my process, this is optional and they don't have to tell me what they did when I wasn't there. One client remarked, "You chose this space on purpose!" when I returned from the pause due to the sheer volume of works which spoke to them about their question in the particular gallery I had invited them to reflect in. It is *never* my intention to interfere in such a direct way, simply choosing spaces that are relatively quiet at the start of section two. I firmly believe that clients who are open to the process will see what they need to see; in the previous example, this was a lot of stimuli leading to profound revelations, but it could be nothing. An exploration of what's missing or how they know nothing here is 'right' can be an equally fruitful discussion.

A certain level of innocuous intrusion is common during explorations in public galleries, particularly when you are sitting down in dialogue. It is important in my sessions that the client retains agency in deciding whether to continue, pause, stop, or even relocate when intrusions occur; however, as coach, I also retain accountability for the privacy of the discussion and the safety and comfort of the client – these are critical aspects of contracting the session at the very beginning and throughout. Remember that in utilising public spaces for coaching or supervision, you are never in control of the environment, only of the session within it.

Case study

This case study took place at The Whitworth in July 2023. For an outline of the session's flow, see the "Practice" section in this chapter.

The client, Alex (not their real name), came to coaching after having recently changed roles within their organisation, moving from a department where they had spent much of their career to a brand-new position in a completely new department. From the exploration call, their chosen topic was around a feeling of 'stuckness' in their past work, which they felt was preventing them from fully embracing their new role. As we were meeting at 10 a.m., the time the gallery opened, this left no time to scope the space immediately prior to the session. I had instead visited the previous day to make a note of the current exhibits and to consider where our coaching might take place.

We entered the gallery together, making our way to the *Office of Arté Util* – a mixed-use workspace and common room that is free to use for visitors. During this initial conversation, we explored Alex's topic in more detail, generating a metaphor of one foot stuck in the 'mud' of the past, with the other leg trying in vain to move forwards. A family with young children came into the space and lingered whilst we were talking, at one point joining us on the sofas where we sat. Holding my belief that Alex would make any decisions about their comfort to continue, and after a brief pause, we resumed our dialogue until we reached a question which reflected a rock-climbing metaphor Alex had used: "*How can I find stability to avoid feeling like I am hanging on by my fingertips?*" I walked with Alex to a different space in the gallery, an exhibition on the work of Albrecht Dürer.

The gaggle of pupils I had spotted on my walk up to the gallery provided our second obstacle. I witnessed approximately 30 uniformed teenagers walking straight into the quiet space where I had just left Alex. I stopped, considering whether I might turn back and invite Alex to reflect in another space, but remembering our clear contracting and my belief that Alex would make the right choice for themselves about the space they occupied, I made my way to linger in the gift shop for 15 minutes.

Alex did indeed move galleries. When we reconvened, they took me on a short tour to talk me through their wandering, most of which took place in an exhibition entitled *Traces of Displacement*. Upon leaving the Dürer exhibition, Alex's attention had been immediately drawn to some books that lay open in glass cases. It was interesting to note in their reflections that whilst Alex didn't understand the text, they felt they could use the illustrations and the gallery labels to build their understanding of what was written. Furthermore, Alex noted that they could go on to learn the language of the text and fully develop their understanding should they wish. There was a moment of laughter here as Alex realised that the books themselves were a strong symbol of their previous role and the irony that these were the first items that captured their attention when their desire was to look to the future.

Following a further walk around the available spaces, their attention had settled on a painting, *Le Cirque au Cheval Blanc* by Marc Chagall, noting that they found additional comfort in an old favourite, *Man's Head (Self Portrait I)* by Lucian Freud, nearby. The ideas that the books and the paintings generated were helpful starting points for an exploration that we continued on a bench near the café – a space which has a glass wall looking out to the neighbouring park and a distinct absence of artwork. In particular, the themes which we discussed that supported Alex's initial questioning were the following:

• The opportunity to build knowledge, even if you were starting from a very basic understanding (from the books)
• The idea of performance at work (from the Chagall painting)
• The relief of finding something familiar back on display, but noticing that it had never really left; it was just 'in storage' (from the Freud painting)

This last exploration led to the broader idea of 'curating' one's knowledge and experience, choosing what was on display and what remained in the archives for future reference. The reflection that Alex was left with was that they had 'closed the door' on their past knowledge and experience in a bid to 'start afresh' – they had revealed during the session that whilst they had chosen to move on to a new opportunity, the 'ending' of the last role had been painful. In shutting everything away, albeit in a 'glass room' that others could see into but not access, Alex was navigating their new role without the skills and experience they had gained in another context. Considering how to open the door and access this previous experience was a huge shift for Alex in recognising that they had a lot they could bring from their previous work into their new space to support their feelings of sure footing and stability.

Discussion points

• How might you use an art gallery or public building to support your own reflective practice?
• What do you believe public buildings could offer to a coach or supervision space?
• What does your own philosophy of coaching lend in terms of designing your own experimental coaching session in a gallery?
• How might you effectively scope the environment in advance of the coaching session?
• Reflecting on your self-knowledge, how might you be impacted by interruptions and intrusions in the space, and how could you mitigate their impact?

Suggested resources

Bown, C. (2023). *Resources*. Thinking Museum. https://thinkingmuseum.com/visible-thinking-in-the-museum/resources/

References

Anderson, D. (1999). *A common wealth: Museums in the learning age: a report to the Department for Culture, Media and Sport* (2nd ed.). The Stationery Office.

Andre, L., Durksen, T., & Volman, M. L. (2017). Museums as avenues of learning for children: A decade of research. *Learning Environments Research, 20*, 47–76. https://doi.org/10.1007/s10984-016-9222-9

Binnie, J. (2013). Does viewing art in the museum reduce anxiety and improve wellbeing? *Museums & Social Issues, 5*(2), 191–201. https://doi.org/10.1179/msi.2010.5.2.191

Blake, S.-C. (2022). *'Zensation': University Student Wellbeing*. University of Cambridge Museums & Botanic Garden. https://www.museums.cam.ac.uk/blog/2022/11/07/zensation-university-student-wellbeing/

Burns, A. S., & Passmore, J. (2022). Outdoor coaching: The role of attention restoration theory as a framework for explaining the experience and benefit of eco-psychology coaching. *International Coaching Psychology Review, 17*(1), 21–36. https://doi.org/10.53841/bpsicpr.2022.17.1.21

Camic, P. M., & Chatterjee, H. J. (2013). Museums and art galleries as partners for public health interventions. *Perspectives in Public Health, 133*(1), 66–71. https://doi.org/10.1177/1757913912468523

Causey, A. (2011). Corporate training in museums. *Journal of Museum Education, 36*(1), 91–102. https://doi.org/10.1080/10598650.2011.11510687

Chatterjee, H. J. & Camic, P. M. (2015). The health and wellbeing potential of museums and art galleries. *Arts and Health, 7*(3), 183–186. https://doi.org/10.1080/17533015.2015.1065594

Cotter, K. N., & Pawelski, J. O. (2021). Art museums as institutions for human flourishing. *The Journal of Positive Psychology, 17*(2), 288–302. https://doi.org/10.1080/17439760.2021.2016911

Dodd, J., & Jones, C. (2014). Mind, body, spirit: How museums impact health and wellbeing. https://le.ac.uk/-/media/uol/docs/research-centres/rcmg/publications/mbs.pdf

Fears, A. (2011). *The museum as a healing space: Addressing museum visitors' emotional responses through viewing and creating artwork*. [Master's Dissertation, Boston University College of Fine Arts]. Boston University Institutional Repository. https://hdl.handle.net/2144/2419

Fineberg, J. D., & Milliken, J. B. (2015). *Modern art at the border of mind and brain*. University of Nebraska Press

Fuster, J. M. (2013). *The neuroscience of freedom and creativity: Our predictive brain*. Cambridge University Press. https://doi.org/10.1017/CBO9781139226691

Group for Education in Museums. (2023). *GEM is for everyone interested in learning through museums, heritage and cultural settings*. https://gem.org.uk/

Global Code of Ethics. (2021). *Global code of ethics for coaches, mentors, and supervisors* (2016, amended effective May 9, 2018, and July 15, 2021). https://emccdrive.org/Lt09zkFBBdd6FPMpT31q1BzI3UKLmWftZLCbLprM

Ivaldi, A. (2023). Understanding and restoring the self in nature for well-being: A phenomenological analysis of walking coaching experiences. *The Humanistic Psychologist, (pre-publication - 16th Feb 2023)*. https://doi.org/10.1037/hum0000314

Ioannides, E. (2016). Museums as therapeutic environments and the contribution of art therapy. *Museum International, 68*(3–4), 98–109. https://doi.org/10.1111/muse.12125

Lomas, T. (2016). Positive art: Artistic expression and appreciation as an exemplary vehicle for flourishing. *Review of General Psychology*, *20*(2), 171–182. https://doi.org/10.1037/gpr0000073

Louis, D., & Fatien Diochon, P. (2018). The coaching space: A production of power relationships in organizational settings. *Organization*, *25*(6), 710–731. https://doi.org/10.1177/1350508418779653

Magsamen, S., & Ross, I. (2023). *Your brain on art: How the arts transform Us*. Canongate Books Ltd.

Manchester Art Gallery. (2021, January 1). *The mindful museum*. https://manchesterartgallery.org/the-mindful-museum/

McManus, B. C., & Giraldez-Hayes, A. (2021). Exploring the experience of using music and mark-making as a reflective tool during coaching supervision: An Interpretative Phenomenological Analysis. *Philosophy of Coaching: An International Journal*, *6*(2), 22–46. http://doi.org/10.22316/poc/06.2.03

Meltzer, C. & Schwencke, E. (2020). Arts-based learning in vocational education: Using arts-based approaches to enrich vocational pedagogy and didactics and to enhance professional competence and identity. *Journal of Adult and Continuing Education*, *26*(1), 6–24. https://doi.org/10.1177/1477971419846640

Metz, R. F. (2010). *Coaching in the library: A management strategy for achieving excellence*. American Library Association.

Mills, L., & Lomas, T. (2021). Mortality awareness in the context of positive psychology coaching: An interpretative phenomenological analysis of client experience. *The Coaching Psychologist*, *17*(1), 38–47. https://doi.org/10.53841/bpstcp.2021.17.1.38

Museums Association (2020). *A manifesto for museum learning and engagement*. https://www.museumsassociation.org/campaigns/learning-and-engagement/manifesto

Passmore, J., & Lai, Y. L. (2020). Coaching psychology: Exploring definitions and research contributions to practice. In J. Passmore & D. Tee (Eds.), *Coaching researched: A coaching psychology reader for practitioners and researchers* (pp. 3–22). Wiley. https://doi.org/10.1002/9781119656913.ch1

Ritter, S. M., van Baaren, R. B., & Dijksterhuis, A. (2012). Creativity: The role of unconscious processes in idea generation and idea selection. *Thinking Skills and Creativity*, *7*(1), 21–27. https://doi.org/10.1016/j.tsc.2011.12.002

Shim, Y., Jebb, A. T., Tay, L., & Pawelski, J. O. (2021). Arts and humanities interventions for flourishing in healthy adults: A mixed studies systematic review. *Review of General Psychology*, *25*(3), 258–282. https://doi.org/10.1177/10892680211021350

Thomson, L. J. & Chatterjee, H. J. (2015). Measuring the impact of museum activities on well-being: developing the Museum Well-being Measures Toolkit. *Museum Management and Curatorship*, *30*(1), 44–62. https://doi.org/10.1080/09647775.2015.1008390

Turner, A. (2022). Coaching through walking. In D. Tee, & J. Passmore (Eds.) *Coaching practiced* (pp. 363–369). John Wiley & Sons. https://doi.org/10.1002/9781119835714.ch39

Tishman, S. (2017). *Slow looking: The art and practice of learning through observation*. Routledge.

van Nieuwerburgh, C. (2016). Towards a philosophy of coaching? In C. van Nieuwerburgh (Ed.), *Coaching in Professional Contexts* (pp. 249–255). SAGE. https://doi.org/10.4135/9781473922181

Vicars, M., & Senior, K. (2013). Making a visible difference: overcoming barriers using arts-based learning. *Education Action Research*, *21*(1), 59–71. https://doi.org/10.1080/09650792.2013.763410

Chapter 9

From pluralistic sand-tray therapy to sand-tray coaching

Doreen Fleet

Introduction

Sand-tray therapy is a profound method for delving into the intricacies of human emotion and cognition. This chapter embarks on a journey to unravel the essence of sand-tray therapy and its multifaceted applications in coaching.

Sand-tray therapy, facilitated by a trained professional, harnesses the power of a simple tray filled with sand and an array of symbolic objects. From representations of human diversity to abstract entities, these objects serve as conduits for clients to navigate their innermost struggles and complexities. As they sift through the sand, selecting objects that resonate with their experiences, a profound exploration of their emotional landscape unfolds.

Diverse theoretical orientations have embraced sand-tray therapy, each imbuing it with unique perspectives and methodologies. From the pioneering work of Margaret Lowenfeld to the depth psychology of Jungian Sandplay, this chapter delves into the rich tapestry of theoretical frameworks that underpin sand-tray therapy.

Moreover, the chapter navigates the interface between professional therapy and coaching, elucidating the distinctions and overlaps between these modalities and exploring how they empower clients to generate change and foster self-growth. Through collaborative dialogue and goal setting, clients embark on transformative journeys guided by skilled professionals.

Furthermore, this chapter introduces the concept of Pluralistic Sand-Tray Therapy (PSTT) and its adaptation to coaching. By integrating structured sand-tray sessions into coaching frameworks, practitioners offer clients a dynamic space for exploration and reflection.

What is sand-tray therapy?

In sand-tray therapy, the therapist helps the client explore their emotional and psychological distress by using a tray filled with sand and a range of symbolic objects. The therapist needs to have a good range of quality objects available for the client to search through: objects representing human diversity, nature,

DOI: 10.4324/9781003453437-10

animals, religion, and spirituality; manufactured objects (boats, cars, etc.); fearful objects like monsters; and abstract objects (Fleet, 2022, pp. 76–78). It is essential to realise that providing an object for every issue is impossible. Usually, clients searching for a target object will choose an abstract object if they do not find what they are looking for and make it fit (Fleet, 2022).

The powerful medium of sand, combined with the objects representing a client's intrapsychic experience (their inner world), their inter-relational experience, and sometimes their broader cultural and spiritual/religious issues, can bring a powerful experience for the client.

The therapist will sit alongside the client as they engage with the process, and with the sand tray acting as a natural container, the client can explore issues without becoming overwhelmed. It is as if they can take one step out of their pain without losing connection to thought and feeling; they become the observer-experiencer (Fleet et al., 2023b; Fleet, 2022).

Various approaches to sand-tray therapy

Sand-tray therapy has been adopted by various theoretical approaches, with each orientation using the sand-tray in therapy to fit the specific underpinning theory associated with that particular approach. Margaret Lowenfeld is acknowledged as the first therapist to have used sand trays in her work with children and established her World Technique (1979). Lowenfeld argued how this intervention helped the child express their feelings physically when struggling to express their verbal experience. More recently, Jungian Sandplay, named to distinguish it from Lowenfeld's work, identified archetypal content and symbolic processes in sand-tray work (Kalff, 1980). The core message of this approach is to help the client express conflicts still in the unconscious mind.

There is other literature on other orientations, such as person-centred or solution-focused therapy, that use sand trays in therapy. However, this usually focuses on how this intervention is applied rather than explaining the underpinning theory. In addition, other publications tend to focus on sand-tray therapy with children rather than adults.

From my experience as a chartered psychologist, therapist, and researcher using sand-tray with clients, I argue how it can be a powerful and effective way of working with a wide range of clients. My multiple case study research established a pluralistic theoretical framework of sand-tray therapy with adult clients (Fleet, 2019, 2022; Fleet et al., 2023b).

Differences between professional therapy and coaching

Coaching, a helping profession but distinct from professional therapy (psychotherapy, counselling psychology, counselling), is also an approach to promoting mental health and well-being. A primary difference is that professional therapists help clients focus on their childhood experiences to unpack past issues that may be influential to their current emotional and psychological distress, whereas a coach would not. Jordan and Livingstone (2013) stated that in mental health coaching, "[R]eports of past trauma or abuse should be empathetically acknowledged but not explored" (p. 4). Similarly, Hart et al. (2001) stated how "the exploration of depth issues is perceived as outside the boundaries of coaching for non-clinically trained coaches" (p. 230). Forge (2022) stated that "the emphasis is on a forward-looking focus" (p. 23), which occurs more often in coaching than with many therapeutic approaches. Furthermore, dealing with unconscious issues may be a significant feature of professional therapy depending on the theoretical orientation but would not be relevant for coaching (Hart et al., 2001) that focuses on a client's present or future concerns.

Another difference between these two professions is that a therapist often deals with severe mental health issues such as suicidal thoughts, post-traumatic stress disorder (PTSD), or trauma from abuse, in contrast to a coach who would not work with complex clinical problems. Jordan and Livingstone (2013) provide a list for health coaches indicating "a client's underlying condition" that "might be a no-entry zone" (p. 27) when a referral may be in order. For example, a coachee experiencing unresolved and prolonged grief, suicide ideation, and eating disorders would most likely be referred to a professional therapist.

Similarities between the pluralistic therapeutic approach and coaching

A pluralistic therapeutic approach (Cooper & McLeod, 2007) considers the strengths of other orientations as helpful to meeting the client's goals for therapy. Cooper and McLeod (2007) argued how various therapeutic approaches could offer insights into how to work in different ways to help "different clients at different points in time" (Cooper & Dryden, 2016, p. 3). For example, breathing techniques used in cognitive-behavioural therapy (CBT) can help anxious clients manage their anxiety between therapy sessions. Furthermore, after therapy is completed, they have these skills to draw on in the future.

Similarly, mental health coaching also draws on CBT by guiding the coachee on how to adopt breathing techniques when stressed or anxious and, at times, giving homework so that the coachee can develop their skills to manage their mental health.

A further similarity between the pluralistic therapeutic approach and mental health coaching is based on the belief that a client in therapy and a coachee in coaching have the inner resources to bring change. A collaborative process between them and the professional fosters autonomy and self-growth, likely promoting the client's and coachee's mental health.

The pluralistic approach is founded on the understanding that working collaboratively with the client in a shared decision-making process via dialogical conversation is both a "helpful and healing experience in itself" (McLeod, 2018, p. 49). Such turn-taking and sharing of ideas between therapist and client affirm the client's knowledge and experience. McLeod (2018) views this purposeful communication, involving the therapist asking purposeful questions, as 'metacommunication' facilitating a "standing back from the ongoing flow of conversation, reflecting on (or inviting reflection on) the intentions and/or reactions of the speaker and/or listener" (McLeod, 2018, p. 83). This process recognises that the client has a valued contribution, resulting in shared decision-making between therapist and client (McLeod, 2018).

Similarly, Bishop (2018) views the coachee in coaching as having the knowledge and capacity to make desired changes, with the coach empowering them to find their own way as they move towards health and well-being, which is a collaborative process. In coaching, motivational interviewing techniques involving open questions help the coachee explore their obstacles to change (Bishop, 2018). This strategy can be compared to the purposeful questions used in pluralistic therapy to help the client take a reflective approach and engage in more profound discovery.

Goal setting is another process that exists in the pluralistic approach and mental health coaching. McLeod (2018) views goal setting as a flexible term in therapy; the client can have a concrete goal, such as wanting to cope with their panic attacks or an open goal of "I just want to feel happier in my life". Furthermore, a goal hidden in the unconscious may emerge during therapy, so it is necessary to return to goal setting when required to meet the client's needs and expectations.

Goal setting is also a feature of mental health coaching; Bishop (2018) described how the coach would support coachees in drawing upon their strengths and abilities, empowering them to make life changes and work towards their personal goals.

Pluralistic sand-tray therapy and adapting this approach to coaching

In PSTT, different methods and tasks are agreed upon between the therapist and the client depending on their goals and expectations for therapy, which is done by engaging in a purposeful collaborative discussion (McLeod, 2018).

For example, a client may have the goal of managing their panic attacks, and a breathing strategy in line with CBT might be adapted to suit the client. Furthermore, the same client might need to address an issue of unresolved loss, and this would be explored by using the sand tray and symbolic objects.

PSTT helps the client explore and express their inner world experience (including previously unconscious experience beginning to emerge into awareness for processing), personal relationships, and their relation to the wider world. Often, this involves a deep exploration of their past, present, and future concerns.

In PSTT, the sand tray is not simply a therapeutic aid but is more integral to the therapeutic process (Fleet, 2019, 2022; Fleet et al., 2023b). I describe it using a theatre metaphor, the sand tray being the stage where clients can present their experience by using symbolic objects to create a picture in the sand. It is a dynamic space "where the individual strives to understand, perceiving their inner world and external events in their own unique way" (Fleet, 2019, p. 161).

As the client engages with PSTT, a phenomenological shift (Fleet, 2019; Fleet et al., 2023b) can occur regarding the client's inner world perceptions of I think, I feel, I believe, I am. This change often brings a reduction in psychological and emotional distress for the client.

Unstructured and structured sand-tray sessions

The therapist can adjust their approach to help the client begin to engage with the sand tray. For example, some clients will want to take the lead in the very first session, working in an unstructured way. The therapist may guide the client to search through the objects and, once chosen, to place them in the sand.

For example, it may help a client experiencing complicated grief to work in this way to explore their phenomenological experience and emotions.

The objects will likely represent various people in their lives in relation to their loss. In addition, objects can symbolise their thoughts and their emotions, such as sadness, loneliness, and anger. By exploring their grief in this way, with the therapist offering empathy and compassion, the client may reach a stage where they move towards accepting that the deceased person/s is gone, and they can begin to think of a future without them. Telling their story can be therapeutic, and expressing their loss can help them overcome barriers in the grief process (Fleet et al., 2023b).

Although an unstructured approach works well when a client explores their intrapsychic experience, this free-flowing process may be too challenging for some clients needing more guidance. Therefore, the therapist may suggest a more structured way of working.

PSTT has a range of structured approaches (Fleet et al., 2023b) depending on the client and the issue to be focused on. For example, the 'Life Space' (Fleet et al., 2023b) is a structured sand-tray strategy that can be offered to a client who is overwhelmed with so much responsibility that they cannot cope and feel exhausted when caring for others combined with other responsibilities, such as work.

The therapist will ask the client to choose objects representing each responsibility and other things in their life contributing to feeling overwhelmed. Once the client has placed the objects in the sand, they can be guided to draw a space around each object to symbolise how much space this takes up in their life.

Once the client has talked about each experience represented by the objects, the therapist can ask a helpful question: "Where is the space for you in all this?" (Fleet et al., 2023b, p. 63). The aim here is for the client to realise they also have needs as well as the people they are caring for.

The second question asked, "What do you need to do to make space for some relaxation/peace/quiet for yourself?" (Fleet et al., 2023b, p. 63) can help the client recognise that something must change so that they can factor in some self-care and manage their responsibilities without becoming overwhelmed and burnt out.

Two example structured sessions for sand-tray coaching

Addressing Karpman's drama triangle in sand-tray coaching

This structured session can be adopted when a coachee is trying to explore a conflict in a work situation between themselves and others. Often, in such conflicts, Karpman's drama triangle (1968) is at play, which is a destructive interaction between people in that social situation. The interaction involves the people involved taking the role of persecutors, victims, and rescuers, and often, the issue of focus is unaddressed.

An example scenario

A coachee (Jane, the supervisor) is describing difficult relationships at work with herself, her supervisee (Sarah), and their manager (Karen). Jane describes how similar situations have come up between Karen being too direct and critical with Sarah, and Jane feeling like she is left to somehow smooth things over.

At this point, the coach could invite Jane to represent each person in the conflict, including herself, by choosing objects and placing them in the sand and then beginning to talk about the most recent conflict.

Jane begins talking:

> Well, we had a meeting between my manager (Karen), myself as Sarah's supervisor, and Sarah. Karen, who is always so direct, really went in on Sarah and began criticising her yet again for not completing a task she was asked to do. Karen went a bit too far, and I could see Sarah getting upset. It wasn't long before she began to cry, and I felt really sorry for her. So, I handed her a tissue and said, 'Don't worry, it's alright'. Then Karen turned on me and said, 'How can I do my job when you always jump in like this?' I then got angry and criticised her for being so hard; that's when she stood up, picked up her papers, and said, 'The meeting's over', and walked out in a huff.

In this scenario, the coach could consider how Jane has a tendency to rescue and, by asking appropriate open questions, could help Jane to see how her intervention neither helped Sarah, Karen, or the situation, which remained unresolved.

Helpful open questions asked by the coach:

"How do you think you could have responded differently to Sarah than trying to rescue and reassure her that everything was okay?"

"Instead of becoming angry with Jane, your manager, what could you have asked her to help Sarah (supervisee) to improve the quality of her work and become more responsible?"

These open questions help the coachee to look at their own behaviour rather than focus on what was happening with the other people involved, helping them to see that they can change. Placing objects representing the people in the conflict into the sand can give a clear picture to help the coachee explore the conflict and their part in it.

The processes of touch, movement, and the spatial arrangement of objects can really help the coachee unpack the issue and explore other possibilities, such as exploring the perspectives of other people in the conflict, facilitating change.

"I just want to be happy" – the quest for joy using sand-tray coaching

When working with a coachee who says, "I just don't feel happy and haven't felt happy for months", it may help if the coach guides them to be specific about the things in their life that are currently making them unhappy. This can be done by using the sand-tray and objects, with the coach inviting the coachee to identify specific things making them unhappy and choosing objects that represent each issue, placing the objects in the sand.

The following scenario is an example:

Coach

"Maybe it will help to focus on the things that make you feel unhappy and choose objects to represent those different issues".

Coachee

"Well, I hate my job. I can do it, and it pays my rent, but I am so bored with it!"

Coach

"So what object could represent that? Maybe choose an object and place it in the sand tray".

Once the coachee has placed the object in the sand, the coach could ask open questions:

"So, what needs to happen to bring change?" Or, "What steps do you need to make to bring change?"

The coachee may respond,

"I need to find a new job", or " I need to ask my manager how I can progress".

The coach can then state,

"So that sounds like a goal".

A second issue could be that the coachee picks up an object and says,

"This object represents me wasting my free time, watching reality TV pro-grammes and TikTok videos on my phone all the time, and although I like that, after, I feel so guilty because I have wasted my time".

Coach

"Okay, so what needs to change so that you don't feel so guilty by wasting your free time?"

Coachee

"I need to do something that makes me feel good, like going back to the gym maybe".

Coach

"So, I wonder how you would feel if you achieved that goal?"

Coachee

"Hopefully, it is good that I have done something active that makes me feel better about myself".

Coach

"So, maybe if you choose an object representing you are feeling happier that you have gone back to the gym and placed the object in the sand".

Once again, the coach could respond with,

"That feels like you've identified another goal".

When the coachee has identified the things that are currently making them unhappy in their life, the coach could invite the coachee to remove all the objects symbolising the things that are currently making them unhappy and then ask them how they would feel if they were gone from their life.

This symbolic action can help the coachee see the future, incorporating other possibilities that can bring some happiness as long as they strive to meet their established goals.

Further sessions can focus on how the coachee is incorporating these changes into their life and any shift in their mood towards feeling happier.

Addressing low self-esteem using sand-tray coaching

Self-esteem can be described as a person valuing, including the extent to which they approve, appreciate, or prize, themselves (Greenberg, 2008; Rogers, 1959).

Smith and Petty (1996) suggested that individuals with low self-esteem experience negative emotions and generalise negative feedback on one particular area to parts of their self-concept, resulting in a low desire to try new things or change.

In comparison, a person with high self-esteem will have confidence, can face challenges in their life, and at times be more equipped to accept failure and unhappiness (Rogers, 1959, 1980).

Some studies (Kuster, Orth & Meier, 2012; Orth, Robins & Roberts, 2008) link low self-esteem with mental health issues such as depression. Similarly, prior research by Rosenberg (1979) suggested that the majority of clinicians view high self-esteem as benefitting healthy living with less risk of developing anxiety and depression.

Although some coaching research suggests coaching is about working in the present and having future goals, the question, "What were you good at when you were younger?", or "What did you enjoy doing when you were younger?" asked by the coach can help a coachee to identify things that made them feel good about themselves before their self-esteem began to diminish.

This can be a good way of working with the sand tray and objects to explore what the coachee can reintroduce into their lives. The objects will symbolise the things that gave them a good feeling, such as running, poetry, drawing, dancing, singing, writing, hill-walking, socialising with friends, or going to church. The physical picture in the sand has a tendency to solidify the coachee's thoughts, feelings, and motivations.

New goals can be set to incorporate such positive activities in the present, and the steps required can be identified in order to bring some fun and positive energy back into the coachee's life.

Such self-care is essential for someone who has low self-esteem, and a step-by-step process to building self-confidence can change a person's perspective as they begin to bring some joy into their life.

Discussion points

- How does sand-tray coaching leverage symbolism and metaphorical expression to facilitate client exploration and insight?
- In what ways does sand-tray coaching differ from traditional talk therapy approaches, and what unique benefits does it offer to clients?
- What role does the sand-tray coach play in guiding clients through their exploration of the sand tray? How do coaches balance providing gentle direction and allowing clients the freedom to express themselves authentically?

Suggested resources

Exploring Sandbox Therapy with Dr Doreen Fleet. Retrieved from https://www.youtube.com/watch?v=1ad8uN8aZBI

Fleet, D., Reeves, A., Burton, A., & DasGupta, M. P. (2023a). Transformation hidden in the sand; a pluralistic theoretical framework using sand-tray with adult clients. *Journal of Creativity in Mental Health, 18*(1), 73–91.

References

Bishop, L. (2018). Coaching has great potential in the world of mental health. *The Psychologist, 31,* 62–64.

Cooper, M., & Dryden, W. (2016). *The handbook of pluralistic counselling and psychotherapy*. Sage.

Cooper, M., & McLeod, J. (2007). A pluralistic framework for counselling and psychotherapy: Implications for research. *Counselling and Psychotherapy Research, 7*(3), 135–143.

Fleet, D. (2019). *Transformation hidden in the sand: developing a theoretical framework using a sand-tray intervention with adult clients*. Doctoral thesis. Staffordshire University. Stoke-on-Trent. Available from Ethos STORE – Staffordshire Online Repository. https://eprints.staffs.ac.uk/id/eprint/5763

Fleet, D. et al. (2023b). Transformation hidden in the sand: A pluralistic theoretical framework using sand-tray with adult clients. *Journal of Creativity in Mental Health, 18*(1), 73–91. 10.1080/15401383.2021.1936738

Fleet, D. (2022). *Pluralistic sand-tray therapy. Humanistic principles for working creatively with adult clients*. Routledge.

Forge, J. (2022). *Coaching in mental health service setting and beyond: Practical applications*. Open University Press.

Greenberg, J. (2008). Understanding the vital human quest for self-esteem. *Perspectives on Psychological Science 3*(1), 48–55.

Hart, V., Blattner, J., & Leipsic, S. (2001). Coaching versus therapy: A perspective. *Consulting Psychology Journal: Practice and Research, 53*(4), 229–237. https://doi.org/10.1037/1061-4087.53.4.229

Jordan, M., & Livingstone, J. B. (2013). Coaching vs psychotherapy in health and wellness: Overlap, dissimilarities and the potential for collaboration. *Global Advances in Health and Medicine, 2*(4), 20–27.

Kalff, D. (1980). *Sandplay: A psychotherapeutic approach to the psyche*. Temenos Press.

Karpman, S. B. (1968). Fairy tales and script drama analysis. *Transactional Analysis Bulletin, 7*(26), 39–43.

Kuster, F., Orth, U., & Meier, L. L. (2012). Rumination mediates the prospective effect of low self-esteem on depression: A five-wave longitudinal study. *Personality and Social Psychology Bulletin, 38*(6), 747–759.

Lowenfeld, M. (1979). *The world technique*. Allen & Unwin.

McLeod. (2018). *Pluralistic therapy. Distinctive features*. Routledge.

Orth, U., Robins, R. W., & Roberts, B. W. (2008). Low self- esteem prospectively predicts depression in adolescence and young adulthood. *Journal of Personality and Social Psychology, 95*(3), 695–708.

Rogers, C. R. (1959). A theory of therapy, personality and interpersonal relationships, as developed in the client- centered framework. In S. Koch (Ed.). *Psychology: A study of science* (pp. 184–256). McGraw Hill.

Rogers, C. R. (1980). Client-centered psychotherapy. In H. I. Kaplan, & B. J. Sadock (Eds.). *Comprehensive textbook of psychiatry*. Lippincott Williams & Wilkins.

Rosenberg, M. (1979). *Conceiving the self*. Basic Books.

Smith, S., & Petty, R. (1996). Message framing and persuasion: A message processing analysis. *Personality and Social Psychology Bulletin, 22*(3), 257–268.

Chapter 10

Dancing and movement in coaching

Alexandra Baybutt

Introduction

This chapter introduces and contextualises movement coaching by identifying its interconnections with somatic movement education and dance. An example of movement coaching is presented through the Laban/Bartenieff Movement System (LBMS). Foundational principles of the coaching relationship include respect for existing knowledge and the unique movement of a client rather than establishing an expert/novice hierarchy and ideal type of movement. Playful exploration comes to matter as bodily co-presence, observation, and affect contribute to the space of learning for both client and practitioner. With process understood as affecting the outcome and, therefore, equal to it, movement coaching welcomes processes of discovery, iterative methods of working, and a spirit of adventure.

Theory, histories, context

The epistemic position in creative somatic movement coaching considers personhood as not fixed nor reducible to any sociological or demographic categorisation. This is important for emphasising the possibility of learning and personal growth and attempting to make movement coaching available to anyone interested. This perspective considers that a client has agency, sensitivity, and creativity, although in many cases, they may be blocked from accessing these because of beliefs, habitual patterns, or lack of sensorial awareness. In this context, the role of a coach is to guide and respond to their specific aims and interests through movement propositions and ongoing reflective dialogue, providing tools for increasing access to new awareness and alternative choices or strategies. Through sessions held individually or in small groups, maintaining this perspective of clients' agency foregrounds their embodied experience of themself in the world, and the coach works with and responds to what is already present or arising.

Creative movement coaching involves respect for the creative capacity of both individual clients and coaches to mobilise ideas and images. Responding

DOI: 10.4324/9781003453437-11

to different interests, needs, bodies, aims, and goals means creating schemes of work that consider any outcome contingent upon a process rather than prescribing an already-assumed route. It means listening to what is said but also listening through the body. It means being ready to adjust a plan based on how a session unfolds. It means trusting in the unknown and being prepared to be wrong. Its philosophies of practice cohere with philosophies of immanence rather than transcendence. Movement and the body are not conceptualised as separate categories. Philosophies of transcendence mean 'going beyond' human experience, and some religions underpinned by this philosophy seek to first split off the bodily experience in any voyage. As a philosophy of immanence, creative movement coaching generates a space of encounter with the immaterial or the virtual in the material, where human experience is already here to be explored within. But this is not a chapter about philosophy (for that, see, for example, Deleuze, Manning, Massumi, Grosz or Whitehead). Movement is approached as life itself. Each of us, whether client or coach, constantly makes adjustments to our inner sensorial experience and perception of the outer world in ongoing processes that make movement as adjustment entirely ubiquitous, as general at the same time it is specific.

In this chapter, creative movement coaching operates mainly synonymously with somatic movement education in order to refer to a variety of practitioners who work in a person-centred way and in which sensation and awareness are vital. A somatic approach favours individuals' capacity to sense themselves from the inside (interoception) and from the outside (proprioception), and it often includes working on the floor, working slowly, increasing ease of breathing, relating to gravity, and the use of touch. During coaching, following examples of movement or copying shapes might be part of an experience, but importance is placed upon an individual's own expression of a movement concept or embodied idea rather than replicating a specific form or technique to resemble the way it was shown.

Key developments of movement coaching require understanding the overlapping and similarly interdisciplinary fields of practice that inform its methods and values. Following the coining of the concept 'somatics' by Thomas Hanna in the 1970s, Martha Eddy identified three branches of the somatic world: somatic psychology, somatic bodywork, and somatic movement (Eddy, 2009, p. 7). 'Somatics' helped to create an umbrella title for process-orientated approaches to working practically with body-mind, emerging through practitioners in or moving between Europe and North America in the 20th century who drew on a vast range of influences, including practices from Africa and Asia. Somatic movement education and therapy found a home in the International Somatic Movement Education and Therapy Association (ISMETA), which acts as a regulatory body for recognising various kinds of training and methodologies, attempting to support a multiplicity of practices centred around health, healing, self-discovery, social justice, creativity, and movement.

Creative movement coaching intersects with histories of modern and post-modern dance appearing in the 20th century to challenge expectations and codifications of the moving body. Eddy traces how modern dance and somatics developed together via figures including Laban, Wigman, Dalcroze, Delsarte, h'Doubler, and Duncan. As largely secular, often anarchic practices, modern and postmodern dance, as well as somatics, trample on the problematic implications of a mind/body split and address the hierarchisation of mind over body that begets other violent dualisms. Experimental performance practices deploy a myriad of choreographic processes, including improvisation as a method of making as well as performing (see Midgelow, 2019). Creative methods to develop bespoke practices and techniques in service of choreographies not only demonstrate important legacies of questioning and rejecting which movements may be framed as dance beyond existing codified dance styles, genres, and techniques, and which people may dance. They also respond to the individuals present in that process: to their bodies' affordances (*pace* Spatz, 2015, after Spinoza) and their histories, identities, and imaginations.

Similarly, a principle in creative movement coaching is to meet people where they are rather than assume a certain 'level' or that coaching requires a certain kind of prior experience. To respond to and work with the techniques and knowledge people bring into the room echoes inclusive methods in dance, as well as some histories of contemporary performance practice. A social model of disability underpinning inclusive dance practices recognises that notions of ability are predicated upon how societies operate differently to exclude or include certain ways of moving, sensing, and being in the world that impact upon participation in life. Intersecting factors exacerbate inequity and create barriers to accessing education, work, networks, and health care. Creative movement coaching requires working inclusively, not only to question existing biases in movement expression and communication but to be part of a persistent movement in the activist sense against the erasure of differences broadly conceived.

Somatic movement education is interested in supporting people learning how to learn and to become their own coach, not simply imparting set strategies or sequences. Coaching is helpful at any time in one's work and life in the context of being seen and supported in a non-judgemental, supportive way. However, somatic movement education's epistemic basis of empowering and increasing facility with tools for learning is also underpinned by the humility to recognise that you might not be needed in a room eventually. Against the notion of the expert and the novice, movement coaching is most effective when mutual learning takes place, and the ongoing creative practice of a coach is, therefore, vital for sustaining awareness that there will always be more to discover and reflect upon. Learning how to learn entails transmission through lived knowledge where knowledge itself is in motion, and there are no fixed methods.

In movement coaching, somatic movement and improvisation are key tools for a dynamic interplay that interweaves self-connection and connection with the world. Coaching might be informed by a mix of the individual practitioner's training and experience and might take place in private practice, in public workshops or classes, and in healthcare contexts. It is more or less formalised regarding it happening spontaneously or as a scheduled event. Movement coaching broadly conceived also appears in peer learning contexts like hip-hop and skateboarding or in rehearsal rooms between actors and movement directors. It requires presence, though it can take place in the same room or via online video communication platforms. I will shift to writing from 'I' to better differentiate one approach from a myriad of approaches. I draw on my background in contemporary performance dance, improvisation practices, and the LBMS, a system for movement observation, analysis, and experience. At its foundation is the awareness that what is experienced by a person and what is observed by another are different but connected. LBMS shares with other somatic practices an emphasis on perception, felt sense, and movement awareness. Less common in other somatic movement education and therapy, LBMS also includes approaches to space that extend experiences of sensing connections in one's own body to relationships with the space around one's body, referred to as the Kinesphere. The Kinesphere, a concept presented by Rudolf Laban, helps to organise movement observation and experience by identifying where movement is happening in the space around an individual person, for example, in specific directions, pathways, reach space, zones, and levels. LBMS is particularly versatile for coaching as it supports processes of observing movement phenomena, as well as conceptual tools to respond with, combine, interrogate, play with, and discard. Movement coaching involves supporting a person to better understand the ways they already move and consider what changes or expansions of that 'signature' might be possible or desirable. Observation of movement to identify reoccurring features, patterns, and absences is supported through LBMS that, although not intended to cover all aspects of being, is wide enough to help mitigate against biases of an observer.

Movement analysis training is premised upon the argument that in order to develop and expand observation skills, it is vital to increase one's own range of movement. Even if you cannot do actions like backflips, handstands, or tightrope walks, you can in your own body visit or approximate their patterns of phrasing, body organisation, dynamic progressions, or breath, for example. LBMS supports observation of the infinite ways elements of movement can arise and helps to illuminate already existing ways of moving or a movement signature. Each of us has preferences and habitual ways of movement that can affect our ways of seeing and perceiving ourselves and others. Elements of movement are regularly repackaged as labels to judge someone or oneself as being 'lazy', 'uncoordinated', 'inefficient', or 'ugly'. LBMS offers a way to take distance from such interpretations to explore other ways of thinking and moving. Learning to select 'lenses' to deliberately look through at one's movement, or the movement of others, helps to alleviate being at the mercy of one's habits or preferences and means meeting the edges of what is known alongside all that we don't know we don't know.

Carrying this sensibility into working with clients involves strategies for noting observations, such as using movement coding sheets to record what is arising. But these are a reminder to look for elements of movement that might not be so dominant in the observer's movement signature. Movement coding sheets vary based on the practitioner, though observation generally includes attuning to and looking at what, where, how, and ways of relating. These refer to what LBMS identifies as the four foundational components of movement. The 'what' refers to which body parts are used, for example, and where movements begin or initiate from, or how movement travels through the body. 'Where' is movement happening means paying attention to their Kinesphere. Asking 'how' leads towards defining qualitative aspects of movement, and ways of relating means observing how a mover accommodates themselves, others, and the environment they are in through ongoing adjustments. Recording patterns, durations, and frequencies of movement help to synthesise a client's movement signature and identify areas they wish to expand, as well as changes throughout the duration of coaching. Coaching is in relationship to the LBMS taxonomy, but the taxonomy itself does not indicate how to use it. Sometimes it is interesting and useful to share with clients the use of the symbols used in LBMS as part of defining concepts that clarify something about movement experience. I use words and symbols as part of my ways of recording, planning, and reflecting in between sessions.

Working with clients

Speaking in terms of movement includes a vast range of phenomena such as the whole body, body parts, and movements of memory, of vocalisation, and of the vibration of cells. As a facilitator, I act as a guide. Whilst there is expertise in holding space and asking the most supportive question at the right time, being a companion to someone's coaching process means not imposing upon it an agenda that would be paradoxical to the aims of the client and assumes more than can be known. To support this sensibility, LBMS relies upon conceptualisations of thematic pairs, sometimes referred to as pairs of opposites or dualities, like Mobility/Stability, to articulate movement experience. These help to organise some understanding of shifting perception and relating (for example, standing on one foot opens an experience of stability and mobility, with both required). Though they allude to a binary, it is rather their wholeness that is important for non-dual praxis.

Using the thematic pair Function/Expression in relationship to one client's process of recovery from a complex hip joint replacement meant considering how the new functionality of the joint affected the expression of sitting, standing, and walking. Understanding the kinetic chains affected through new access to muscular activity included a realm of feeling, shifts in self-perception, awe, and grief. The newly affected part of this client's body affects the whole of their experience of their functionality and expressivity, and movement coaching created a space to integrate, discover, and test out new possibilities of shifting weight that had implications for lying, sitting, standing, walking, balancing, and dancing. Function/Expression, capitalised as part of the LBMS lexicon, serves to continually decentre biomechanical facts or the emotional response towards surgery as the most important part of the experience. These parts are understood to be entangled. Occasionally teasing them apart for clarification included, for example, realising discomfort was an impingement of bone and nerve that needed a new movement cue or intention. Or tracing the appearance in sense memory of being berated for not doing the movement in a dance class the same way as everyone else. Movement coaching means the stories of the body are welcomed and not made irrelevant because of any prevailing epistemic primacy or hierarchy. Often, clients who have had surgery and then receive an exercise plan from a physiotherapist struggle with motivation for engaging in repetitive activity despite knowing it makes for better healing. For this client, an outcome of sessions together was being able to better self-direct movement exploration beyond their diligent undertaking of physiotherapist's exercises with less anxiety about doing damage. In addition, sessions supported an increase of self-compassion in a long process of healing. Movement coaching attempts to get closer to what is meaningful for a person beyond, but including, a part of the body that might be very readily in the foreground of attention, as is the case with injury or ongoing conditions.

A consultation process includes discussing goals and interests, moving in the room through walking or other movements if welcomed, and participating in floor-based movement sequences that engage different kinetic chains, breathing, patterns of body organisation, level change, and so forth. The way these are done reveals areas of the body that might be more held or passive, how the parts relate to one another, and through observation and conversation, how the client experiences such actions. Any images, associations, ease, discomfort, and emergent questions help to shape the working methods of subsequent sessions as I respond to how the aims or goals of the client correspond with how they are already moving. A plan for sessions includes tasks that may be more or less 'open' – for example, a few instructions initiate a movement improvisation – or a more specific action such as 'heel rocking' (Hackney, 2002: 108–109). Sometimes I move with a client for the possibility of mirroring what they are doing, or doing something qualitatively different, or to be a sense of companionship in the room where we are both engaged and active rather than having a still observer watch a moving person. Observing through moving together is possible through how peripheral vision is activated. Attuning to one another through breath and bodily co-presence can create increased trust: we affect and are affected.

A typical arc of a session might include floor-based practices leading into improvisation to then set a short, repeatable phrase. This becomes material to continue adapting by changing various parameters of movement (for example, its space, phrasing, time, body initiations, dynamics, levels). Making a movement phrase generates the conditions of exploration from which discoveries can inform other tasks and activities related to the client's goals. Movement coaching is a route for self-discovery, which requires giving consistent, close attention to the changing experience of the client, or what performing artists might call 'being present'. As the method requires following discoveries and creatively responding, sometimes the aims of both the client and myself, as the practitioner, shift. Whilst goals are important, a goal could be to stay present to the unknown. Like contemporary choreographic practices that work with improvisation, my task is to create the conditions for something to happen. A client's process of reflection is included within a session through movement itself, as well as other forms such as speaking, drawing, and writing. I offer tasks for in between sessions to help the client develop their personal practice and sometimes include films of them and/or me.

Rather than elaborate upon one specific case study, I wish to emphasise how goals and motivations to seek movement coaching vary along the continuum that can be summarised through Function/Expression. One cluster of clients includes students and graduates of Dance Movement Therapy programmes or related psychotherapeutic disciplines seeking to supplement their observation skills and tools for personal practice (indicating that the provision in these trainings is not always substantial). Other clients include a nanny looking to better understand his movement on a journey towards therapeutic training, a yoga teacher seeking creative practices and poetic routes towards movement away from codified movement, a singer wishing to find more confidence in being seen when performing, a PhD arts and humanities student wanting more tools to identify her movement signature and increase range to support some of the methods used in her research, an actor wanting to understand his habitual ways of moving prior to characterisation, and someone terrified of attending group yoga classes for fear of not 'doing it right'. These examples highlight how movement coaching can respond directly to specific needs that might be less possible in group movement classes.

Discussion

Irmgard Bartenieff was a dance artist and, later, a dance movement therapist and physiotherapist. LBMS includes movement sequences based upon fundamental components of locomotion, level change, and developmental progression from birth to walking, derived from Bartenieff's work with children with Polio. In this context, her ambition was not only to activate neuromuscular chains but also to motivate individuals. This holistic approach to personhood does not view the body as a collection of parts and does not adhere to some physiotherapeutic methods that only work on a part of the body. Bartenieff did not conceptualise movement only in terms of biomechanic functionality but took an expansive approach that made space for spontaneous movement expression.

Creative movement coaching shares aspects with Dance Movement Therapy/ Psychotherapy (DMT/P) and related psychodynamic body therapies interested in the integration of body and mind, healing and wholeness. Working through the body can bring up memories, and there are differences between how practitioners might work with those stories based on their frameworks of training and education – for example, drawing upon archetypes. As a coach, it is important to know in advance health histories, including injury, trauma, and any existing conditions, to know how to work with clients and what to expect, but creative movement coaching is not necessarily claiming to be therapy in the sense that it is understood as a psychological field (though nor is DMT/P). The articulation and inclusion of the therapeutic dimensions of movement, however, are not simple to define or delimit to one field of practice more than another. ISMETA accredits both somatic movement educators and somatic movement therapists, and discussion ranges over who chooses to identify their work with the term 'therapy' and/or 'education' and why. There are many trainings and forms of education, some emphasising group dynamics and psychotherapeutic theory, as DMT/P does. Each form of training has specific histories and implications for where one can work and with whom, with context-specific connotations that affect questions of insurance, ongoing training, and supervision expectations. What is at stake in creative movement coaching overlaps with somatics, somatic movement repatterning, DMT/P, and performing artists' training concerns four main points: communicability to a non-specialist audience or clients as being recognisable, which matters for the futures of such practices; safety for clients and coaches; freedom for practices to develop and meet the needs of changing knowledges and contexts; and preservation of practices, ethics, and epistemologies. For movement coaching, the community of ISMETA is crucial for robust, though lightly held standardisation within a multiplicity. With many performance and movement practices trade-marked and parcelled into specific economies of knowledge, often making them inaccessible, and the concept of 'embodiment' appearing more frequently in mainstream spaces, I argue that it is important creative movement coaching remains a frame through which to see a plural field of interpersonal movement practices and creative learning rather than claim narrow specialisation, despite coaches and clients' specific methods, goals, and outcomes.

Creative movement coaching might relate to 'body language', but I wish to emphasise some differences. Theories of body language can be limited through emphasising static postures rather than the movement into and out of postures, which is how perception of movement takes place. Theories of body language may start from conclusions about movement's possible impact or communicative power movement, with assumptions of it being, for example, 'distracting'. This is problematic in that it perpetuates an ableist, ethnocentric view of the body and movement. In some contexts, 'body language' skills are taught to equip people with tools to feel more confident, which overlaps with the aims of movement coaching, as does recognising habits in one's ways of moving. However, the goal of some body language training is to 'neutralise' individual traits in order to attempt to minimise other people's possible interpretations or assumptions about a person. In situations when you want to pass, be taken seriously, or want to fit in, to be able to modulate your speed, length of step, eye line, and gestures might well be a tactical advantage, albeit a defensive starting point. But it also assumes all bodies could arrive at such a reductive, even nebulous notion of 'neutral', which risks the perpetuation of conservative approaches to bodies and movement, and limits an embrace of the diversity of human expression in which more confidence to inhabit oneself need not flatten the differences between us. LBMS, in this regard, decentres a 'normative' or 'neutral' body through a politics of practice that acknowledges cultural hegemonies but without the desire to keep serving them.

Creative movement coaching opens discussions of what it means to 'pass', how creative agency is shaped, and what authenticity might entail as part of individual growth in relationships. The briefly sketched examples of movement coaching in one-to-one contexts allowed the possibility to closely follow one person's process, needs, and aims. Such creativity and care are also found in practitioners who work with groups, and many dance practitioners working in health care and community settings do similar work to follow needs and aims. Creative movement coaching sounds general. But as I have illustrated, it approaches highly specific goals and works well in situations of recovery when conditions are no longer acute, as well as even a mode of intervention in institutions (see Dowling in Peck, forthcoming). Movement is often lumped into conceptualisations of only functional aims (movement to 'fix' the body) or pleasure and recreation (dancing for fun; sports for challenge/competition). Somatic creative movement coaching encompasses all of it. The vast range of approaches to movement and dance are its advantage but also grounds for confusion and misinterpretation. There remain gaps in understanding and appreciating the value of engaging in creative responses to individuals and individuals' capacities for creative responses through movement. Fighting for subsidising and increasing access to such spaces of connectivity also requires advocating for an expanded approach to movement as life, not only function or expression.

Discussion points

1 Movement coaching is the practice of having a plan and being ready to deviate from it, partly because of the emphasis on presence to sensation and articulation of experience. This semi-improvisatory approach appears in

other forms of coaching, as well as creativity, and opens questions of control in how processes modulate. Turning to the body and movement helps to recognise these capacities of being and being-with where attunement might be easily taken for granted or glossed over as part of how a relationship is formed or renegotiated.

2   There is bodily co-presence as part of any coaching relationship, even if the focus is not on or through movement. It can be helpful to reflect further upon the nuances of one's physical presence and responsiveness. This might simply be out of curiosity, though it is more urgent if there are specific blocks, reoccurring comments, or questions about how you work or come across to others.

3   Playful exploration of one's own movement can be for preparation, as well as recuperation. Such a relationship towards one's movement serves one's work with others and one's own longevity. Through movement, 'creativity' might be welcomed or even reified as an everyday mode rather than deferred to others.

Suggested resources

ISMETA, https://ismeta.org/join
LBMS, https://wholemovement.org/what-is-the-laban-bartenieff-movement-system-lbms/
ADMP UK, https://admp.org.uk/

References

Eddy, M. (2009). A brief history of somatic practices and dance: Historical development of the field of somatic education and its relationship to dance. *Journal of Dance and Somatic Practices*, *1*(1), 5–27. doi: 10.1386/jdsp.1.1.5/1

Hackney, P. (2002). *Making Connections: Total Body Integration through Bartenieff Fundamentals*. Routledge.

Midgelow, V.L. (Ed). (2019). *The Oxford Handbook of Improvisation in Dance*. Oxford University Press.

Spatz, B. (2015). *What a Body Can Do: Technique as Knowledge, Practice as Research*. Routledge.

Thanks to Susan Scarth, Paola Napolitano and Karen Studd for their feedback.

Chapter 11

"Yes, and..." What coaches can learn from improv

Julie Flower

Introduction

What does it feel like to step onto a stage, having no idea what you and your teammates will co-create? That's improv comedy.

What does it feel like to step into a room with a coaching client, having no idea what you will co-create? That's coaching.

Improvisation can be described as "creativity, adaptation and innovation under time pressure" (Ratten & Hodge, 2016, p. 149) and, as it translates to the theatre and comedy (improv), a style of unscripted performance in which players creatively collaborate in the moment to create characters, scenes, and stories. Coaching, as a relational, dialogic activity concerned with partnering and co-creation, in the moment, is inherently improvisational (Read, 2013). In addition, the fast-moving, uncertain environments and systems in which clients' organisational and personal lives operate call increasingly for improvisational skills and behaviours.

In this context, the time is ripe to explore the conceptual and practical relevance of improv to coaching. Improv training exercises have an emerging evidence base as a simple, yet powerful, form of experiential learning, including concerning improved flexibility of thinking, self-awareness, psychological safety, and collaborative creativity (Kirsten & Du Preez, 2010; Felsman et al., 2020). Improv principles and exercises may support coaches in their development towards coaching maturity, offering self-awareness and skills to support a more present, spontaneous, and emergent way of coaching. They also offer practical ideas for the integrated and eclectic coach to incorporate into creative partnership with their clients.

Theory, basic concepts, and key developments

What is improvisation?

Long associated for television audiences with the comedic programme *Whose Line Is It Anyway?*, performance improv actually encompasses a variety of

DOI: 10.4324/9781003453437-12

different formats and genres with a wide emotional range. As a form of spontaneous creativity, it relies on performers being 'in the moment', listening actively, and building on 'offers' made rather than blocking others' ideas or expressions (Johnstone, 1979). This is the principle of "yes, and". Training exercises derived from improvised theatre and comedy (improv exercises) have been used widely within corporate training and team development over the last two decades, promising to build collaboration, confidence, spontaneity, and creative thinking (Koppett, 2001b; Leonard & Yorton, 2015). This aligns with more recent thinking which has recognised the importance of improvisational skills for leaders, teams, and organisations, particularly in the face of uncertain and rapidly changing external factors (Hadida et al., 2015).

How is improvisation relevant to coaching?

Coaching is a dynamic, dialogic practice which can be viewed, in many ways, as an inherently improvisational activity (Read, 2013). The International Coaching Federation (ICF) recognises the importance of a creative partnership, defining coaching as "partnering with clients in a thought-provoking and creative process that inspires them to maximise their personal and professional potential" (ICF, 2019). The coaching literature and professional competency frameworks highlight the need for coaches to develop skills, behaviours, and ways of being associated with improvisation, even if it is rarely mentioned by name. These include the following:

- Presence (being in the moment; being aware of, and using, our own emotions; avoiding judgement; sitting with uncertainty)
- Co-creation (spontaneity, creativity, building on and making 'offers', taking risks)
- Active listening (with all our senses, maintaining an open curiosity)

Read (2013) introduced the concept of improvisation to the coaching literature. His research with experienced coaches highlights the relevance of improvisation, as a behavioural concept, to coaching, with recognition of a number of 'improvisational moments' within coaching. "Professional coaching is improv" remarked one participant in Read's qualitative study of how far coaches improvised within their own practice (2013, p. 50). The study found that improvisation, defined by him as "a spontaneous and creative attempt at finding a new way of doing things" (Read, 2013, p. 56), was used extensively by coaches and 'often' in the five coaching practices of conversations, sessions or practices, delivering feedback, team building, simulations, or rehearsals (Read, 2013: 52). Seventy-three percent of the 113 respondents identified improvisation as very important or essential, leading him to conclude that it is a crucial skill within coaching (Read, 2013).

The relevance of improvisation has been recognised to a greater, though still limited, extent within the literature on therapeutical professions. For Kindler (2010, p. 222), considering improvisation from a therapeutic perspective, it "embodies the idea of a cooperative effort at keeping the play, or creative conversation, going forward" (p. 222), and for therapists, it is an important concept and skill to facilitate learning and growth in the therapeutic relationship. Romanelli and Tishby (2019) draw direct parallels between improv theatre 'guidelines' and competencies, behaviours, and skills relevant to clinical social work. Building on their qualitative study of therapists' experiences of improvisational or 'spontaneous peak moments' in therapy, Romanelli et al. suggest they are "not radical or wild uncontrollable actions when therapists lose control of themselves, rather they are out-of-the-box, creative, and surprising interventions and interactions occurring within the framework of the therapeutic encounter" (2019, p. 297).

What is the evidence base for the use of improv exercises?

Training exercises derived from improv usually take the form of short paired and group activities or 'games', supported by facilitated reflection to draw out the learning. They do not usually involve any need to 'perform' or for participants to have acting or comedy experience. Although the empirical evidence base for the application of improv exercises in non-theatre settings remains low (Ratten & Hodge, 2016), it is increasing in both quality and quantity, as well as in areas that are increasingly relevant to the practice and aims of coaching. Lewis and Lovatt (2013) demonstrate potential positive cognitive benefits for divergent thinking, including fluency, originality, and flexibility, for those who had engaged in improv exercises, compared to a control group, in their quantitative experimental study. More recent work by Felsman et al. (2020) replicates Lewis and Lovatt findings and demonstrates improvisation could improve positive affect and increase uncertainty tolerance. Studies in the realm of team development and interpersonal skills also point to some promising findings that may be relevant to the developing field of team coaching. A quasi-experimental study by West et al. (2017) shows that creative teams who engaged in improv training demonstrated increased playfulness and creativity. A previous quasi-experimental study by Kirsten and Du Preez (2010) suggests that engaging in improvised theatre training was beneficial for teams through the creation of climates for innovation, drawing out impact in areas such as trust and support, acceptance, and listening and awareness.

From a practitioner perspective, qualitative research in the field of therapeutic social work indicates an increase in flexibility, open-mindedness, therapeutic presence, self-disclosure, and self-awareness for practitioners who engaged in improv training (Romanelli et al., 2017; Romanelli & Tishby, 2019; Romanelli et al., 2019). The well-designed mixed-methods study looked at the impact of a semester-long improv theatre course for clinicians on flexibility and therapeutic presence amongst 35 graduate-level social work students (Romanelli et al., 2017; Romanelli & Tishby, 2019). Whilst the quantitative analysis showed significant improvements in both flexibility and therapeutic presence, compared to a control group, the impact was not maintained at the three-month follow-up. The parallels with coaching suggest there may be a benefit in exploring how such exercises could impact on coach development.

My own qualitative research into how coaches experience engaging in improv exercises provides promising findings with respect to:

- The development of coach presence (including emotional self-awareness and empathy)
- The strength and speed of connection and relationships
- A desire to be more experimental, creative, and playful within coaching; and
- The potential for direct practical application of improv exercises within coaching encounters (Flower, 2021).

Practice

Coaching is a relatively young and eclectic profession, which draws widely on a range of philosophies and disciplines, benefiting hugely from the integration of evidence-based learning and practice (Hardingham, 2006; Passmore, 2007). Given the modern client context and the increasing evidence base around the benefits of engaging in experiential improv exercises, the time is ripe to take improv more seriously. Yes, improv can be great fun, *and* it can also offer coaches and clients (both individuals and teams) the chance to develop their self-awareness, relationships, and skills in a safe, creative, and experimental environment.

The implications for practice appear to be twofold:

- The potential of improvisational theatre exercises as powerful experiential learning for *coach development*, promoting greater self-awareness and presence, empathy, rapport-building, and comfort with co-creation, creativity, and the unknown in coaching
- The opportunity for direct application of improvisational theatre concepts and exercises as part of an *eclectic approach to coaching*, offering powerful client learning through a playful, creative, and experimental approach

Coach development

"Playfulness is largely about your willingness to play, to be curious, experiment, explore, prepared to not know and improvise, creating the space to enable your clients to do so" (Wheeler & Leyman, 2023, p. 198). The coaches involved in my research indicated an increased willingness and motivation to experiment and be creative in coaching, for the benefit of clients, after engaging in improv activities (Flower, 2021). For many of them, the visceral, emotional experience of taking part and reflecting on the experience increased their self-awareness and interest in occupying a more emergent, uncertain, and playful space within coaching, even if it sometimes feels uncomfortable or exposing.

This can take many forms and overlaps with a range of psychological fields and creative approaches within coaching. An example from my own practice is inviting a client who described herself as "being all at sea" to physically inhabit a rowing boat and go for a voyage within the room. With parallels to creative experiments within Gestalt coaching (Bluckert, 2015), this activity had an improvisational quality, "yes, and-ing" the client's metaphor in order to explore complex emotions and make discoveries through an experiential, in-the-moment exercise. Similarly, another client's repeated mention of a "bag of snakes" led to a virtual, metaphorical game of snakes and ladders, exploring a challenging work situation through a playful, co-created game based on an invitation to experiment.

To invite and enable exploration in such ways requires a strong coach presence and a safe and trusting, yet challenging, relationship. Improv exercises may support coaches in developing such skills and ways of being. Bachkirova (2021, p. 43) explains presence as a level of self-understanding, which enables a coach to use themselves as instruments and "notice their own emotions, hunches and subtle messages from their body as they occur and utilise them in the session". She suggests coaches practise developing the focus of attention outside direct coaching relationships, including potentially through using exercises in the Gestalt tradition. It could be argued that exercises derived from improvised theatre could also be powerful and effective ways to develop such self-understanding.

An eclectic approach to coaching

The direct application of improvised theatre techniques within coaching sessions is also a potential area of fruitful discovery and future exploration. Given that the application of improv theatre exercises is associated in the literature with positive intrapersonal development in areas such as presence, creativity, trust, self-awareness, and flexibility, as well as collaborative team behaviours (Ratten & Hodge, 2016), they may be naturally aligned with many of the aims of coaches in their work with clients. This includes in the context of greater uncertainty and a need for leaders and teams to build their improvisational capabilities.

Kolb and Kolb (2006) argue that an increasing body of evidence demonstrates the effectiveness of experiential learning in enhancing students' metacognitive abilities, their capacity to apply newly acquired skills and knowledge to real-life situations, and the ability to become self-directed learners. This is relevant to coaching, which is effectively a form of reflective development that seeks to impact areas such as affective outcomes, including emotional improvements, and skills, such as leadership and interpersonal skills (Jones, 2021). Coaching is a profession that draws on a wide range of evidence-based approaches, as well as many intuitive ones, and so the emerging literature around the potential benefits of improvised theatre techniques may well support their inclusion in an experienced coach's repertoire.

Practical exercises to experiment with

Four simple, practical exercises are outlined in the following sections. They can be used both as experiential exercises in coach development and for use with clients within coaching sessions. All can be adapted for use with individuals, groups, or teams and can be used equally well online as in person. They are based on my own practice but particularly build on the influential performance work of Johnstone (1979) and applied workplace examples of Koppett (2001b). The most important consideration is the reflection on the experience: the 'what?', 'so what?', and the 'now what?' (Driscoll, 2007). Through active reflection, including thoughts, feelings, physiological reactions, and behaviours, learning from the experience can be translated into action and behavioural change.

Naming things

Great for getting present and building skills of attention and flexibility of observation and thinking.

Firstly, walk around the room pointing at things and naming them (e.g., chair, curtains). Then, walk around pointing and naming the things something (anything) that they're not (e.g., elephant, swimming pool, capitalism – really, anything!). (You can add a round in between where you point at things, but say the name of the thing you previously pointed at.) It is surprisingly difficult.

"Yes, and..." – planning a day trip

Building on the principle of "yes, and", this is great for exploring accepting and blocking behaviours.

In pairs, one partner initiates with "let's… [go on a day trip or a team away day or something similar]". The partner responds with "yes, and let's…" each time, building specifically on the last offer, alternating and building each time. The story does not need to be within the bounds of possibility. In fact, the more fantastical, the better!

With more time, experimentation can take place with the difference experienced when responding with "yes, but…" instead. Participants can reflect on whether they are truly listening and "yes, anding" the previous suggestion or whether they are trying to control the conversation and move it around to their own 'great' idea.

Expert interview

This is a great exercise for building confidence, comfort in 'thinking on your feet', and resourcefulness, as someone is asked to embody being an 'expert'. It is also usually very playful and fun.

One person is endowed with being an 'expert' in a seemingly nonsensical subject, such as "teaching squirrels to tap dance". They are then 'interviewed' about their specialist subject by another participant or the coach. As the interviewer, it's great to probe deeper into the 'how' of what they did, as well as encourage them to reflect more widely (in character) on the learning and insight they gained from their 'expert experiences'. An additional stretch in this exercise is then to use the same format in a follow-up round, this time using a 'real' subject, such as a hobby, their work, or as if they were looking back on a future achievement, helping to build confidence, commitment, and resourcefulness.

Gift giving

This simple yet powerful exercise is all about dealing with uncertainty and accepting, making sense of, and building upon 'offers' made by another person. By being physical as well as verbal, it helps us connect in different ways.

In partners, one person starts by making a clear physical offer and saying, "I got you a gift". The gift-giver should take time in the passing of the gift to demonstrate something of the size, shape, and weight of the gift, or potentially how they feel towards it, without describing it in words and without necessarily knowing what object they think they're offering.

The recipient should take a moment to receive the gift as it was given, again exploring its properties. They then respond, "Thank you for the [naming what they think it is or could be]", tapping into how they feel about receiving the gift (usually a positive response). The gift-giver then briefly justifies why they chose that particular gift, trying to be as specific as possible. The justification can be completely imaginary but should be relevant to what they just heard. For instance, the recipient says, "Thank you for the inflatable flamingo", and the gift-giver responds with, "I thought you'd love it for the new swimming pool you've just installed in your garden".

Case studies

As a coach

My introduction to improv was during the COVID pandemic; I took part in two 6-week improv comedy classes and then another more specialised course building on the work of Brené Brown, all online. A while later, a memorable experience was a day-long, in-person mask workshop based on improvisation. While my initial motivation for taking the classes was to find a way to have some fun, be playful, and connect to others, they allowed me to experiment with and experience a different way of interacting and being. Improv allows me to experience in a very real way what it is to co-create and how quickly rapport can be built by working in the moment in true partnership and creating something which none of us would have come up with on our own. This act of presence and co-creation is often described as necessary for coaching mastery, and yet in more traditional coaching training, I was often left with the question, "But how?!" Improv is a jigsaw piece of moving from theory to practice on this.

For me, two other jigsaw pieces are my explorations of playfulness in coaching and my continuing learning journey into Relational Mindfulness. In many ways, the three are very similar: to play at the edge of not knowing, embrace the willingness to set aside all pre-formed ideas and assumptions, to be completely present, make space, and be willing to work with whatever is coming up internally (emotionally, somatically, intellectually) for us and our co-creation partner in that moment. There is rich learning here for the balancing of the 'doing' and 'being' in both our life and the coaching dance.

Stephanie Wheeler is an individual and teach coach, as well as author, working with coaches to access their playfulness.

The leadership team of a rapidly growing charity

The senior leadership team of Dads Unlimited took part in simple exercises from improvised comedy/theatre training as part of some team coaching sessions. These included creative storytelling exercises which used the concept of "yes, and", followed by personal and team reflection. This powerful experiential learning was then applied to the work of individuals and the team, enabling active experimentation in the real life of running the charity during a period of rapid expansion.

> Exploring the concepts of 'yes, and' and 'yes, but' came at a pivotal point in our journey as a leadership team. As a rapidly growing charity we are keen to generate and implement new ideas, and this needs to be balanced with the time and resources we have available. We took part in 'yes, and' exercises as part of a series of team coaching sessions. The experience has made a huge impression on us as a leadership team. We all have much greater awareness of our own behaviours and their impact on others, including how they can both encourage and stifle creativity and innovation. It now just feels like part of our culture that we call ourselves and each other out by saying, 'that felt like a yes, but'...or 'how can we make that into a yes, and?' This is a simple yet powerful intervention that is helping us innovate, constantly expanding and improving what we offer.

Nav Mirza is chief executive of Dads Unlimited, a charity improving the lives of children of separated parents.

Final considerations

It could be argued that the coaching profession has always known about the importance of improvisation at the level of both theory and practice but has never used those words. In fact, it may be at the heart of advanced coaching or coaching maturity. Passmore (2021, p. 322), in his work on integrative coaching, recognises the importance of coaches being able to "blend different approaches, flexing their approach to meet the needs of the individual client or the specific presenting issue". This has parallels with the definition of improvisation as "the conception of action as it unfolds...drawing on available material, cognitive, affective, and social resources" (Cunha et al. 1999, p. 302). Coaching is an inherently resourceful and creative activity which requires a person-centred, adaptive approach.

The challenge for coaches is how to develop both the skills and the underlying way of being to operate effectively in that improvisational space. The initial evidence suggests that improv exercises may offer a simple, effective, engaging, and, often, fun form of coach development. A number of professional bodies have run one-off training sessions using improv exercises, and articles have begun to appear, although little coach-specific research has been carried out. 'Improvisation and coaching' has recently been included on the syllabus for the Henley Business School MSc in coaching for behavioural change as part of the development of advanced coaching practice. This is all part of a wider movement to explore and acknowledge the potential of playfulness and creativity coaching.

Using and adapting improv exercises within coaching sessions may also add further choices to an eclectic coach's repertoire, offering greater behavioural flexibility and range. The small, though growing, evidence base points to their potential benefit in a range of client situations. However, most studies are based on the initial reported impact of engaging in a small number of exercises. More work is required to consider whether benefits are sustained over time and to assess what level of (repeated) engagement with improv activities is required. There is also always the risk that the use of a shiny new 'tool' is more for the coach's benefit than the client's (Passmore et al., 2021). Coaches should tread carefully when actively incorporating improv exercises; the strength of the relationship and quality of trust and safety are paramount. Some of the exercises may be easier to use in group or team settings by a skilled coach, although all can be adapted in some way to one-to-one coaching scenarios. The difference between using these exercises in a coaching rather than a training environment is likely to be the emphasis, quality, and focus of the reflection to evoke awareness and enable clients to use the experience to learn and grow for themselves.

Interdisciplinary research opportunities within coaching could be fruitful, particularly with respect to improv exercises and the emerging research fields of playfulness and creativity in coaching. This could include quantitative and qualitative work, considering the impact of both coach and client engagement in such exercises. Concepts such as psychological safety and flow may also present interesting theoretical frames for advancing understanding of how improvised theatre may benefit coach and client learning.

As practitioners, the emerging evidence suggests that our ways of both 'doing' and 'being' can potentially be enhanced by engaging with improv concepts and by taking part in improv theatre exercises ourselves or by using them with our clients. What could be dismissed as merely 'silly play' or 'just a bit of fun' is, in reality, supported by a growing empirical evidence base as a powerful form of experiential learning. Enjoy experimenting with the fun and the fear of improv!

Discussion points

- How can being more improvisational in coaching sessions help clients?
- How can the improvisational mindset enhance coaching, particularly in encouraging creative problem-solving, expanding perspectives, and facilitating breakthrough moments for clients?
- How would you use improv in your own coaching practice?

Suggested resources

Reading

Flower, J. (2022) Acting on instinct. *Coaching at Work*, *17*(2), 40–43.
Koppett, K. (2001a). *Training to imagine: Practical improvisational theatre techniques to enhance creativity, leadership, teamwork and learning*. Sterling: Stylus Publishing.

Audiovisual

Association for Coaching (2022). *Coaching Conversations: Thinking on your feet*. LinkedIn Live conversation between Julie Flower and James Bridgeman. Oct 2022. https://www.linkedin.com/events/accoachingconversations-thinkin6982740955049140224/comments/

Training

There are many improv training schools all over the world. Hoopla! is a well-established school, offering a range of well-taught courses and programmes covering many different aspects and formats of improv, from beginners' to advanced. Both in-person in London and online. Hoopla! also runs an improv venue in London with many different shows on offer. https://www.hooplaimpro.com

References

Bachkirova, T. (2021). Understanding yourself as a coach. In J. Passmore (Ed.), *The Coaches' handbook* (pp. 39–47). Routledge.

Bluckert, P. (2015). *Gestalt coaching: Right here, right now*. Open University Press.

Cunha, M., Cunha, J., & Kamoche, K. (1999). Organisational improvisation: What, when, how, and why. *International Journal of Management, 1*(3), 299–341.

Driscoll, J. (2007). *Practising clinical supervision* (1st ed.). Baillière Tindall Elsevier.

Felsman, P., Gunawardena, S., & Seifert, C. M. (2020). Improv experience promotes divergent thinking, uncertainty tolerance, and affective well-being. *Thinking Skills and Creativity, 35*, 1–9.

Flower, J. (2021). *Everything's an offer: An IPA study of how Coaches experience engaging in improvised theatre exercises* (Unpublished master's thesis). Henley Business School.

International Coaching Federation (ICF). (2019). Updated core competencies. https://coachfederation.org/core-competencies

Hadida, A. L., Tarvainen, W., & Rose, J. (2015). Organisational improvisation: A consolidating review and framework. *International Journal of Management Reviews, 17*(4), 437–459.

Hardingham, A. (2006). The British Eclectic Model of Coaching: Towards professionalism without dogma. *International Journal of Mentoring and Coaching, 4*(1), 11–14.

Johnstone, K. (1979). *Impro: Improvisation and the theatre*. Theatre Arts Books.

Jones, R. J. (2021). *Coaching with research in mind*. Routledge.

Kindler, A. (2010). Spontaneity and improvisation in psychoanalysis. *Psychoanalytic Inquiry, 30*(3), 222–234.

Kirsten, B., & Du Preez, R. (2010). Improvisational theatre as team development intervention for climate for work group innovation. *SA Journal of Industrial Psychology/SA Tydskrif vir Bedryfsielkunde, 36*(1), 1–9.

Kolb, A., & Kolb, D. (2006). Learning styles and learning spaces: A review of the multi-disciplinary application of experiential learning theory in higher education. In R. R. Sims & S. J. Sims (Eds.), *Learning styles and learning: A key to meeting the accountability demands in education* (pp. 45–92). Nova Science Publishers.

Koppett, K. (2001b). *Training to imagine: Practical improvisational theatre techniques to enhance creativity, leadership, teamwork and learning*. Stylus Publishing.

Leonard, K., & Yorton, T. (2015). *Yes, and: How improvisation reverses "no, but" thinking and improves creativity and collaboration*. HarperCollins Publishers.

Lewis, C., & Lovatt, P. J. (2013). Breaking away from set patterns of thinking: Improvisation and divergent thinking. *Thinking Skills and Creativity, 9*, 46–58.

Passmore, J. (2007). Integrative coaching: A model for executive coaching. *Consulting Psychology Journal: Practice and Research, 59*(1), 68–78.

Passmore, J., Day, C., Flower, J., Grieve, M., & Jovanovic Moon, J. (Eds.). (2021). *Coaching Tools: 101 coaching tools and techniques for executive coaches, team coaches, mentors and supervisors: WeCoach!* Volume 1. Libri Publishing.

Ratten, V., & Hodge, J. (2016). So much theory, so little practice: A literature review of workplace improvisation training. *Industrial and Commercial Training, 48*(3), 149–155.

Read, M. J. B. (2013). The importance of improvisation in coaching. *Coaching, 6*(1), 47–56.

Romanelli, A., Moran, G. S., & Tishby, O. (2019). I'mprovisation – Therapists' subjective experience during improvisational moments in the clinical encounter. *Psychoanalytic Dialogues*, *29*(3), 284–305.

Romanelli, A., & Tishby, O. (2019). 'Just what is there now, that is what there is'—The effects of theater improvisation training on clinical social workers' perceptions and interventions. *Social Work Education*, *38*(6), 797–814.

Romanelli, A., Tishby, O., & Moran, G. S. (2017). 'Coming home to myself': A qualitative analysis of therapists' experience and interventions following training in theater improvisation skills. *Arts in Psychotherapy*, *53*, 12–22.

West, S., Hoff, E., & Carlsson, I. (2017). Enhancing team creativity with playful improvisation theater: A controlled intervention field study. *International Journal of Play*, *6*(3), 283–293.

Wheeler, S., & Leyman, T. (2023). *Playfulness in Coaching*. Routledge.

Chapter 12

The use of film in coaching

Nefeli Soteriou

Introduction

The notion of using film in coaching arises from what is known as *Cinematherapy* (Berg-Cross et al., 1990), which harks back to the late 1980s. With this approach, the coach and client discuss the relevance of one or more commercially successful narrative films to the client's area of current concern. The idea is proposed that the client might elect to view the film(s) independently or with trusted others. Such a film can ignite curiosity, educate, inform, and promote discussion or debate. Narrative films tend to be favoured, given their tendency to inspire action, providing clients with what often turn out to be a set of meaningful insights. After all, from an early age, many of us are introduced to fairy tales and perhaps sit through oral histories and myths at a summer campfire. For example, in a narrative film's typical story structure, the protagonist faces a personal challenge, and her way forward is somehow blocked. As she takes steps to overcome her issues, she finds support from trusted others (Vogler, 2007). Aside from the story itself, such a film's creative inspirations include narration, setting, costume and make-up, lighting, staging, editing, and sound. As such, the use of film in coaching can thus extend far beyond plot and life lessons into reflection on the craft of cinema and its various conceptual frames (Kolker, 2015b). The coaching conversation is led by whatever is collaboratively considered to broaden the client's view of her circumstances and the world.

An introduction to theory, basic concepts, and key developments

A brief history can be helpful in our understanding of what the broader world gained from the birth of cinema and its impact on science and technology. Motion pictures emerged from the Industrial Revolution and the invention of photography. Before the end of the 19th century, photographer Edward Muybridge pursued the study of motion by capturing a galloping horse on film. His pioneering work led to the design of a Kinetograph box (1892), a

DOI: 10.4324/9781003453437-13

contraption which allowed the first-ever motion picture projections onto a screen. When still photographic images are played in succession, as Muybridge demonstrated, they can create the illusion of movement. A great many images tend to be required, given that just one second of a motion picture film is said to contain 24 still images.

The first quarter of the 20th century was a particularly active period of creativity at all levels. The Hollywood studio system was established, later proving to be an incredibly efficient business model. Cinema moved from one-person camera work to a complex collaborative endeavour. Motion pictures evolved into being far more relational to human nature with story-generating content. They offered unparalleled attraction to viewers across a range of economic and social classes (Bordwell et al., 2008b), perhaps more than literature, painting, or photography. As early as the 1920s, the study of films found its place in academia as a means of theoretical research, a trend which continues to the present. Film analysis as a discipline has advanced into an area of continued interest in university studies, whereby educators now use them as tools to inform, ignite curiosity, and engage in debate or discussion in the classroom (Uhlin, 2014). Television channels were launched over networks as early as 1939, albeit initially with limited viewership. Pioneering countries with early TV stations include the United States, the United Kingdom, Germany, and the former Soviet Union. By 1965, even the Vietnam War was being featured on television. The film was quickly transferred to be developed, edited, and offered into the lives of millions of Americans who owned a television set (Manovich, 2001). As the global community of filmmakers and scholars has grown over the years, films are now appreciated as vital historical records. For example, the US Library of Congress today holds the world's largest and most comprehensive collection of audiovisual works, with more than six million moving images, sound recordings, and related documentation (Library of Congress, n.d.).

The use of colour in motion pictures grew at first by a method of hand drawing. Later, it was embedded in the film strip made from celluloid, colourised by means of a chemical process. Animation in moviemaking was shaped gradually, from Walt Disney's two-dimensional *Fantasia* (1940) to today's computer-generated animated films. The technology has been afforded with various leaps and bounds along the way. An example is George Lucas's *Star Wars Episode IV: A New Hope* (1977), widely considered to have changed the game in the animation industry. Fast forward to Pixar's *Toy Story* (1995), where audiences enjoyed the first 3D animation which was entirely computer-generated (Prince, 2012). Despite the advances in both technology and approach, it is worth noting that until the 2000s, film screening in cinemas was enacted entirely by photochemical means. The most profound leap in any of our lives, aside from those involved in the film industry, was the arrival of digital technology, whereby filmmakers embraced an entirely new set of tools in a manner which elevated the mechanics of the production of narrative filmmaking, making it both easier to produce, store, and screen, but also more affordable and thus arguably accessible to wider audiences.

The notion of viewing films to understand life's issues has been enabled greatly by the democratisation of access to them, all by means of the internet. For example, the popular *Cinema Therapy Show*, launched on Patreon as well as a YouTube channel in 2019, features licensed therapist Jonathan Decker and professional filmmaker Alan Seawright breaking down the themes of many of what will no doubt be some of your favourite films. Alan Seawright typically offers a brief analysis of the art and craft of commercially successful narrative films, whilst Jonathan Decker tends to comment on character behavioural dynamics (The Cinema Therapy, n.d.). This show remains enduringly popular, with more than 1.5 million subscribers. Other examples abound whereby psychology meets technology in the form of mobile phone apps and wearable devices. Such devices are already able to create convincing three-dimensional experiences, which most of us perceive as multisensory. Such technology is already finding its way into various interventions using cognitive-behavioural therapy, where patients with phobias and anxieties work through their problems in a controlled environment instead of an actual exposure (Cardos et al., 2017). The future will make our technology-enhanced experiences more realistic with the passage of time. Technologies, such as virtual and augmented reality, will continue to evolve in ways we probably do not even imagine.

Learning how to integrate the use of film into coaching

A vast array of creative choices made by filmmakers will affect what eventual viewers will experience and how they are likely to respond. Various stylistic elements comprise the result of a blockbuster film intended for wider audiences. By interrogating their impact through careful analysis, even if not expert analysis, you can engage your client in what are often quite meaningful conversations (Kolker, 2015b). There are many directions which can be taken in such a co-considered interrogation, some of which are presented below:

Narration, in the form of voiceover dialogue. Whether implicit or voiced over by an actor, a film's narration signifies how the story unfolds within its plot structure, connecting various elements or providing insight into the unobservable mindset of a protagonist. An important consideration might be to ask about your client's language preferences before suggesting a film and to learn of the client's rationale. For example, some individuals prefer to watch a film in its original language, assisted by subtitles in a chosen language, as opposed to the once common practice of 'dubbing' the dialogue for multiple-language distribution.

Setting provides the filmmaker with a much-needed container for the acting, and it takes shape largely through the location in which the film is shot.

Aside from animations, filmmakers may use purpose-built sets, an actual living room, an office building, or even a location setting such as a motorway. For example, in the comedy-drama *On the Rocks* (2020), Sofia Coppola chose to set the location in two countries: the United States and Mexico. We watch the protagonist in her apartment in lower Manhattan, working at her desk, visiting her husband's office, and going to their children's school. At one stage, she and her father visit Mexico and stay at a seaside resort, which gives an intentionally distinct feel to the unfolding drama. Within the overall backdrop of a film's setting, filmmakers will often introduce symbolic props which later prove to be crucial to aspects of the narrative's unfolding plot. Iconic examples include the time machine in *Back to the Future* (1985) and the briefcase in *Pulp Fiction* (1994).

Costume and make-up guide the viewer's attention to the character. In the romantic comedy *Pretty Woman* (1990), the costume and make-up are used to depict the progressive transformation of Julia Roberts' character from a professional escort to the girlfriend of the businessman played by Richard Gere. When she first meets him at the film's inception, she wears an off-white sexy tank top, a sports bra attached to a blue mini skirt, and sets it all off with a round buckle at her belly button. Her above-the-knee boots are conspicuous in black leather, and the whole ensemble is flourished by a brown jacket wrapped casually around her waist. Her make-up and free-spirited hairstyle appear to complement her role as an escort. As the film unfolds, however, the new outfits bought for her serve to advance and drive the unfolding plot. The evolving transformation charts for the viewer a developing narrative in which, inevitably, they fall genuinely in love.

Lighting in cinema creates both mood and connotation. The art of cinematography, or what may be termed 'painting with light', tends to shape the contours and the detail of our sense of the space as viewers of a film's various *tableaus*. The work involved in the execution of a filmmaker's vision involves technical skills, mechanical and electrical knowledge, and creative prowess. Artificial and natural light are often combined, whilst others use light filters to create illusions through the selection of camera lenses and placement, and there is much else involved, as well. Two contemporary films to consider watching purely as an interrogation of the effects of light and shade are Roger Deakins' *Empire of Light* (2022) and Mandy Walker's *Elvis* (2022).

Staging. The director orchestrates the movement and performance of all animals, puppets, and props, as well as the actors themselves, all within what is known as the 'screen space'. Blockbuster movies are large-scale productions with secure budgets. They are backed by the Hollywood studio industry or by independent companies that adhere to the same production value system. As such, an enquiry into staging can draw from multiple films whose layered approach has involved the talent and consideration of many.

Editing is the process by which the various aspects of a film are ultimately assembled. Nowadays, as would be expected, all editorial decisions are digitally worked on a computer. The process includes a consideration of motion graphics titles, colouring, masking, music, transitions, and special effects. You can learn to notice the simple editorial decisions made in what results in the final cut of a film, often doing so even as you watch it. For example, when you see a change in a scene, mark it with a dot or a straight line on a notepad with a pencil. Over time, you will discover the pace and how quickly or slowly certain scenes are cut. Another way is to simply count the shots of a film. Some films require fewer shots than others (Bordwell et al., 2008b). There is a whole array of possibilities when it comes to ways in which it is possible to consider and discuss a film's editing process.

Sound in film comes in different forms, such as the music composition, the speech, and the background noise. With focused attention, you can sharpen your awareness of the sound as you watch a film. For example, you might simply ask yourself the following questions: Where is the sound coming from? In the story space or outside of it? On the screen or offscreen? How does the sound influence you as to what you are seeing? Does it sound realistic, or are you perceiving it a certain way? When does it take place? Are there sound repetitions, and where? What is your outcome as the viewer with a particular film's sound?

Mapping a film's narrative to specialised areas of interest

If you are a coach specialising in a certain area of interest, it would only take you some online searching to find films which appear to be based on your speciality. For example, if you are a finance coach, search for "films on financial literacy" or "top ten films in finance". The same applies to the "top ten films about addictions", etc. If you work were more of a general nature, for example, as a life coach, you might wish to inspire a client who can't seem to overcome her despair over a temporary health challenge. You might enquire as to whether this client had heard of the film *The Miracle Worker* (1979). If so, or even if the client was intrigued by the mention of the film, an invitation might be made to consider watching it, with a view toward discussing what they liked or what it made them think about in an upcoming session.

Inducting your client to the use of film in coaching

Sometimes a client struggles with the notion of working with film in a coaching session or cannot quite grasp the point of doing so. You can often co-create a brief experiential exercise which does not map to an area of interest or to the client's coaching goals as a means of introducing the overall concept. For example, it might work for you and the client to both agree to some simple practice on sharpening your individual observational skills. A film's stylistic approach might be a great way to start, as it does not involve a lot of personal interpretation. It would be easy to conduct an online search and locate the film trailer for the classic romance film *Casablanca* (1942), starring Humphrey Bogart and Ingrid Bergman. A comparison could be made to the trailer of the recent release of *Barbie* (2023) with Margot Robbie and Ryan Gosling.

Everyone knows that a film trailer is an attempt to entice potential audiences with the highlights of the film in its entirety. You can certainly use the sharply contrasting trailers to practice having a view of the stylistic approach of both these films, whether you have seen the full-length feature or not. Knowing that your client will be doing the same, you, as the coach, might find yourself writing down various observations for each film. These may entail what you noticed regarding impressions of the likely story (narration), setting, camera, lighting, acting, sound, and editing. You might agree with your client to describe a sentence or two for each element and then, when finished, compare notes and impressions. This simple exercise can give an experiential sense of working with film, which can be expanded upon. An example of doing so is presented in the case study with a client referred to as "Dora."

Case study

When the coach started to work with Dora, it soon became apparent that Dora was a recent film school graduate who was keen to break into the entertainment industry. She held a part-time position at a neighbourhood bakery on the outskirts of New York. Due to the low income of her salary, Dora lived with her parents. Dora's brightness stood out early on and continued to shine through with each coaching session. Various between-session exercises were agreed upon, but it seemed to be a pattern that Dora seldom got them done. An attention deficit hyperactivity disorder diagnosis and a hypersensitivity to light were agreed to be a challenge, but Dora also shared how she feared growing up. For example, at one stage she shared that she never planned to move out of her parent's basement. In addition, the coach observed what is known as 'filtering the positive' and a constant adverse comparison between herself and her peers. Although her parents had arranged a family gym membership, Dora rarely attended. It soon became apparent that, instead, she tended to overeat, snack on pastries, and to drink too much coffee, and both smoked marijuana and drank alcohol in a manner that was reported as secretive and excessive. As such, Dora complained of headaches and insomnia.

Time and space were agreed, which was to be dedicated to talking about films at each session. This arrangement turned out to be meaningful to Dora, and it built a great deal of trust in the coaching alliance. Given Dora's interest in the film industry, the conversation often involved no more than a simple mention of a new release, an actor stepping into a new role, or an observation about a film influencer. It transpired that Dora found it natural and validating to describe film scenes as examples which could be used to make a point about her own life and struggles. For example, when she considered becoming a children's teacher, she mentioned a scene from *Kindergarten Cop* (1990). Dora recounted the scene in which the film's villain, Crisp, was setting about to harm the school children. In this part of the film, John (famously played by Arnold Schwarzenegger), as the children's teacher but at the same time an undercover policeman, saved them. Dora shared confidently that she now realised that she could enjoy such a job, remarking, "An evil person must never be allowed to work around children". By associating herself with this film's hero, Dora started to rethink her possibilities, widen what she would consider as career choices, and interrogate the competing desires to not ever grow up versus to do so by embracing a fulfilling career. This included initiating a programme of more mindful eating, attending the gym, and working with an accountability partner.

Conclusion

In conclusion, the integration of film in coaching represents a dynamic and innovative approach to personal development and self-discovery. Stemming from the principles of Cinematherapy, this technique leverages the power of narrative films to spark curiosity, promote reflection, and foster meaningful discussions (Berg-Cross et al., 1990). By selecting commercially successful films which seem to be relevant to an individual's concerns, coaches can guide clients through interventions involving exploration, insight, and action. The significance of narrative films lies in their ability to provide a relatable platform for the client's storytelling and reflection. Through a film's typical journey of overcoming challenge and finding support, viewers can gain valuable insights into their circumstances (Vogler, 2007). Furthermore, understanding the stylistic elements of filmmaking enables coaches to engage in deeper conversations with their clients (Kolker, 2015b). By analysing these elements within the context of a film, clients can explore themes, emotions, and motivations relevant to their personal growth. By harnessing the power of storytelling through the visual medium of film, individuals can gain valuable insights, cultivate self-awareness, and take meaningful steps towards positive change.

Discussion points

- To what extent do you consider that narrative films accurately reflect real-life experiences, and how does this influence your views on their effectiveness in coaching?
- How might cultural and linguistic differences impact the effectiveness of using narrative films in coaching sessions, and what strategies might coaches use to address these challenges?

- Consider your five favourite films and reflect on how they relate to given clients. Which films depict what amounts to a Hero's Journey, and which of your clients would most identify with the narrative of your favourite films? After considering these matters, it is interesting to search online for a review of your favourite films to ascertain if others have shared your sense of the narrative arc, the Hero's Journey, and the closeness to one or more of your client's coaching aims.

Suggested readings

The following texts provide the reader with a useful overview of film studies, giving the interested reader a grounding in what is possible with the use of film in coaching:

Kolker, R. (2015a). *Film, form, and culture*. Routledge.
Bordwell, D., Thompson, K., & Smith, J. (2008a). *Film art: An introduction* (Vol. 8). McGraw-Hill.

References

Berg-Cross, L., Jennings, P., & Baruch, R. (1990). Cinematherapy: Theory and application. *Psychotherapy in Private Practice*, 8(1), 135–156.
Bordwell, D., Thompson, K., & Smith, J. (2008b). *Film art: An introduction* (Vol. 8). McGraw-Hill.
Cardos, R. A. I., David, O. A., & David, D. O. (2017). Virtual reality exposure therapy in flight anxiety: A quantitative meta-analysis. *Computers in Human Behaviour, 72*, 371–380.
Kolker, R. (2015b). *Film, form, and culture*. Routledge.
Library of Congress. (n.d.). About the library of congress. Retrieved 23 March 2024 from https://www.loc.gov/about/
Manovich, L. (2001). *The language of new media*. MIT Press.
Prince, S. (2012). *Digital visual effects in cinema: The seduction of reality*. Rutgers University Press.
The Cinema Therapy. (n.d.). *The cinema therapy*. YouTube. Retrieved 23 March 2024 from https://www.youtube.com/@TheCinemaTherapy
Uhlin, G. (2014). Playing in the Gif(t) economy. *Games and Culture*, 9(6), 517–527.
Vogler, C. (2007). *The writer's journey: Mythic structure for writers*. Michael Wiese Productions.

Chapter 13

The power of place

Integrating environmental psychology and arts-based coaching

Max Eames

Introduction

Research has given a rich language to the nuanced ways in which environmental attributes affect our thoughts, feelings, and actions. For example, matters such as aesthetics, functionality, and symbolic meanings are notionally on our minds when we book a room (or choose a virtual backdrop) for our coaching sessions. The research suggests, however, that rather more ought to be under consideration. Drawing on insights from environmental psychology, this chapter explores the contribution that a better understanding of space and place can make to enhancing the coaching experience. Environmental psychology offers a helpful framework for understanding how we interact with our surroundings, how these interactions can affect our well-being, and how the actual 'setting' of coaching might be a contributing factor in encouraging more helpful psychological and emotional outcomes.

By applying what is offered by the field of environmental psychology, it is hoped that coaches will feel minded to select, adapt, or transform coaching environments so they more effectively align with the specific needs and objectives of their clients. Whether coaching sessions occur in nature, in indoor spaces, or in virtual environments (Riva et al., 2016), an informed approach to setting can lead to more engaging, productive, and transformative coaching experiences.

It is the aim of this chapter to equip coaches with knowledge and skills that encourage them to harness 'the power of place' as a tool for facilitating personal growth. Through a brief introduction to some of environmental psychology's core concepts, the reader is invited to consider strategies for optimising the physical and psychological spaces in which coaching occurs. This is also an opportunity to consider the role of cultural and individual differences in shaping people's responses to setting and place, and to reflect on ways to accommodate such differences.

DOI: 10.4324/9781003453437-14

Environmental psychology and its interest in physical space

Environmental psychology explores the complex relationship between human beings and their environments. As such, it delves into the myriad ways in which physical spaces influence a wide range of human experiences. This field of study is founded on the notion that humans are seldom passive occupants of their surroundings; rather, they are deeply affected by them. All the while, they are actively interpreting and reacting to various environmental stimuli (Gifford, 2014). The foundational principles of environmental psychology thus provide a robust framework for analysing and understanding the psychological effects of environments, from the serenity of natural landscapes to the bustling dynamics of urban spaces.

The insights from environmental psychology permit us to consider the significance of physical characteristics and their impact on psychological processes. In the broadest of terms, for example, spaces that are harmonious and aligned with human needs tend to foster a sense of well-being, whereas discordant environments can lead to stress, distraction, and reduced performance (Steg et al., 2013b). Far more in the way of knowledge, however, is essential for coaches who aim to create or select environments that will more consistently support their clients' goals.

The influence of place and space in human psychology

The impact of place and space on human psychology is a multifaceted phenomenon which intertwines with our emotions, behaviours, and overall mental health. The environments in which we find ourselves can deeply influence our psychological states, ranging from a sanctuary that promotes mental rejuvenation or a challenging setting inducing stress and cognitive overload. This realisation underscores the importance of understanding the psychological implications of physical spaces, especially in contexts where optimising human potential and well-being is the goal.

Kaplan and Kaplan (1989) articulate the restorative benefits of certain environments, proposing that settings can contribute to reducing mental fatigue, enhancing emotional well-being, and promoting cognitive clarity. Their work introduces the concept that spaces are not merely physical locations but are imbued with emotional, symbolic, and practical significance which interacts with the human psyche in complex ways (Kaplan & Kaplan, 1989). Well-considered environments can thus act as conduits for psychological restoration, offering individuals a respite from the demands of modern life.

Often, it is the symbolic significance of settings which plays a central role in how they impact our psychology. Spaces can embody cultural values, personal memories, or social norms, affecting our emotional responses and behaviours. The personal and cultural meanings attributed to different places can evoke a wide range of psychological responses, from a sense of belonging and identity to feelings of alienation and discomfort. Understanding such symbolic dimensions can assist in creating environments that resonate positively with either individuals or groups of participants.

Aside from such matters, the practical significance of spaces should not be overlooked. Environments designed with human needs and behaviours in mind can greatly enhance daily functioning and quality of life. This includes considerations of accessibility, usability, and adaptability of spaces to meet diverse needs. When places are chosen with an awareness of their practical impact, they can significantly contribute to reducing distraction, enhancing inclusivity, and promoting positive social exchanges.

Sensitivity to settings in coaching

The following are some of the many likely considerations involving a coach's need to attend to matters of sensitivity to settings in coaching:

Assessing environmental influences on clients

Throughout this book, various arguments are being made in support of the favourable impact that arts-based interventions can have on the coaching process. In planning such interventions (where the aim is to foster growth and insight through creative endeavours), it may be particularly important to acquire sensitivity to the setting in which coaching takes place. Such sensitivity extends far beyond merely acknowledging the physical attributes of a space. It involves a sophisticated understanding of the psychological impacts certain attributes may have (Hartig et al., 2014) in shaping human emotions, behaviours, and cognitive functioning. As such, arguably, the skill of assessing environmental influences requires a multifaceted approach.

Firstly, it involves the observation of immediate, observable effects of a space on a client's demeanour, engagement level, and comfort. For instance, a coach might enquire whether a client becomes more open and relaxed in a serene, natural setting as opposed to a sterile office environment. Such information can provide insight into the settings which best support the client's ability to reflect, engage, and transform.

Next, it demands an understanding of the subtle, often unconscious psychological processes which are influenced by environmental factors. Drawing on environmental psychology, coaches might wish to consider in detail how setting can affect mood, stress levels, and cognitive clarity (Bratman et al., 2012). For example, research has shown that environments with ample natural light and greenery can boost mood and creativity, potentially making them ideal settings for coaching sessions aimed at brainstorming and visioning.

Finally, coaches are encouraged to consider individual differences in terms of sensitivity to environmental cues. What might be perceived as calming and conducive to one client could be distracting or even unsettling to another. Neurodivergent individuals have inclined architects, workspace planners, and urban designers towards a better understanding of neurodiverse perceptions of space and place. It is argued that our need for such understanding as helping professionals may be equally important, even without our knowing it (Robertson & Simmons, 2013). Given widespread variability, a range of arguments can be made for a personalised approach to choosing coaching environments, taking account of the client's preferences, past experiences, and specific coaching objectives.

As referenced elsewhere in this chapter, the psychological impact of space also encompasses the symbolic meanings which may be attached to certain environments. A setting which holds a particular personal or cultural significance may elicit stronger emotional responses and facilitate deeper engagement with the coaching process. Coaches should be attuned to any such symbolic dimensions, engaging in dialogue with clients to understand the personal narratives and meanings they associate with different spaces.

Ultimately, sensitivity to settings involves a dynamic and ongoing assessment process. As such, coaches should be prepared to adapt and modify their approach as the coaching relationship evolves. The ability to assess environmental influences is arguably a critical competence, requiring a blend of observation, psychological insight, and a personalised approach (Hartig et al., 2014). Such a sensitivity means that, as coaches, we can more effectively support our clients' growth and well-being by harnessing the power of place as a facilitator of change.

Adapting coaching strategies to various settings

The art and science of coaching entails the ability to create a conducive environment that aligns with unique needs and preferences. Recognising that each client will respond to setting and place may be important in crafting interventions which are not only effective but also deeply personalised. That said, the impact of physical settings on the coaching process is often largely unexamined, despite its likely role in shaping the client's level of comfort, openness, and receptivity.

For instance, we can take it as given that some clients find inspiration in the tranquillity of natural settings (such as parks, forests, or bodies of water), inspiring a sense of clarity whilst facilitating deeper introspection. The theories behind this phenomenon are far more interesting than the notion itself. It is said that this response can be attributed to the so-called *biophilic* tendency (Ulrich, 1984; Heerwagen & Orians, 1993), the innate human attraction to life and lifelike processes. Nature's restorative effects might thus be leveraged in the context of arts-based interventions aimed at encouraging reflection and emotional processing.

Conversely, other clients may derive energy and inspiration from the bustling atmosphere of urban environments. The dynamic nature of city settings, with their sensory stimuli and the wide range of human activity, are equally positioned to stimulate thinking and creativity. Such a preference underscores the importance of understanding the psychological impacts of built environments, which can vary based on personal experience, cultural background, and psychological needs.

Adapting coaching strategies to different settings involves more than just selecting the right environment; it also requires modifying the approach and techniques to be used within those environments. For example, coaching interventions held in natural settings might incorporate walking meetings, which not only offer the many benefits of physical activity but also an enhanced capacity for creative problem-solving (Kaplan & Kaplan, 1989). In contrast, coaching sessions in urban settings might leverage a range of unique features (such as art installations or historical landmarks) as metaphors or prompts to facilitate discussion.

Managing the logistical details of arts-based interventions

Importantly, any adaptation of arts-based interventions to different settings must consider the logistical and practical aspects of conducting sessions in these environments. This includes considerations of privacy, accessibility, and the potential for distractions, which can significantly impact the effectiveness of the coaching session. Coaches must remain proactive in anticipating and managing a vast array of logistical details.

Incorporating client feedback and observations into the decision-making process is also important. Engaging clients in conversations about their preferences and how they perceive different environments can provide valuable insights that inform the customisation of a planned intervention (keeping in mind that such matters may be particularly important to neurodivergent individuals). Such a collaborative approach goes a long way toward ensuring that creative and arts-based interventions are tailored to a client's needs, all whilst fostering a sense of ownership and engagement in the coaching process itself.

By tailoring interventions to the client's comfort with various environments, coaches are likely to enhance the relevance, impact, and personalisation of the experience. Keep in mind, however, that adapting an intervention to its setting may prove to be unexpectedly complex – and that doing so is often beset with compromise. It requires a deep understanding of the psychological impacts of environments, a thoughtful consideration of client preferences and needs, and a flexible approach to integrating environmental factors into coaching practices.

Practical application of arts-based interventions

Below are presented some of the many likely considerations involving the practical application of arts-based interventions, as follows:

Transcending the constraints of verbal communication

Particularly when integrated with an awareness of space and environment, arts-based interventions can act as pathways to exploring inner landscapes, unlocking new perspectives, and engaging in what can be profoundly deep emotional expression. The theoretical foundations for these approaches are in many ways grounded in an understanding that creative expression transcends conventional verbal communication (McNiff, 1998b), tapping into non-verbal realms of human experience to foster insight and transformation.

Aligning the setting with coaching objectives

True integration of environmental psychology with the facilitation of creative interventions requires alignment between a physical space and the specific objectives of the art-based activity. For example, a coaching session aimed at fostering creativity might benefit from being held in a space that is colourful, dynamic, and filled with natural light, qualities that are known to stimulate creative thinking (Steg et al., 2013b). Conversely, interventions focused on introspection and emotional healing might be more effective in serene, nature-infused settings that promote calmness and reflection (Hartig et al., 2014).

Exploring complex emotions and unresolved conflicts

The process of creating art, whether it be through painting, sculpting, writing, or performing, offers a unique and profound avenue for clients to explore complex emotions, unresolved conflicts, and personal narratives (McNiff, 1998b). The act of artistic creation, coupled with the supportive qualities of a well-chosen surrounding environment, can facilitate a deep sense of self-awareness and emotional catharsis.

Encouraging cognitive and emotional flexibility

In addition to fostering emotional expression, it is argued that creative and arts-based interventions can enhance cognitive flexibility, problem-solving skills, and the capacity for imaginative thinking. The non-linear, open-ended nature of creative expression encourages clients to think in new ways, challenge existing assumptions, and explore alternative perspectives. Given that cognitive and emotional flexibility tend to be constituent elements of personal and professional growth (Padesky & Kennerley, 2023), such creative expression can assist with coaching goals aimed at adapting to change, overcoming obstacles, and envisioning new possibilities.

Fostering collaboration and mutual support

There can also be significant benefits arising from the social and communal perspective of creative expression conducted in a group setting. Group art-making activities (particularly when facilitated in spaces which encourage collaboration and mutual support) encourage a sense of connection, empathy, and shared humanity. Various social dynamics can amplify the likely transformative effects of an art-making endeavour, providing a rich context for interpersonal learning, feedback, and validation. By intentionally leveraging the expressive potential of communal art within thoughtfully designed spaces, coaches can incline clients towards engaging in various means of self-discovery, emotional healing, and personal growth.

Case studies

The following case study examples are intended to inspire an enthusiasm for attending to space and place when proposing creative and arts-based interventions. Whether drawing upon the tranquillity and inspiration of natural landscapes or harnessing the dynamism of urban environments, coaches can use environmental psychology to enhance the coaching experience. By thoughtfully integrating such settings into their practices, they are much more likely to demonstrate the powerful synergy between place, creativity, and personal growth, offering valuable insights for those seeking to enhance their commitment to self-discovery.

Nature as a canvas

Nature, with its inherent beauty and serenity, serves as a powerful canvas for clients to explore their inner thoughts, emotions, and connections with the broader world. The act of engaging in creative exercises within the tranquillity of a natural setting can foster a deep sense of peace, grounding, and clarity, facilitating moments of profound insight and self-reflection.

The benefits of engaging with nature include improvements in mood, reduced stress, and increased cognitive functioning (Bratman et al., 2012). These effects can be instrumental in instances in which goals are centred around personal growth, overcoming challenges, and fostering a deeper understanding of oneself.

For example, so-called mindful walks in natural settings provide the dual benefit of physical activity and mindfulness. They encourage clients to engage with their surroundings in a manner which promotes mental clarity and emotional balance. The rhythmic nature of walking, combined with the sensory experience of being in nature, can facilitate a meditative state, enabling deeper reflection and insight (Kaplan & Kaplan, 1989).

Outdoor art projects, similarly, can encourage clients to draw inspiration from the natural environment. They might well use creative expression to not only leverage the calming effects of nature but also to foster a connection to the external world, enhancing both well-being and ecological awareness (Kellert & Wilson, 1993).

Leveraging urban settings

The dynamism of urban landscapes offers a contrasting, yet equally inspiring, backdrop for creative and arts-based interventions. The rich tapestry of visual and auditory stimuli found in urban settings can invoke creative thinking and problem-solving efforts, prompting clients to view their personal and professional challenges from new perspectives. The bustling energy of city life, with its diverse architecture, public art installations, and vibrant street scenes, can provide a suitable backdrop for engaging in creative activities which encourage exploration and discovery.

Louv (2011) discusses what is termed *urban advantage*, whereby the dynamism, diversity, and complexity of city environments can provide a setting for interventions aimed at stimulating resilience and adaptability. After all, the challenges and opportunities presented by urban life can mirror those faced in our personal and professional lives, making the city a powerful metaphor for navigating change and uncertainty. Engagement with urban environments in coaching sessions can help clients develop the skills and mindsets needed to thrive in the face of life's complexities.

Activities situated in urban settings might simply include exploratory walks that encourage clients to observe and interact with their surroundings in new ways, drawing parallels between the urban landscape and their internal landscapes. Such exercises can stimulate creative problem-solving and idea generation as clients learn to see familiar environments through fresh eyes (Louv, 2011). Additionally, exposure to diverse cultural experiences and social interactions inherent in urban environments can enhance adaptability and empathy, which are said to be essential skills in both personal development and professional leadership (Florida, 2014).

Integrating natural and urban elements

Many settings lend themselves to a merging of elements derived from natural and urban environments to create a multifaceted setting for creative exploration. One means of doing so might be a workshop whereby participants are invited to engage in a so-called *biophilic* project. In keeping with the thesis advanced by Kellert et al. (2008), participants might be tasked with creating art pieces that integrate natural materials and themes with urban aesthetics. Such a fusion might encourage a consideration of the synergy between human and natural systems. The process of creating art pieces in this vein might well engender various dialogues concerning sustainability, well-being, and harmony between individuals and their environments.

Conclusions and future directions

The intentional use of space can play a pivotal role in enhancing the effectiveness of creative activities. The environment in which art-based interventions are conducted will likely influence a person's openness, comfort level, and overall engagement with the creative process. A well-configured setting can also serve as a catalyst for self-discovery, providing the physical and psychological space necessary for individuals to freely express themselves, explore their emotions, and engage in reflective practice.

As the field of coaching continues to evolve, it is hoped that further research and exploration will delve deeper into the relationship between place, space, and coaching effectiveness. Another promising direction for future research will no doubt be the continued exploration of virtual and digital environments and their potential role in coaching. As technology advances at a rapid pace, various possibilities exist for creating immersive and interactive spaces that can simulate a wide range of environments and settings for coaching interventions.

For the time being, however, we inhabit a largely physical world. The right environment not only serves as a passive setting for coaching sessions but actively contributes to the process by influencing mood, creativity, and cognitive function. It is argued that arts-based interventions which attend to environmental factors are likely to create a more dynamic, effective, and personalised coaching experience. Finally, it is hoped that this chapter has in some way succeeded at stimulating an interest in the role of place and space in enhancing the important work you do with your clients.

Discussion points

- What did this chapter make you think about regarding your own reactions to space and place?
- How does a particular setting tend to affect your mood, stress levels, and cognitive clarity?
- What are some of your reflections on optimising the physical and psychological spaces in which coaching occurs in your practice?
- What are your thoughts on the role of cultural and individual differences in shaping people's responses to setting and place?

Suggested resources

Steg, L., Van den Berg, A. E., & de Groot, J. I. (2013a). *Environmental psychology: An introduction* (2nd ed.). Wiley-Blackwell.
McNiff, S. (1998a). *Art-based research*. Jessica Kingsley Publishers.

References

Bratman, G. N., Hamilton, J. P., & Daily, G. C. (2012). The impacts of nature experience on human cognitive function and mental health. *Annals of the New York Academy of Sciences*, 1249(1), 118–136.

Florida, R. (2014). *The Rise of the Creative Class, Revisited: Revised and Expanded.* Basic Books.

Gifford, R. (2014). *Environmental psychology: Principles and practice* (5th ed.). Optimal Books.

Hartig, T., Mitchell, R., de Vries, S., & Frumkin, H. (2014). Nature and health. *Annual Review of Public Health*, 35, 207–228.

Heerwagen, J. H., & Orians, G. H. (1993). Humans, habitats, and aesthetics. In S. R. Kellert & E. O. Wilson (Eds.), *The biophilia hypothesis* (pp. 138–172). Island Press.

Kaplan, S., & Kaplan, R. (1989). *The experience of nature: A psychological perspective.* Cambridge University Press.

Kellert, S. R., Heerwagen, J., & Mador, M. (2008). *Biophilic design: The theory, science, and practice of bringing buildings to life.* John Wiley & Sons.

Kellert, S. R., & Wilson, E. O. (1993). *The Biophilia Hypothesis.* Island Press.

Louv, R. (2011). *The nature principle: Human restoration and the end of nature-deficit disorder.* Algonquin Books.

McNiff, S. (1998b). *Art-based research.* Jessica Kingsley Publishers.

Padesky, C.A., & Kennerley, H. (2023). *Dialogues for discovery: Improving psychotherapy's effectiveness.* Oxford University Press.

Riva, G., Banos, R. M., Botella, C., Mantovani, F., & Gaggioli, A. (2016). Transforming experience: The potential of augmented reality and virtual reality for enhancing personal and clinical change. *Frontiers in Psychiatry*, 7, 164.

Robertson, A. E., & Simmons, D. R. (2013). The sensory experiences of adults with autism spectrum disorder: A qualitative analysis. *Perception*, 42(5), 123–134. https://doi.org/10.1068/p7499

Steg, L., Van den Berg, A. E., & de Groot, J. I. (2013b). *Environmental psychology: An introduction* (2nd ed.). Wiley-Blackwell.

Ulrich, R. S. (1984). View through a window may influence recovery from surgery. *Science*, 224(4647), 420–421.

Chapter 14

Fires for the cold

The uses of poetry in coaching

Auriel Majumdar

Introduction

Poetry has existed as long as humans have had recourse to language. It is one of the creative ways we express ourselves in words through structured and often rhythmic writing and speaking, using language chosen for its aesthetic qualities, evoking emotions, imagery, or ideas in a condensed and heightened manner to create a distinct and often moving artistic experience. Poetry transcends conventional prose, aiming to evoke feelings, provoke thoughts, and convey meaning through the careful arrangement of words. This chapter explores the use of poetry in coaching. It covers the early roots of poetry and its use in therapy and goes on to present theoretical ideas underpinning the introduction of poetry into the coaching space. The chapter explores how the expressive nature of poetry can deepen self-reflection, spark insight, and enhance the coaching experience. The practicalities of using poems in coaching are considered alongside an illustrative case study. The chapter concludes with a poem intended to prompt further reflection and some reflective questions for coaches and suggests additional resources for coaches wishing to add poetic methods to their coaching repertoire.

A beginning

As a novice coach, my lifelong love of poetry and newly discovered belief in the power of coaching collided as I was introduced to Gestalt theory, in particular the concept of use of self (Siminovitch & Van Eron, 2006). The idea that the coach need not be a neutral party in coaching but could be an instrumental partner to the coachee's reflection was a revelation and prompted me to write my first coaching-related poem, exploring the idea of the coach as an active collaborator:

> They tell me I'm supposed to be a mirror,
> Glassy and reflective, all surface
> But I think, what if I was someone to put my shoulder to yours?

DOI: 10.4324/9781003453437-15

Someone who sees colours when you speak.
Who dreams new stories when you tell me yours?
A deep pool into which you can drop your stones and count the ripples?
Mirrors have their uses but that's not what I'm doing here.
Put your shoulder to mine.

Already interested in adopting creative approaches in my coaching practice, through the experience of writing, reflecting on, and sharing poems with clients and other coaches, I became fascinated by the way poetry helped my clients articulate and understand their experiences, helped to "explain people to themselves" as William Sieghart puts it (2017, p. xviii). As I allowed more of my own poetic self into the coaching space, I witnessed how choosing or writing poetry and reflecting on it as part of the coaching process yielded different results to the conventional dialogic coaching models I was being taught. Clients working with poetry appeared to reach their own understandings and insights much more quickly as they thought about the poems we read together, and I became interested in the power of poetry to transform, to be "a disturbing unit; that, when one goes into that force field, one will come out the other end a changed person" as the poet Paul Muldoon (2024) describes it. In this chapter, I will explore the theoretical underpinnings of the use of poetry in coaching, the benefits and challenges of a poetic approach, and the practical implications for coaches wishing to work in this way.

Deep roots – the history of poetry

The history of poetry is as ancient as the history of human language. The earliest poetry is believed to have been recited and sung to pass on the histories of communities, their beliefs, rules, and family lineages. Early poetry was closely related to musical expression and ritualistic performance and, as much as it was used to convey facts, was also a way for early people to exist beyond the material realm. Poetry is not simply a reporting of an objective 'reality' but subjective interpretation of experience, and the use of poetry in coaching highlights the ever-present debate between rationality and magic – is coaching a logical march towards achievable goals or a meaning-making dance between coach and coachee? I agree with the Bengali poet Rabindranath Tagore, believing as he does that "a mind all logic is like a blade all knife/It makes the hand bleed that uses it" (1919), and poetry is a way for me to include magic in my practice. Jane Hirshfield (2017) says that "poems are like the emotions they awaken in us: not preservable object but living event" (p. 184), and it is this ability of poetry to capture the heightened emotions of lived experience and compress meaning in a concise sentence and a vivid image that allows us to use it to go beyond a logical examination of events and reach for deeper levels of understanding. When we work with poetry, we invite ourselves to feel, hear, think, and see in altered ways. Working with poetry requires us to move beyond the concrete and into the abstract, supporting the client to find their own new sense of things and the action that might arise for them from this.

The roots of poetry therapy are equally ancient. Aristotle's *Poetics* (2013) is widely cited as the most influential book on poetry and proposes the role of catharsis in effecting an emotional cure, suggesting that the role of poetry is to liberate the troubled mind by providing insights and universal truths. This idea of poetry's role in healing through release found its way into modern western practices such as psychotherapy and subsequently into specific forms of thera-peutic practice such as poetry therapy in which poetry is explicitly used to support the resolution of emotional difficulties. Mazza's *Poetry Therapy: Theory and Practice* (2021) offers a comprehensive account of the evolution of this branch of therapy, its theoretical foundations, and its practical applica-tion. In poetry therapy sessions, clients may write, read, or share poetry, either in the session with the therapist's support and guidance or as a way of reflect-ing between sessions. This use of therapy helps to heal through a process of the client becoming aware of and expressing emotions that might otherwise be difficult to acknowledge. Poetry is understood as a vehicle to promote self-reflection and exploration, increase self-awareness, help individuals to take dif-ferent perspectives on their circumstances, and to make sense of their world. Coaching, of course, is not an explicitly therapeutic practice; as coaches, we are not trying to heal but to support the coachee to identify and make the changes they want to. Despite this fundamental difference, however, the aims of heightened self-awareness and meaning-making that lead to change and transformation are similar. This is especially true for person-centred modes of coaching which centre clients' experiences and are committed to the idea that the client already possesses their own resources for growth and are agents of their own destiny.

There is a growing understanding that creative or arts-based coaching meth-ods can "open up new possibilities and encourage a more expansive mode of thinking" (Megginson & Clutterbuck, 2009, p. 101), and this is often attributed to these methods being beyond dialogue. This is most explicit in Sheather's "Coaching Beyond Words" (2019) which explores the uses of visual language to aid the client's reflection and self-expression. In my own practice, I have experienced the power of working with creative methods such as image selec-tion and making, music, and dance, but this idea of working 'beyond words' does provide a challenge for the introduction of poetic methods. Unlike many other arts-based approaches, poetry revolves around words, but its use of evoc-ative images and metaphor similarly invites us to work beyond the logical, lin-ear, and rational and triggers the same sense-making processes as visual arts-based coaching. Visual and poetic arts-based approaches also share a belief that supporting the client to access their creativity through improvisa-tion, playfulness, willingness to experiment, and letting go of perfection is transformational in ways that more conventional coaching approaches are not. In "Coaching Creativity" (2016) Jen Gash, citing Daniel Doherty's research, suggests that writing techniques, including poetry, can "accelerate and deepen the coaching practice" (p. 143) both in the moment and through a process of reflection and sense-making after the event. This is perhaps where the use of poetry is distinct amongst the creative coaching approaches in its ability to persist beyond the coaching session, for "when we employ poetry as a tool for healing and transformation, we come to see that we are not only poets while we are writing; we are poets all the time" (Richo, 2009, p. 9). When I turn to reading and writing poetry as a reflective practice, I find it permeates into my whole life, and I respond to dilemmas with more creativity and flexibility; more options present themselves to my poet's eye.

Jacki McCartney explores poetry's potential for client *and* coach transformation in her paper "Practice and Potential: A Heuristic Inquiry into the Potential of Poetry for the Reflexive Coaching Practitioner" (2018). McCartney concludes that the role of poetry as a 'reflective enabler' offers "space, time and perspective to facilitate deeper reflexive consideration of personal values and beliefs, the influence of self and others in real time and retrospectively, bringing forth choice and opportunity for proactive learning and choice" (p. 151).

Humphrey and Tomlinson (2020) have identified three benefits of poetic approaches in coaching: stimulation of metacognition, enhancement of empathy, and generation of new perspectives. Poetry's ability to support metacognition, or the awareness and understanding of our own thought processes, echoes McCartney's work on reflexivity and highlights the value of imagination, the "dance between thoughts and feelings" (p. 8) as a catalyst for change. Humphrey and Tomlinson also suggest that becoming immersed in fictional writing such as poetry helps us to develop empathy by extending our understanding of the ways that others respond to events that we may never have encountered, which in turn will extend our range of responses to other people. Thirdly, they suggest that the act of reading poems in coaching has the potential to generate new perspectives, allowing the client to see in the images and stories possibilities for themselves that they had not previously recognised.

Poetic coaching approaches are particularly helpful when the client is grappling with existential questions or feels unable to act in the face of complexity and uncertainty. Existential coaching is marked less by clear and precise knowledge and more by uncertainty and change with fewer clear outcomes, and this can prove resistant to orthodox coaching process models driven by goal setting. In this context, poetry can ask hard, unspoken questions, prompting clients to deepen their understanding of themselves and discover their own answers. As poet and essayist Jane Hirshfield writes, "[A] good poem is able both to answer uncertainty and to contain it" (2017, p. 131). Through reflecting on a poem, a skilful coach can help the client raise what is invisible to conscious awareness and support them to face uncertainty with courage or at least hope. Humphrey and Tomlinson (ibid. 2020) bring together John Keat's notion of 'negative capability', the ability to hold "uncertainties, mysteries, doubts, without any irritable reaching after fact and reason" (Keats, 2002 in Humphrey and Tomlinson, ibid. 2020) and the notion of the 'fertile void', the paradox of a space that is simultaneously empty and full. If the coach can tolerate working in this void, without linear process or certain outcomes, then introducing poems as reflective prompts can support "slow unfurling insights as opposed to immediate answers" (p. 13), making the uncertainty at worst bearable and at best, full of creative potential.

It is easy to think of poetry in coaching as a frivolous device, but as contemporary life becomes ever more fractured and perilous, coaches will increasingly need to develop negative capability, a sense of poetry and the ability to tolerate complexity so that they can support clients. These stirring words of Audre Lorde capture the essence of my belief in the uses of poetry to support myself and others in turbulent times:

> Poetry is not a luxury. It is a vital necessity of our existence. It forms the quality of the light within which we predicate our hopes and dreams toward survival and change, first made into language, then into idea, then into more tangible action. Poetry is the way we help give name to the nameless so it can be thought. The farthest external horizons of our hopes and fears are cobbled by our poems, carved from the rock experiences of our daily lives.
>
> (Lorde, 1985, p. 1)

Seeing colours – poetry in practice

Palus identifies three levels of 'artful coaching' (2006) that offer a useful way to think about the practicalities of working with poetry. Level 1 is an entry level in which the coach and coachee pay attention to stories, metaphors, and images but do not explicitly bring art into the session. At this level, the coach or client might spontaneously mention a poem or a line of poetry that generates new thinking or sheds new light. Here poetry is useful but incidental and has not been deployed intentionally.

Level 2 is tool use, where an artefact is intentionally used to support the creation of meaning. With poetry as the 'artefact', there are two choices here:

1 Choosing – either the coach can suggest a poem that has some resonance with the situation being discussed or invite the client to choose one. This requires the coach to have access to a repertoire of poems or feel confident that the client can bring a poem into the space, and, as with any art-based method, this requires clear contracting to frame the work. The client reflects on the choice with the coach's assistance to make connections, notice new insights, and consider implications for action. It is important to resist the urge to make this a literary exercise – the work is to reflect on what the poem provokes rather than to analyse it. The poem does not have to be 'good' or 'worthy' – I have had striking results with limericks, for instance!

2 Writing – this can be a joint effort either in session, before, or after. With
   supervision groups, for instance, I have used the chat function of Zoom
   meetings, asking each participant to contribute a line in response to a
   prompt or a first line from me. We then reflect on the resulting poem as a
   group. Working individually, I occasionally write poetry outside of the session and invite clients to do the same, and we then share the results in our
   coaching sessions and reflect on what new perspectives or insights they offer.
   Sometimes clients who are confident with poetry as a medium share their
   own poems. Again, as with all arts-based approaches, it is important to
   embrace imperfection and resist any need to get it 'right'. Sharing poetry is
   brave work, an act of vulnerability for the client and for the coach. The
   coach is critical in setting the tone here and modelling non-judgemental
   noticing and reflection of our own responses as well as the client's. Of
   course, this creating of Carl Rogers' 'core conditions' (1951) is at the heart
   of person-centred coaching, and coaching with poetry is no different.

Level 3 in Palus' Artful Coaching Framework is World Making in which the
client uses the artful practice to remake the relationship between their self and
the world. In this level of artful coaching encounter, "there is a sense of risk
associated with exploring the unknown and commitment to transformation.
All creative resources are fair game for application toward further development" (p. 265). Practically speaking, poetry in coaching is more reflective
prompt than problem-solving tool, a prism, or a kaleidoscope rather than a
road map. Poetry fits well in a person-centred "let's see where this takes us"
coaching approach where the coach and client are explorers of complicated
landscapes, seeking to support the client to find their own way through. Of
course, not all clients either want or are able to work in this way and may prefer
to work at Levels 1 or 2, but where the context is right, bringing poetry in as
'fair game' to transform the client's meaning-making can have noticeable
results as the case study below illustrates.

*Sarah is the director of a creative design agency and writes poetry for enjoy-
ment and as part of her own artistic practice. She has been grappling with questions about her identities as leader and artist and how the two can co-exist. We
have worked together for six sessions, and as we both write poetry, this has sometimes come up in our work together. In our latest session, we have contracted
explicitly to make poetry the focus. Sarah wants to explore the challenges of her
role and organisational life and the impact this is having on her mood and well-
being. As we talk, Sarah shares several of her own poems at points where they feel
relevant to her. The first poem uses the metaphor of taking up the floorboards and
seeing the 'bad pipes.' This leads to a conversation about Sarah's discomfort with
exposing 'potential for decline and trouble', but this line of enquiry does not seem
to lead anywhere significant for her. The second poem she shares, written on a
journey back from a distant country, contains the lines "The decisions that keep
re-writing themselves/The conversations that feel like surfing/The confluence of*

parts of you that usually shelter in distant stables/The absurdity of what you might have been doing instead", and as we reflect on what she has written, she notices that "poetry seems to lodge somewhere in the gap between noticing some-thing and processing it through the way my brain would normally process some-thing. Sometimes in writing, you realise what it is about, but you can finish a whole poem then only at the end you're like oh yes, it's also about that. It's not literal, and they get to you before your brain gets in the way". This poem helps her realise that her artist identity is somehow in conflict with her leadership identity and the expectations that come with it. The final poem contains the lines "Time's flimsier than it seems/Loosen its seams/Take a novel from Cockfosters to Heathrow and back again", and as Sarah reflects on these words, she picks up the earlier theme of the different parts of herself and her resistance to classification as a conventional leader. She says that what she wants is the "space between her identities" to help her resolve the difficulties she experiences in having a leader-ship persona that is not authentic to her. I ask her if writing poetry is a way of making her situation tolerable, and she replies that poetry gives her the space she needs and that she wants to create more 'breathing room'. She says that by being able to share her poetry with me, someone she trusts, the artist identity "gets more oxygen... so then maybe I'll be able to sit in leadership just as peacefully". We talk for a while about how she might create breathing room but agree that this work "is not for now". As we finish the session, I ask her how it has been to share her poetry and use it to reflect on her situation. She tells me that she has experi-enced the sharing of her poems (and some that I have offered in response) as "little scraps that are an invitation that would allow you and me to both stare at this thing side by side". Sarah leaves without a definitive resolution to her dilemma but knowing that the idea of breathing room connects to "some act of imagining how a life might be configured" in her future.

Ripples in the pool – reflections on practice

This coaching encounter falls into the category Level 3 Artful Coaching, in which Sarah is world building, reflecting on her poems to remake the way she thinks about herself as an artist and as a leader so that she can lead in her own authentic way. As we began, I noticed my own anxiety about whether I would understand her poems or have a useful interpretation to offer, but I was able to bracket this, place it to one side, and focus on creating a safe and supportive space in which Sarah could make her own connections, identify themes and the implications of these. In practice, this is no different to working with poetry as it occurs in Level 1 or Level 2 coaching encounters but what differs is the level of support the client may need. Less confident clients or those who are not familiar with creative practice will need more encouragement from the coach, more structure, and more explicit invitation to reflect. This is true when work-ing with any art-based method which often comes loaded with unhelpful expe-riences and messages from schooldays. Assumptions about the 'correct' form of a poem, whether it needs to rhyme and so on, will need to be addressed in contracting so that both coach and client feel free to experiment with poetry as a medium. That said, it is important not to underestimate clients' willingness and ability to access the poetic, and it is surprising how many people are able to quote a favourite line or verse that has meaning for them. I am continually moved and captivated by the poetry in people's lives.

In this case study, Sarah was working on existential questions of identity that were troubling and which did not lend themselves to neat resolution. The metaphors in her poems were a useful way to explore this hazy landscape – the "bad pipes", "the confluence of parts of you that usually shelter in distant stables" and "loosen the seams" spoke directly to Sarah without her having to translate them for me. They took her directly to a meaning that she had not previously been aware of. As she made connections between her three poems, Sarah noticed his dissatisfaction with being labelled a conventional 'leader' and realised her creative self needs room to breathe so that she can create more balance. Although we did not reach definitive actions in this session, a new insight emerged that in time may shift Sarah's perception of her identity. This required my negative capability as a coach, holding the ambiguity, honouring emergence, and resisting any urge to drive towards some concrete 'result'. As I coached Sarah, I felt drawn to explore the edges of her dilemma, using her poems as anchors to give shape to the conversation, helping her to knit together something meaningful. As we reviewed the session, Sarah told me that realising that her creativity needed 'room to breathe' felt like significant progress, and she left the session with renewed energy and optimism. I am reminded of Jane Hirshfield's question, "Why ask art into a life at all if it not to be transformed and enlarged by its presence and mysterious means?" (Hirshfield, 2017).

Onwards – an encouragement for coaches

For coaches considering bringing poetry into their coaching, I offer the following reflection points in the form of a list poem, inspired by Edip Cansever's "The Table", which I hope captures the sense of anticipation that we coaches feel as we are waiting to meet with our coachees.

> A listener arrives in a quiet room, full of words and wondering.
> Puts her notebook on the table and her special pen next to it,
> Her books that tell her "How to", the list of instructions,
> Memories of her teacher telling her to make it rhyme and scan,
> Memories of her clumsy attempts and red-faced reading aloud.
> She gently places her desire to help next to her fear that she won't be able to.
> She sets down the heavy weight of her own expectation of herself,
> Her need to be logical, to work in sequence,
> The pressure of achieving, of getting somewhere.
> The table is buckling now under the weight of all her doubts.

The listener knows she needs to lighten the load,
She picks up her glittering heart, her trust in herself,
Her flickering vulnerability and willingness to try.
She gathers all the poems she has ever encountered,
But leaves behind the pressure to remember them all.
She gathers up her belief in mystery and magic,
Remembers that she knows how to decide what's needed,
How to and ask and respond,
Remembers that she can smell rain coming, remembers that she is an open-hearted prism.
The door opens and the listener gets to work

I will close this reflection on the use of poetry in coaching with a wondrous reminder from Mary Oliver (1994) "Poetry is a life cherishing force. And it requires a vision…. For poems are not words after all but fires for the cold, ropes let down for the lost, something as necessary as bread in the pockets of the hungry. Yes Indeed". I wish us all vision and faith so that we may warm ourselves with the fire of poetry and send the ropes down for those who may need them.

Conclusion: An invitation to reflect

Poetry may appear spontaneously as we are coaching, but when we are considering being more intentional about introducing poetry into our work, as always, the coachee's needs are paramount. As with any coaching intervention, we must ask ourselves whose needs are being served and how. While poetic flourishes can feel satisfying for coaches, beware of feeding your own ego at the expense of your coachee. My rule of thumb with any creative approach, including poetry, is to first ask myself if the approach is necessary, relevant, or useful and if there is even a shred of doubt, then don't even consider using it!

Poetry is seductive and spellbinding, and it is easy to assume that poetic coaching will be light and enjoyable. However, if we do decide that poetry will enhance the coaching dialogue, remember that poetry, with its ability to hold profound meaning, can take us deep very quickly. Careful contracting and re-contracting are essential to ensure that we are working safely, with the client's consent and a mutual understanding of the potential implications of working in this way. As coaches, we must think carefully about how we will introduce poetry and what impacts we intend or anticipate. It is also important to think in advance about our response if it goes nowhere or takes us somewhere we have not predicted. Of course, none of these reflective questions are unique to the use of poetry, but the prospect of introducing creativity into work is an exciting one, and we need to keep our heads and not be swept away without carefully considering the practical and ethical aspects of poetic work.

For any coach wanting to introduce poetry into their work, I would recommend paying close attention to your own creative capacity. How is your own creative self being tended to outside of the coaching sessions? How is poetry present in your life? What are you reading, writing, sharing beyond the sessions with your coachees? To work effectively in poetic coaching, I believe we need to be surrounded by poetry daily. As part of my own personal and professional development I read poetry every day, write my own poetry and collaborate with others. I go on writing retreats and surround myself with poets who are more advanced in their journey. Immersing ourselves in this way develops a familiarity and ease with poetry's potential to move and illuminate meaning but also ensures that we remain alive to poetry's potency so that we may harness it wisely in service of our coachees.

Discussion points

- How does the historical role of poetry as a medium for self-expression and emotional exploration align with the objectives of coaching in fostering personal growth and insight?
- Can you share examples of how the expressive qualities of poetry can facilitate deeper self-reflection and insight for clients in a coaching setting?
- Drawing from the case study presented in this chapter, how can coaches effectively incorporate poems into their coaching sessions, and what considerations should be considered when selecting and utilising poetry as a coaching tool?

Suggested resources

Developing poetry writing skills:

WLAG – https://writelikeagrrrl.com
Arvon Foundation – https://www.arvon.org/

Finding poems to inspire:

The Poetry Pharmacy – William Sieghart
Staying Alive trilogy – Edited by Neil Astley
National Poetry Library https://www.nationalpoetrylibrary.org.uk/online-poetry
BBC Resources: The BBC's poetry site features poems, poets' biographies, videos, and writing and performance tips from contemporary poets. https://www.bbc.co.uk/programmes/articles/5y4773X4mxPhXGTcbHDxN3J/poetry-resources

References

Aristotle, A. (2013). *Poetics*. OUP Oxford.

Gash, J. (2016). *Coaching creativity: Transforming your practice*. Routledge.

Hirshfield, J. (2017). *Ten windows: How great poems transform the world*. Knopf.

Humphrey, D., & Tomlinson, C. (2020). Creating fertile voids: The use of poetry in developmental coaching. *Philosophy of Coaching: An International Journal, 5*(2), 5–17.

Lorde, A. (1985). Poetry is not a luxury. In *The broadview anthology of expository prose* (pp. 217–220).

Mazza, N. (2021). *Poetry therapy: Theory and practice*. Routledge.

McCartney, J. (2018). Practice & potential: A heuristic Inquiry into the potential of poetry for the reflexive coaching practitioner. *International Journal of Evidence Based Coaching & Mentoring, 16*(S12), 138–153.

Megginson, D., & Clutterbuck, D. (2009). *Further techniques for coaching and mentoring*. Routledge.

Muldoon, P. (2024). *Joy in service on rue Tagore*. Faber & Faber.

Oliver, M. (1994). *A poetry handbook*. Houghton Mifflin Harcourt.

Palus, C. J. (2006). Artful coaching. In S. Ting & P. Scisco (Eds.), *The CCL handbook of coaching: A guide for the leader coach* (pp. 259–285). Jossey-Bass.

Richo, D. (2009). *Being true to life: Poetic paths to personal growth*. Shambhala Publications.

Rogers, C. (1951) *Client-centred therapy*. Houghton Mifflin.

Sheather, A. (2019). *Coaching beyond words: Using art to deepen and enrich our conversations*. Routledge.

Sieghart, W. (2017). *The poetry pharmacy: Tried-and-true prescriptions for the heart, mind and soul*. Penguin UK.

Siminovitch, D. E., & Van Eron, A. M. (2006). The pragmatics of magic. *OD Practitioner, 38*(1), 51.

Tagore, R. (1919). *Stray birds*. Macmillan.

Chapter 15

Together in electric dreams

Stephen Brown

Introduction

In the wake of the global pandemic of 2020, the landscape of coaching underwent a significant transformation, with a notable shift towards online platforms. This chapter delves into the ramifications of this shift in the practice of creative coaches, offering insights into how they have adapted their methodologies to thrive in the digital realm.

We embark on a journey to understand the nuances of online coaching and its impact on the creative process. From exploring the technological advancements that have revolutionised the coaching industry to showcasing innovative approaches tailored for digital delivery, we uncover the multifaceted dimensions of this evolving landscape.

Drawing from my experiences as a practitioner, we present first-hand how creative coaches have navigated the digital terrain, reimagining traditional methods and embracing fully digital solutions. Through illuminating examples and case studies, we dissect the intricacies of coaching in the virtual sphere, shedding light on ethical considerations and professional standards that guide practitioners in this new paradigm.

At its core, this chapter serves as a comprehensive guide for creative coaches seeking to harness the power of digital platforms, offering practical insights and actionable strategies to elevate their practice in an increasingly online world.

The digital world and our evolving industry

Our digital lives undeniably accelerated in March 2020 as the coronavirus pandemic shifted how we all worked, socialised, and interacted. Lockdowns normalised digital interactions in an unprecedented way, changing the way we communicate and collaborate forever. Four years on, in 2024, it felt like we were still emerging from that period, but people were generally back in the workplace, and life was returning to some form of normality, yet the practice of many professional coaches remained online, a lot of the time, if not entirely.

DOI: 10.4324/9781003453437-16

Looking further back, beyond the past decade, we have also seen the prominent rise of digital technologies such as social media, internet-of-things, and artificial intelligence (AI). Technologies that differ from earlier generations, such as the internet and email, in their editability, flexibility, and transfigurability (Shao et al., 2022).

AI has exploded into public consciousness in recent times and is being heralded as one facet of the Fourth Industrial Revolution (McKinsey & Company, 2022). A long-established view is that it won't replace 'people jobs' or the creative sector (Hambly & Bomford, 2018). But that view is being challenged with each passing year given the sudden rise of generative AI and machine learning. In Marcus du Sautoy's book *The Creativity Code* (2019), he shares how developers are now determined to undermine Ada Lovelace's first descriptions of the creation of code in 1843, that "machines can only do whatever we order them to do" and have shifted their focus to a 'bottom-up' approach, encouraging computers to chart their own path. Despite these developments, there are those who see limits to AI and machine learning and maintain that human functions such as creativity, shared understanding, and empathy – in other words, areas of social cognition – will prove resistant to mathematical equations.

No doubt the debate will continue, and perhaps coaches are safe from the rise of the machines, for now. However, it may be prudent to integrate new technology into our practice sooner rather than later so that it becomes a partner, not a threat (Grabmann & Schermuly, 2021).

Amid this technological advancement, a new term has emerged within the coaching industry: 'CoachTech'. A collective term which broadly captures any piece of technology which forms part of or enables a coaching conversation. This could be anything from tech that schedules your coaching sessions to virtual reality-enabled interactions and AI (Isaacson, 2021).

Virtual and augmented reality (VR/AR) technology has for some time now been adapted for use in coaching, introducing a whole new world of creativity. From designing your own avatar to crafting a unique and immersive virtual location for a coaching session, the possibilities are literally endless. However, despite VR/AR technology being more affordable than ever, it still has a relatively high cost to entry and brings with it some technical hurdles to overcome. This seems at odds with the main benefits our shift to digital working has provided, such as increased accessibility, flexibility, and cost-effectiveness (Kanatouri, 2020).

How effective is it to coach online?

The efficacy of online coaching is an important factor to explore, and it's true there were reservations about coaching in the digital realm when this was enforced upon all coaches in 2020; however, a 2021 survey of over 1,300 coaches found more benefits to coaching this way than downsides. Benefits include convenience, safer personal space, and cost reduction. Conversely, around a third surveyed found coaching online to be less intimate, harder to build relationships, and less enjoyable, but perhaps most importantly, the findings show that 83% of those surveyed stated their clients would prefer to work this way (Passmore, 2021).

Similarly, in the therapeutic world, counsellors have in the past generally viewed working online as less effective when establishing a therapeutic alliance. But as counselling pivoted online during the pandemic, a reasonably large body of studies were developed to suggest this is not necessarily the case. Clients consistently rate the therapeutic alliance online as moderate to high, equivalent to face-to-face interactions. Research also found that clients experienced a higher degree of safety and comfort in their own homes to access private aspects of their inner selves when compared to a counsellor's office. This includes using supplies, objects, and toys from the clients' environment for art and play therapy (Barker & Barker, 2022).

Despite this, many coaches feel working online blocks their creativity and struggle to bring their creative selves online, but much of the anxiety around becoming a successful online creative coach stems from using technology itself rather than coaches' ability to communicate their ideas (Anthony & Nagel, 2021).

If the use of technology is a potential area for growth, then those who value self-development will bring the same passion for learning, experimentation, and improvement as they would to other aspects of their practice. As the EMCC states, "A critical part of a professional coach's competency is the commitment to self-development, of course through supervision, but also through deliberate action and reflection".

A digital creative practice

In the interests of full disclosure, I'm passionate about technology. I follow trends. I'm curious about how technology can be used and adapted, and it's the platform for my own creative background in electronic music. Whilst I accept that this provides a solid platform on which to base my digital creative coaching practice, I don't believe this to be a prerequisite.

Despite the perceived advantage of being tech-oriented (finally being a geek paid off!), I was faced with many familiar questions when first coaching online at the start of the pandemic:

- How will working digitally affect my ability to make a connection with a coachee?
- Will my technology be stable?
- How will I coach creatively?

In my own practice, certain coaching capabilities have been heightened due to the reduced sensory data experienced in the digital domain, such as enhanced listening and the ability to notice shifts in tone of voice and body language (Kanatouri, 2020). Similarly, adjustments have had to be made during contracting to acknowledge that both coach and coachee exist in their own individual space, recognising how that may impact confidentiality, for example. However, the skills mastered by coaches, such as the ability to remain present, engage in appreciative inquiry, and be guided by intuition, remain highly relevant and clearly transferrable to the digital domain. The greater challenge was how to bring a creative approach to an online coaching session.

First, let's adopt a broad view and consider creativity in coaching. Jen Gash (2016) separates the method of creative coaching into process and product, with process being the act of thinking creatively and product the creative activities used during the coaching process. Simply by asking our clients to answer reflective questions we are encouraging them to be creative – bringing something new to form. However, if we feel it's right to introduce a creative or arts-based 'product' into an online coaching session, what would that look like?

I now propose two further distinctions of creative coaching products, analogue and digital. Analogue products are physical, real-world tools, techniques, and objects that can be simply adapted for use in a digital setting. For example, when working with picture cards, this could be adapted by holding the cards to your webcam for your coachee to observe. For a higher fidelity experience, picture cards could be scanned into a computer and shared on-screen, not to mention the fact that tools such as Unsplash.com can increase a coach's picture library into the millions with a few simple clicks of a mouse.

A first-hand experience of analogue tools in a digital setting came when I attended a group creative, reflective exercise involving mark-making to music. Our coach and fellow contributor to this book, Beth Clare McManus, demonstrated the exercise by utilising a second camera positioned to focus on the piece of paper in front of her. A simple change to the camera settings between cameras 1 and 2 provided a seamless transition between the experiment and the speaker. It was very simple yet highly effective – an approach accessible to most coaches (additional webcams are available at very reasonable prices).

Likewise, when I spoke to contemporary artist, educator, and creator Paul Merrick about working creatively with groups online, he had to adapt his use of objects and improvisation and think tactically about asking groups to find 'universal' items in their own space to work with – e.g., something to cut with, some paper, something heavy/light.

This presents the first opportunity for coaches to work creatively online by considering how they can take their favoured creative approach and adapt it for online work. Equally, this provides the first opportunity for development, that being the fluent use of your chosen online platform. Microsoft Teams and Zoom dominate and therefore have significant free resources available to learn about the finer elements of their functionality. For your analogue creative product to work well in the digital domain, it's likely you will need to know how to enable and work with features that permit screen sharing, sound sharing, attachments, chat, etc. It's not desirable to be aimlessly cycling through menus, options, and features when the environment you're trying to create is one of improvisation, experimentation, and flow. Your chosen online platform should remain the 'silent partner' in the coaching system.

Going digital

In the same way that the music industry has embraced digital tools, making a shift from the use of analogue musical equipment to working completely 'in the box' with software and moving from physical media, such as vinyl and CDs, to downloads and streaming services, I would like to invite you to consider how your own creative product could 'go digital'. In this section, I won't be recommending specific technology, but I will share how you can begin to establish a digital coaching toolkit to complement your in-person techniques.

In her book *Coaching Beyond Words* (2019), Anna Sheather describes one of the most frequently asked questions about coaching creatively: "How do you know what exercise to use?" For me, the answer to this question emerged from my own experiences of using sound and music as part of my reflective practice. Through supervision, I was encouraged to experiment, utilising my background in electronic music composition. The result was highly meaningful and inspired me to investigate how I could provide a similar experience for my clients. However, producing sound and music requires access to the right tools and the skills and know-how to use them. This created a necessity to find a tool that anyone with a mouse and keyboard could engage with.

In seeking an accessible digital option to fit the creative need, the initial research was no more complicated than a Google search: 'create music online'. I'm sure if you substituted the word 'music' in that search string with another art-based approach, you will be introduced to a world of graphic/sound design experiments, digital artworks, and websites designed for education or simply for fun. However, many of the digital assets that you will discover won't have been created with coaching in mind. Therefore, in the same approach described earlier, some adjustments may be required.

By creating time to purposefully explore what's out there, it's possible to quickly establish an inventory of interesting digital tools. The question is, then, how can they be developed into a fully formed digital creative product for use in a coaching situation? Here's the fun part: experiment! Being open-minded and deliberately playful will help you evaluate whether your digital tool will be effective as a vehicle for deeper reflection and creative thinking. Once you've explored it yourself, share it with peers and with your supervisor, and gather as much feedback as possible. Why not use a digital tool to aid your own reflections? After all, "reflective practice is an iterative, open-ended, creative process" (Lucas, 2023).

Of course, a Google search is only the beginning; you may need to deepen your research in your quest to find the perfect digital creative product. Blogs, newsletters, and podcasts are all great places to hear from prominent voices in creative coaching and CoachTech and will generate more ideas and inspiration. What you discover through your curiosity and experimentation could be completely unique to you and your coaching practice, as Rick Rubin puts it in the 2023 book *The Creative Act*, "There is no wrong way, only your way".

Your professional and ethical practice, online

Best practice tells us that creative experiments should be introduced by invitation during a coaching session. This aspect of in-the-moment contracting ensures agency for the coachee and comfort for the coach that they remain in their non-directive space. As part of this, we must also take time to consider our coachees feelings and proficiency with technology in the same way we have considered our own. Does the prospect of positioning cameras and clicking links to access online products create any unwanted barriers or anxieties that may inhibit the coaching process? If your coachee is the meeting organiser, for example, they may take on the responsibility of cycling through menus to enable the correct functionality. Have you considered whether your coachee has adapted their workstation in any way? Do they rely upon the use of physical or software-based tools to support the use of their PC, such as magnification apps for the visually impaired? Leave nothing to assumption.

Being aware of any organisational contexts may also be a key factor in avoiding any pitfalls with technology, particularly when adopting digital products. There would be nothing more disheartening than providing a link to your chosen tool only to find the site is blocked by the organisation's security protocols. If that did happen, what is your plan b?

Fundamentally, part of providing a professional coaching experience is the safety that is engendered in the relationship, which in turn creates an environment of trust, enabling meaningful conversations and positive outcomes. Introducing a creative digital tool into that environment can bring with it excitement and intrigue, but with it a new risk – data security. Files can contain viruses, sites capture data, and although Microsoft Teams and Zoom offer end-to-end encryption, we should consider all aspects of online interaction. The purpose of this chapter is not to provide thorough advice on data security but to raise the question of how you will ensure the safety of your coachee's data and technology when working digitally. Both the Global Code of Ethics and the International Coaching Federation (ICF) Code of Ethics describe in detail our responsibilities around confidentiality and data in relation to relevant laws, with the ICF specifically referencing the use of emerging and growing technologies in coaching and how their ethical standards apply to them.

You may need to research further how to ensure websites are safe, but some basic principles such as using sites that have a secure connection as well as positive reviews and ensuring everyone involved in the process has up-to-date security software on their devices would be a good starting point.

If you're reading this, knowing your proficiency with technology is an area for development, then this may add to the size of the task at hand, but fear not, by becoming well-versed in staying protected online, you're providing a safe experience for your clients, and your own online safety will improve in tandem. Coachees gain benefits when a variety of tools and techniques are presented during coaching, but as Alison Hardingham suggests when describing an eclectic coaching approach, "they need that choice and variety served up by a coach who is a master of their craft and can select and present a range of tools with confidence wisdom and finesse" (Passmore, 2020).

Case study

Helen (not their real name) is an experienced practitioner who was keen to learn more about coaching creatively online and wanted to explore a current topic and challenge in a new way. Helen and I had an existing relationship, which was established during the pandemic, and as a result, we had never met face-to-face, meaning this was our expected way of interacting with each other.

At the beginning of the session, I informed her that there would be an invitation to work with sound and visuals, and after a period of contracting, Helen shared her topic and was 'curious' to accept the invitation to experiment.

The tool introduced was patatap.com – a soundboard/digital graphic design website – the web address was dropped into the chat box of our online platform, and Helen was invited to open the link. She was then encouraged to share her screen and sound so that we could both experience the outputs of the experiment.

Having previously experienced creative coaching through physical objects, Helen's initial feeling was one of underwhelm, as she had simply been asked to access a website. That feeling quickly disappeared, however, when she was encouraged to press keys on her keyboard, which resulted in the generation of sounds, shapes, patterns, and colours. Helen was handed complete control of this tool, with the freedom to experiment, which quickly engendered a sense of expression and playfulness, with me, as her coach, a keen observer.

After a period of purposeful play, Helen began gravitating towards certain sounds, shapes, and colours, and through questioning, we explored those choices. The circular shapes she was drawn to represented how she viewed her current situation; the sounds she was creating were light in tone, representing a desired future state, and some outcomes of the experiment were discarded due to memories dating back to childhood.

Guided by Helen, we agreed when the experimentation had reached its conclusion, and together, we moved towards what Jen Gash (2016) describes as a process of contraction which follows an expansive creative period, the aim of which is to move towards action through the integration and synthesis of ideas and reflections.

In the debrief that followed, Helen shared that this experience had reminded her of her original coach training, where she was encouraged to try new things and experiment but had somehow now reached a point where she felt she needed permission to be playful – particularly given most of her interactions take place online. She shared the comfort that was felt experimenting with sound and visuals this way and how the experience helped her see her topic "from the third person".

It also emerged that, unprompted, Helen began drawing circles on the pad in front of her during the experiment. A physical extension of this digital creative activity. She then recounted a song which had carried meaning for her in the recent past. I took the opportunity to open Spotify, share my computer's sound, and conclude the session by playing the song, resulting in a noticeable shift in energy and emotion.

Discussion points

- How would you assess your level of confidence and comfort coaching online? How does the idea of introducing a creative exercise impact this?
- With some adaptation, how could you take your creative product online?
- What research will you undertake to find a digital equivalent of your chosen creative approach? What value would be gained by finding one?
- What areas do you need to upskill to get the best out of your technology?
- What investments would enhance the experience or simply reduce the risk of things going wrong? Higher-resolution cameras, noise-cancelling headphones, and higher bandwidth/more stable internet connection may all be useful additions.
- How will you measure the effectiveness of your new approach?

Suggested resources

"Never. Stop. Experiment – Crate digging for creative coaching tech" – Stephen Brown's newsletter on digital coaching tools - https://tinyurl.com/4886ck28

"Coaching with Sam Isaacson" – Newsletter from author Sam Isaacson regularly featuring developments in CoachTech - https://tinyurl.com/59m4eata

Let's Make Coaching Creative – Podcast Series by the Association for Coaching - https://www.associationforcoaching.com/page/Lets_Make_Coaching_Creative_Series_Page

National Cyber Security Centre – Features security advice and guidance for individuals, families, and businesses - https://www.ncsc.gov.uk

References

Anthony, K. and Nagel, D. M. (2021). *Coaching Online*. 1st edn. Taylor and Francis.

Barker, G.G. and Barker, E.E., (2022). Online therapy: Lessons learned from the COVID-19 health crisis. *British Journal of Guidance & Counselling*, *50*(1), pp. 66–81.

du Sautoy, M. (2019). *The Creativity Code*. HarperCollins Publishers.

Gash, J. (2016). *Coaching Creativity*. 1st edn. Taylor and Francis.

Grabmann, C. and Schermuly, C.C., (2021). Coaching with artificial intelligence: Concepts and capabilities. *Human Resource Development Review*, *20*(1), pp. 106–126.

Hambly, L. and Bomford, C. (2018). *Creative Career Coaching*. 1st edn. Taylor and Francis.

Isaacson, S. (2021). *How to Thrive as a Coach in a Digital World*. Open University Press.

Kanatouri, S. (2020). *The Digital Coach*. 1st edn. Taylor and Francis.

Lucas, M. (2023). *Creating the Reflective Habit*. 1st edn. Taylor and Francis.

McKinsey & Company. (2022). What are Industry 4.0, the Fourth Industrial Revolution, and 4IR.

Passmore, J. (2021). *Global Coach Survey*. Henley Business School

Passmore, J. (2020). *The Coaches' Handbook*. 1st edn. Taylor and Francis.

Rubin, R. (2023). *The Creative Act*. Canongate Books.

Shao, Z., Li, X. and Wang, Q., (2022). From ambidextrous learning to digital creativity: An integrative theoretical framework. *Information Systems Journal*, *32*(3), pp. 544–572

Sheather, A. (2019). *Coaching Beyond Words: Using Art to Deepen and Enrich Our Conversations*. Routledge.

Chapter 16

Coaching with collage

Andréa Watts

Introduction

In this chapter, we will answer the question, "How does coaching with collage facilitate better self-expression for clients? And why does this expression help them achieve the changes they seek?" To do this, we start from the premise that self-awareness and self-expression are inextricably linked, each informing and influencing the other. From here, you are taken on a journey through the three-stage creative process of the Collage Coaching Technique™ (CCT). Key concepts covered include projection, metaphors, external visualisation, and narrative storytelling. At each stage, the theory and practice demonstrate how coaching with collage enables simultaneous development of self-expression and self-awareness.

At its core, self-awareness is "the ability to see ourselves clearly – to understand who we are, how others see us, and how we fit into the world around us" (Eurich, 2017, p. 3).

This insight includes understanding your values, passions, drivers, behaviours, and triggers. It involves a perception of your internal landscape and how this manifests externally as you engage with others and express yourself outwardly.

However, true self-awareness is rare. Therefore, so is authentic self-expression, where you unapologetically show the world who you are and what you believe and think. Instead, you may mimic and borrow from others or conceal parts of yourself. Ultimately, this distorted version of self-expression is not beneficial.

The Collage Coaching Technique™ allows expression of all aspects of the 'self', including the painful, uncomfortable, and challenging. In a psychologically safe and creatively constructive space, clients can work with and through all they present (Watts, 2023b), reaching a place where self-expression empowers positive change with self-belief, resilience, creativity, love, and confidence.

DOI: 10.4324/9781003453437-17

Cultural context

In Western society, self-expression is of paramount importance. It is a way of demonstrating your uniqueness, distinguishes you from others, and reflects your personal thoughts, belief systems, values, feelings and so on. The concept is closely related to positive attributes such as confidence, creativity, self-assurance, authenticity, well-being, and a sense of freedom. Multiple research studies support these as outcomes of positive self-expression. Consequently, finding ways to express yourself as an individual is encouraged.

Acknowledging the difference across cultural contexts, for the purposes of this chapter, the theory and practice are written predominantly from the Western perspective. From the Eastern viewpoint, the self is largely viewed as interdependent of the collective (Kim & Ko, 2007).

The science beside the art

The theory and practice of coaching with collage are like the hand and mind connection (Jones, 2006; Rich, 1999). Being integral to the function of the other, they seamlessly collaborate, taking turns to lead and respond, inform, and influence each other. As such, and to reflect how collage combines different materials into a coherent whole, this chapter blends theory and practice together. The focus is on those most relevant to using the CCT to enable better client self-expression.

Self-awareness and self-expression|Two sides of the same coin

The CCT is a powerful tool for simultaneously increasing self-awareness and enabling self-expression. It does this by facilitating client exploration and reflection of their internal landscape through outwardly expressing their thoughts and emotions. Significantly, as a co-dependent process, increased self-awareness enables better, more authentic self-expression and vice versa. This creative process helps clients know, define, and express themselves better. Essentially, to be clear of their identity. Without this clarity, clients struggle to be seen, heard, and understood, to influence and make an impact at a personal or professional level. For this reason, providing them with a means to improve their self-expression is an important facet of coaching. For coaching to reflect the client's journey, self-expression and self-awareness benefit from exploring, understanding, confronting, and embracing the spectrum of human emotions and experiences, from the uplifting, joyous, and fulfilling to the challenging, uncomfortable, or upsetting.

Coaching with collage allows both ends of the spectrum to be felt and heard in a psychologically safe and creatively constructive space. Taking this holistic approach enables them to be worked with and through in a way that facilitates the truest expression of all that the client presents, from a place of acceptance rather than judgement.

The collage coaching technique™

The CCT is a three-stage framework comprising the following:

1 Gathering
2 Creating
3 Storytelling

Working with images as the language of the mind, the approach first takes clients on a journey into the unconscious to access and gather from the wealth of information held there, including unearthing thoughts, values, emotions, and memories that have been forgotten, ignored, hidden, edited, or denied. This material finds creative expression as visual metaphors and symbolic imagery (Watts, 2023b).

The creating stage then facilitates meaning-making through external visualisation and projection. Once available at a conscious level for evaluation and reflection, clients play with and manipulate images while constructing their collages. During this activity, they simultaneously construct internal knowledge in their minds (Ackermann, 2001). As a projective technique that allows uncensored material to find expression through external objects (Branthwaite, 2002), their collages embody the client's inner voice, ideas, judgements, and feelings.

Being visible, they can explore, reflect on, and understand these thoughts and emotions, and, in turn, express these to others. The first opportunity for this comes at the storytelling stage as clients share the meaning and story with the coach. Because the collage holds personal expression as visual metaphors and symbols, it bypasses the editing and judgement of verbal-centred approaches and the conscious mind. As such, clients articulate their emotions and experiences honestly, often describing and expressing themselves using language that is rich, authentic, detailed and even poetic (Watts, 2023b).

The artistic-creative process

Introducing an Arts-Based Method (ABM) in coaching generates helpful and often unexpected insights by causing the brain to work in unfamiliar and diverse ways. With the CCT, a profound shift in cognitive processing occurs by

• using images instead of words as the initial form of expression
• working with unconscious knowledge

The unconscious internal exploration is beneficial as, according to Kim and Ko (2007), "Core aspects of self are those that come from within a person, such as thoughts, values, preferences, feelings and beliefs" (p. 5). Coaching with collage equips clients with the materials and methods to uncover, explore, and present these aspects of themselves from a different perspective.

Furthermore, "Artistic expression always involves two forms of self-expression. One is a deliberate and conscious external creative endeavour. The other occurs because the process of creating something always unconsciously reveals aspects of the 'self'" (Watts, 2023b, p. 20). As an ABM, a benefit of working with the CCT is that these aspects of self find a voice in multiple ways. Not just visually but also physically, spiritually, and verbally.

Accepting that choice is also an expression of the 'self', whether clients choose to create a classic (magazine) or digital collage, their decision is another opportunity for personal expression as they determine how to experience the artistic, creative process.

Stage 1|Gathering

Clients have complete agency as they engage with the first stage of the CCT and follow the guidance to gather images that resonate with them. As clients do this, they reveal parts of themselves that may not usually find expression, including drawing up past experiences that affect how they currently express themselves. This discovery happens as they allow themselves to 'feel' something and trust and respond to that feeling, however, and wherever it manifests, whether emotionally, physically, or otherwise.

The ability to remain open and curious about the process is imperative, as it improves the client's chances of honest self-expression. Coaches support this experience through further guidance which helps clients move beyond the default state of rationalising, editing, and dismissing at this early stage. Instead, they are encouraged to be present and allow full expression of all that is showing up for them. As a non-threatening activity, cutting and tearing images from magazines or cutting and pasting online with a mouse, clients get into a flow state. The concept of flow was developed by Mihaly Csikszentmihalyi. He describes it as "the mental state of operation in which a person performing an activity is fully immersed in a feeling of energised focus, full involvement and enjoyment in the activity" (Csikszentmihalyi, 1990, p. 35). As such, outside distractions recede, and clients are often unaware of the emotional depth at which they are working. "It wasn't until I started creating my collage that I realised how much the images were revealing to me on a deeply personal level" (Rachel).

As clients steadily look through the magazines, they must slow down physically and cognitively. The guidance (and music) helps them transition into a state of relaxation where they can more easily access their unconscious minds.

Music without words and a slow tempo are chosen, as research shows this influences the human brain by lowering defences and slowing the heart rate, in turn engendering a state of calm and well-being (Bush, 1995, as cited in Beebe & Wyatt, 2009). This slower pace allows clients, through the images, to connect to aspects of themselves that are neglected, often due to external time pressures. The gathered images provide the foundation for what follows in the creating stage. Despite not understanding what they all mean, seeing and feeling something of themselves in an image starts the process of external self-expression and internal self-awareness.

Stage 2|Creating

For many clients, coaching with collage will be the first time they have used their hands to intentionally create something to explore and express aspects of themself. Therefore, as they begin creating their collage, emphasis is on reassuring them that its appearance is unimportant. Clients may come to their coaching session with a negative art story. As such, clarifying that their collage is an outward expression of themselves, rather than artwork, releases them to create without reservation or fear of judgement. There is also an invitation to playfulness and curiosity which contributes to the sense of freedom and negates artistic expectation. With this permission to work without restraint, it is unsurprising that most clients express deep pride and joy in their completed collages. As an outcome of using an ABM in coaching, this is invaluable for inspiring visual self-expression beyond the coaching context and renewing clients' belief in their creative ability.

While composing the collage, there is a dance between the hand and mind. This is stimulated as the client makes decisions concerning which images to include or omit and how they will appear on the final piece. Each small decision, whether to cut or tear, add or remove material, move an image up or down, left or right, duplicate or resize, is a gesture of self-expression. Through this activity, the client captures their present state and their hoped-for future self.

This is only possible because of external visualisation, where thoughts, values, emotions, experiences, and beliefs are represented physically through images, with the ability to move these around in a physical space (Martin & Schwartz, 2014). Here the dance between the hand and the mind enables questions and responses. So, as they create, the emerging collage says, "This image represents my core value, and this colour reflects my passion which I'll move to the middle. Over here, I'll place my unfulfilled dream, while the gap beside it speaks to my stuckness. But that doesn't feel right. I wonder what it would feel like to move the unfulfilled dream?" Re-organising the 'self' to find different expressions and meaning empowers clients to shift their sense of identity and how they choose to represent themselves.

As the images start to work together, the story emerges from the page. The final collage will be unique to the individual, capturing and preserving aspects of themselves at the time of creation. Affected by internal models and external experiences, the appearance changes every time they create another one, reflecting how human thoughts, emotions, and mindsets are dynamic and constantly shifting. With the collage as a source of reflection, over time, clients can see the changes and similarities in how they understand and express in relation to others and themselves, further deepening their self-awareness.

The coaching collage is also a resource for clients to continue learning about themselves and experiencing different forms of artistic-creative expression. For example, clients are encouraged to use their collages for reflection through journaling. Others have used theirs as inspiration for poetry and drawing, as well as bringing symbols and colours from their collages into their physical environment. As a tangible expression of the 'self', a collage's potential use beyond the coaching session enhances the value of using collage as a coaching tool.

Storytelling

At the storytelling stage, clients are invited to share the meaning of their collage. With similarities to narrative therapy (Standish, 2013) clients are encouraged to find their own voice and tell their story in their own words. They are given as long as it takes and follow the path they choose. This stage is sacred and not intended for the coach to gather information and consider what questions to ask. Instead, clients are reassured that they will not be interrupted, and notes are not taken. With an understanding that the client is the expert, the role of the coach is to focus entirely on the client, listening and hearing to understand rather than respond while holding a psychologically safe space. Rarely is anyone heard in that way without an agenda or judgement. "This is the longest I've spoken without interruption; it felt weird but good" (Inaya).

As an extension of how clients are or wish to show up in the world, the telling is an opportunity for them to experience themselves through their collage. Sharing empowers them to make decisions about how they will express themselves in the telling, with expression coming not only through language but also tone, order, pace, metaphors as embodied cognition (Lakoff, 2012), and physical reactions. Additionally, as they speak and hear themselves, establishing and understanding their identity, clients have the option to own or re-author all or parts of their story. Building on the meaning-making as they gathered and created, this process helps them consider if there are new expressions and awareness for them in that moment. "It wasn't until I spoke it out that I realised I had a choice in how I saw my relationship with my sister" (Robert). In recognising that they can be and feel differently, clients report experiencing a palpable shift in that spoken moment of awareness.

After storytelling, the coaching conversation begins. The client leads, deciding where they want to focus, while the coach remains curious about the story. The coach's role is to help the client elicit further meaning through questions, reflections, observations, and holding the silence (Watts, 2023b). Teasing out the meaning is an intricate and delicate process that should not be forced or rushed. Using the collage as the vehicle for sharing enhances the tradition of oral storytelling by providing a visual reference from which to share. For example, the clients will interact with their collage as they speak, perhaps tracing their fingers repeatedly around an image. As they do this, the coach notices on the client's behalf and can ask about these physical responses. The purpose of the questions is to help clients generate experience, memories, and knowledge of themself rather than to gather facts (Knowles et al., 2012).

Storytelling is emotive, natural, and fluent when elicited from images that originate from the unconscious (van Schalkwyk, 2010). Drawn to the surface, this honest reflection of the 'self' finds expression by overriding edited, learnt, old, superficial, and people-pleasing language that can pass as the client's own. Consequently, when using reflection, the coach ensures they paraphrase using the client's own words or actions. As best practice, this technique avoids the coach projecting their meaning into the dialogue while also honouring the client's meaning-making process. For the client, hearing their words echoed back helps clarify and consolidate their thoughts and decisions. "As you reflected back what I said, I realised I've made huge progress, more than I'd thought" (Jessica).

Clients can continue to share their stories with others beyond the life of the coaching session. In this way, the collage remains a source of expression, learning, and growth, as each time the story will evolve.

Client reflection

Yolanda created her collage while attending Collage as a Creative Coaching Tool training (see Figure 16.1). After completing the training, she chose to sign up for a 12-session coaching with collage programme. Her generous contribution to this chapter is a very short excerpt from an otherwise detailed and comprehensive exploration of her experience.

When I was first attracted to coaching with collage, I didn't know what it would wake in terms of expressing my feelings and thoughts. However, during the session, I began to understand the unconscious becoming conscious. Having that awareness and self-expression allowed me to become open to the process. I began to ask myself questions like, "What am I good at? What am I hiding or not expressing? Why am I doing certain things?"

Whereas I think traditional coaching is directional and would ask, "What about the picture on the left, do you want to say something about it?" the Collage Coaching Technique™ (CCT) asks questions differently, thus permitting the

Figure 16.1 Yolanda Fernandes|First collage created on 23 June 2022.

person being coached to follow whatever pathway is being evoked in them in that moment. So, coming back the next time, another side of your collage is talking to you and saying, "This is what I was trying to express". This was an amazing navigating and discovery process, including coming to the self-awareness that I express myself better visually.

The CCT also helped me think deeper, connect, and really address some of the challenging conversations I need to have with myself. In showing connections and the gaps (as white spaces), you think, "What's in the white spaces? There's something there, something I'm unable to express, and what's behind that: Is it guilt? Is it shame? Is it whatever?"

The CCT creates a container for you to be in that space of uncertainty. So that I've become comfortable with self-expression as allowing me to surrender being in this space where I'm not looking for answers, but I'm allowing myself to be with the messy bits. This self-expression allows me to step into the unknown with confidence and courage, knowing that understanding emerges the more attention you pay to what you're seeing and not seeing. For example, I would look at something on the collage, then see it again the next day and think, "I didn't notice that colour, shape, etc., before". Or, where I've started going for meditative walks, I look at things differently, and as I take photos,

I think, "What if I take it from this angle? What are the different perspectives looking at the same thing? What do I see when I change the way I'm doing things?"

Whereas before, I would experience something and move on, now I think about what I've gone through, and even when I feel bad about it, to then understand why I'm feeling bad. So, it's about slowing down and paying attention to create that deeper connection which I wouldn't have had before. And actually, with something like crying, coming to appreciate that there can be tears of joy, sadness, pity, or anger. Rather than say, "Oh stop crying, come on, get tough". I think, "Just let me sit with this", so then I connect to a different emotion that is talking to me and ask what has triggered this feeling. Rather than deny it, coaching with collage has taught me that unless you work through it and become aware of it or the expression of it, then it's going to come up again and again, and you don't change the patterns of how you respond. (Yolanda Fernandes).

Conclusion

Self-expression is about knowing and showing the world who you are with confidence and without apology. To achieve this requires self-awareness. Coaching with collage enables both by moving clients away from editing, rationalising, and denying their thoughts and feelings. Facilitating this involves working with images – the unconscious and slowing down enough to allow what is felt to be heard, explored, and expressed. This new information increases client's self-awareness, enabling them to understand themselves better and, subsequently, how they want to show up in the world. As a starting point, in allowing multiple modes of expression, the CCT is an empowering and creative approach for clients to begin this journey.

Discussion points

• Working with the unconscious, what ethical considerations should coaches consider when using collage as a coaching tool?
• AI is increasingly used as a tool in coaching, and many coaches are concerned about the impact, particularly with more traditional verbal-centred approaches. What role might arts-based practices contribute to the changing face of coaching?

Suggested resources
Book

Watts, A. (2023a). *Collage as a Creative Coaching Tool: A Comprehensive Resource for Coaches and Psychologists*. Routledge.

Website

www.unglueyou.co.uk – The chapter author's website with information about coaching with collage. Including blog posts, free resources, details of her accredited training programme, and other services.

References

Ackermann, E. (2001). Piaget's Constructivism, Papert's Constructionism: What's the Difference. *Future of Learning Group Publication*, 5(3), 438.

Branthwaite, Alan. (2002). Investigating the Power of Imagery in Marketing Communication: Evidence-based Techniques. *Qualitative Market Research: An International Journal* 5, 3, 164–171.

Beebe, L. H., & Wyatt, T. H. (2009). Guided Imagery and Music: Using the Bonny Method to Evoke Emotion and Access the Unconscious. *Journal of Psychosocial Nursing and Mental Health Services*, 47(1), 29–33. https://doi.org/10.3928/02793695-20090101-02

Csikszentmihalyi, M. (1990). The Domain of Creativity. In M. A. Runco & R. S. Albert (Eds.), *Theories of Creativity* (pp. 190–212). Sage Publications, Inc.

Eurich, T. (2017). *Insight: The Power of Self-Awareness in a Self-Deluded World* (First). Macmillan.

Jones, E. G. (2006). The Sensory Hand. *Brain*, *129*(12), 3413–3420. https://doi.org/10.1093/brain/awl308

Kim, H. S., & Ko, D. (2007). Culture & Self-Expression 1 Culture and Self-Expression. https://www.researchgate.net/publication/267794252

Knowles, J., Cole, A., & Weber, S. (2012). Visual Images in Research. In *Handbook of the Arts in Qualitative Research: Perspectives, Methodologies, Examples, and Issues* (pp. 42–54). SAGE Publications, Inc. https://doi.org/10.4135/9781452226545.n4

Lakoff, G. (2012). Explaining Embodied Cognition Results. *Topics in Cognitive Science*, 4(4), 773–785. https://doi.org/10.1111/j.1756-8765.2012.01222.x

Martin, L., & Schwartz, D. L. (2014). A Pragmatic Perspective on Visual Representation and Creative Thinking. *Visual Studies*, 29(1), 80–93. https://doi.org/10.1080/1472586X.2014.862997

Rich, G. J. (1999). The Hand: How Its Use Shapes the Brain, Language, and Human Culture: The Hand: How Its Use Shapes the Brain, Language, and Human Culture. *Anthropology of Consciousness*, 10(1), 62–64. https://doi.org/10.1525/ac.1999.10.1.62

Standish, K. (2013). Lecture 8 narrative therapy|PPT. https://www.slideshare.net/kevins299/lecture-8-narrative-therapy

van Schalkwyk, G. J. (2010). Collage Life Story Elicitation Technique: A Representational Technique for Scaffolding Autobiographical Memories. In Qualitative Report (Vol. 15, Issue 3). http://www.nova.edu/ssss/QR/QR15-3/vanschalkwyk.pdf

Watts, A. (2023b). *Collage as a Creative Coaching Tool: A Comprehensive Resource for Coaches and Psychologists* (First). Routledge.

Chapter 17

Ethical considerations in using arts-based tools and approaches in coaching

Andrea Giraldez-Hayes, Wendy-Ann Smith, and Max Eames

Introduction

The use of art tools and approaches in coaching has become increasingly popular in the last 15 years. However, despite a growing interest in the field, as demonstrated by several publications and workshops, more needs to be considered about the ethical dimensions of these practices. Compared to art therapy, a recognised profession in many countries, the use of art in coaching is very much in its infancy. It is easy to feel attracted by the idea of integrating art and creativity into various aspects of working with coaching clients. It is argued that there is considerable potential for unintended harm without an awareness of the ethical implications of such interventions. Awareness of potential dilemmas that may arise before, during, and after the coaching include but are not limited to informed consent, voluntary participation, confidentiality, the potential for harm, and a consideration of whether the coach has the requisite knowledge and competencies to facilitate art-based coaching interventions. Although the questions and answers may differ, all coaches should contemplate these ethical quandaries. This chapter will examine several ethical issues relevant to coaches when using arts-based and creative methods.

Considerations for an ethical arts-based coaching practice

To the uninitiated, arts-based coaching interventions may appear to be a soft, unintrusive, non-threatening method of exploring the psychic experience or of facilitating the awareness and intentions of a coaching client. On the contrary, arts-based methods have the potential to elicit highly emotive, and often unexpected, responses. Furthermore, arts-based methods may create a diverse range of unique ethical dilemmas due to the specific and complex nature of artistic mediums available and the multimodal nature of application (e.g., images or music) and interpretation. For example, listening to a piece of what is generally understood to be a soothing/relaxing piece of music may in one client aid

DOI: 10.4324/9781003453437-18

relaxation and enhance creativity, whilst another client may have uncomfortable or repressed traumatic memories attached to that same piece of music.

In the realm of therapy, there is a clear distinction between art therapy and "creative counselling" – that is, the practice of professional counsellors choosing to incorporate art resources and tools in their interventions. Whilst art therapists adhere to a code of ethics – for example, the ethical code provided by the British Association of Art Therapists (2019), there is no equivalent for counsellors in the use of non-verbal forms of expression such as visual art, drama, or music as a means to help clients explore and communicate their inner world.

The parallel with coaching is easy to identify. Various professional bodies, such as the International Coach Federation (ICF), the European Mentoring and Coaching Council (EMCC), and the Association for Coaching (AC 2021), have their own codes of ethics. Still, there is no specific professional body or interest group, and, therefore, no ethical guidance for coaches using arts and creative tools in their practice.

Including arts and creativity into existing ethical codes could prove to be a reasonable first step. That said, it is essential to consider, as suggested by Lowman (2013, cited by Garvey and Stokes, 2023), that ethic codes within professional contexts can be problematic and limited, as they are usually based on normative approaches or presented as a set of 'rules'. In this respect, Stokes et al. (2023), as well as Iordanou et al. (2017), address a highly relevant issue regarding the practicality of implementing such codes whilst inviting us to consider whether a clearly outlined set of explicit guidelines can accommodate the variety of individuals and, consequently, the unique ethical challenges which coaches are likely to encounter in their coaching practice.

Furman (2013) makes a distinction between what she terms mandatory and aspirational ethics. According to this author, "[M]andatory ethics dictate a minimal standard, generally reflecting legal guidelines by which one must practice" (p. 17). Conversely, aspirational ethics "go beyond what is simply legally compliant to encompass all aspects of practice which affect the wellbeing of the client" (p. 18). Aspirational ethics have particular significance for arts-based coaches due to the intricate and emotive nature of their practice. As with all coaching practices, the integration of art within coaching demands a thorough and nuanced examination of ethical considerations. Inherent to artistic endeavours are complexity and involve subjectivity, which require a more profound exploration of ethical principles. Relying solely on standards of practice is insufficient to address the myriad ethical issues arising.

Although the lack of specific ethical guidelines for arts-based coaching can be a limitation, much more can and needs to be done to consider the ethics of arts-based coaching, including actively integrating ethics in coach education (Garvey & Giraldez-Hayes, 2023). Smith and Clutterbuck (2023) suggest coach educators role model their ethical deliberations, decision processes, and reflections, whilst also ensuring coaches engage with critical reflexivity processes and supervision. After all, every activity and situation presents opportunities for 'technical' decisions, and coaches must adopt an ethical position with each choice made along the way. It is worth noting that using arts in coaching can trigger unexpected emotional responses (Hammond & Gantt, 1998), as described earlier in this chapter. Therefore, coaches should be cognisant of the rich and unexpected potentiality of unconscious experiences, attended by an array of thoughts and emotions that may arise at any moment in time. The coach must be competent in responding to the coaching client's reactions to the process of creating art and, if appropriate, the resultant artwork itself. The question is, Are all coaches trained to do this? If not, would it then be appropriate to engage in art-based practices and facilitate, through deep questions, the surfacing of deep emotions but without effectively supporting the client in processing them? Visual arts, music, dance, drama, or photography are specific forms of communication. In the same way that coaches are trained to understand the nuances of verbal and non-verbal communication, it seems reasonable that they should have at their disposal the knowledge and expertise to understand the subtleties of the thoughts and emotions triggered when using arts-based interventions/methods. Additionally, coaches should have an emotional regulatory capacity to sit with and hold the emotional space for the client to feel safe when powerful insights emerge in the context of arts-based interventions.

As arts-based coaching is a specific way of working that, as discussed, may trigger unexpected responses, the coach's knowledge and competence are essential, but various other ethical issues should also be taken into consideration. Among them, contracting, informed consent, voluntary participation, confidentiality, the potential for harm, and competence and practice within the coach's scope are worth mentioning.

Contracting, informed consent, and voluntary participation

Establishing a contract is crucial in coaching, as it allows the clarification of the foundational guidelines for the coaching relationship and the use of various interventions within the coaching. Such clarification ensures that both the client and the coach understand what they are committing to. Contracting involves collaboratively setting the parameters of the coaching relationship, including goals, expectations, and the boundaries of confidentiality and being cognisant of the assumptions that each party has in the relationship. Importantly, it also involves making such matters explicit (McLean, 2023). The contract serves as a roadmap, guiding all parties through the creative journey ahead. In the context of using arts-based interventions, it is also an opportunity to discuss the nature of the artistic processes involved, the intended outcomes, and any potential challenges that may arise.

When using an arts-based approach (or when the coach plans to use arts-based tools), either systematically or occasionally, it is essential to share this aim with the client and to clearly explain the rationale behind such an approach.

Contracting allows the coach to comply with the requirement of informed consent – that is, sharing sufficient and detailed information with the client about the nature of the coaching process, the artistic mediums that may be used, and any potential risks involved so that the client can make an informed decision about their participation, empowering them to actively engage in the coaching process with a clear understanding of what it entails.

It is the client's choice to embrace or decline an invitation to engage with arts-based approaches. Even if such approaches are agreed upon in the contract, it is good practice to ask for permission before using a specific tool or technique to guarantee voluntary participation. Clients should feel free to express, at any juncture, their preferences and concerns regarding the use of artistic approaches without any pressure for agreement. By seeking such permission, the coach respects the client's autonomy and ensures that the coaching process aligns with the client's preferences. Establishing a clear and comprehensive contract is foundational to arts-based and creative coaching approaches.

Confidentiality and records

Confidentiality in coaching conveys a sense of security that the conversation will remain private and operate within defined boundaries. An essential feature of the coaching relationship, confidentiality must be consistently and consciously understood and maintained. Keeping confidentiality is thus paramount in arts-based coaching, just as in traditional coaching settings. Given the personal and often intimate nature of the creative processes involved, clients must feel they can trust that their creations and interactions will remain confined to the agreed boundaries of confidentiality in the same manner as the verbal exchanges that occur in all coaching modalities.

Coaches should establish clear guidelines for handling artistic products and documentation. Whilst the coaching codes of ethics do not contemplate the use of arts-based approaches, the ethical standards for art therapists – for example, those provided by the British Association of Art Therapists (2019) – refer to the obligation to keep records of the materials produced during the sessions. Moreover, it is expected that they are "named, dated, and ideally safely stored throughout the therapeutic relationship". Likewise in coaching, the coach and client should reach mutually agreed decisions on how and where the artwork will be stored during the coaching process. It is typical to consider that the client retains sole ownership of the artwork, including its utilisation and disposal decisions. If mutually agreed, the coach and the client can decide to digitalise and save some or all artistic productions. The coach should in this instance attain permission to include some of those materials in their notes. When this is the case, the same considerations toward keeping session records apply (see Iordanou et al., 2023, Chapter 11, for an in-depth consideration of record keeping in coaching), including compliance with GDPR requirements (Rogers, 2023).

It is not uncommon to attend a workshop or presentation, or read a book or published paper, in which a coach has elected to feature a given client's artistic work. Although sharing such materials can be of interest to others from an educational perspective, from an ethical standpoint, coaches should not show nor share such materials if they have not previously obtained permission to use them. The same should apply to verbal interactions or written reflections related to those materials. In either instance, coaches are obliged to obtain written consent.

Potential harm

Coaching is a developmental endeavour, positive and growth and learning-oriented in nature. At first glance, one would expect there to be little room for harm. However, with the emotive nature of art, the potential for harm is increased. Therefore it is imperative that coaches be cognisant of the potential for such harm and work to minimise any harm for the benefit of the coaching relationship (Smith & Arnold, 2023) and the client's well-being. Whilst the arts offer a powerful means of self-expression (Gerber et al., 2018), there is potential for harm, particularly when the coaching process is not carefully managed. Coaches must be aware of the emotional impact of creative activities and interventions. Sensitivity to potential triggers and the emergence of intense emotions is an expectation of those facilitating arts-based interventions, and coaches should be prepared to suggest or provide additional support or alter the course of coaching if necessary. Furthermore, most ethical guidelines suggest that coaches should only engage in practices within the scope of their professional competence and practice. The coach is responsible for acquiring the necessary knowledge and skills before engaging in specific practices and informing clients about their experience level (Furman, 2013).

Identify your limits: Competence and practice within the coach's scope of experience

Integrating the arts into coaching, like all other coaching modalities and methods, requires the coach to have a degree of competency (Iordanou et al., 2017). It should be noted, however, that arts-based coaching demands a very specific level of competence in the context of a solid understanding of the challenges and opportunities innate to both traditional coaching principles and arts-based modalities.

For example, arts-based coaches should feel equipped to encourage clients to create visual, auditory, or kinaesthetic representations when verbal communication becomes challenging or when the client encounters difficulties describing something. Additionally, a proficient coach should be capable of engaging in helpful and supportive discussions with a client about a piece of art produced or presented during a session. In such instances, the artwork should be approached much like one would approach a metaphor or any reported experience.

Moreover, even highly experienced coaches may need to prepare themselves for the intense emotional responses often triggered by art, including the use of specific art materials. They may also need help understanding how to use artistic processes effectively whilst simultaneously managing strong emotional reactions.

A key concern is the interpretation of artwork. Such interpretation is at the purview of the coaching client, not the coach. The attempt by the coach to interpret raises various ethical considerations, notably harm through distorting, influencing, or intrusively entering the client's intrapsychic world, with the potential to destabilise their sense of self in areas the client may not be psychologically grounded enough to delve into. Such interpretations would require training in arts-based coaching interventions and a comprehensive familiarity with artistic processes, art history, and graphic, auditory, or motor symbolism. Here it is recommended to approach with the mindset of asking curious questions to elucidate meaning and understanding.

All this means that coaches who wish to use arts-based interventions should continuously operate within their scope of competence (see ICF, 2021; EMCC, 2021, codes of ethics), seeking ongoing professional development and support, such as supervision, to enhance their skills and knowledge. Additionally, the coach should continuously work to be as aware as possible of their own biases and limitations, maintaining a commitment to professional competence and humility.

In conclusion, ethical considerations are integral to the success and integrity of arts-based coaching. By prioritising contracting, informed consent, voluntary participation, confidentiality, awareness of the potential for harm, and competence, coaches can create a coaching environment that encourages exploration, expression, and self-awareness whilst safeguarding the well-being of their clients. Upholding ethical principles ensures that arts-based coaching remains a potent and responsible approach to fostering personal growth. Ethical awareness and conduct in arts-based coaching involve recognising how the intricate interplay of competence, the artistic process, the therapeutic relationship, and the art space converges to shape what can be a rich and rewarding client experience, one that can facilitate deep personal insight.

Case studies

Case study 1: Showcasing client's creations

This case study explores a scenario in which a coach faces ethical challenges using a client's drawings during a presentation.

During their sessions, an experienced arts-based coach invited his client to create drawings to self-express and explore thoughts and emotions. The drawings have been instrumental in uncovering insights and facilitating meaningful discussions. Recognising the transformative potential of these artworks, the coach at one stage decides to showcase them in a presentation about the effectiveness of arts-based coaching at a coaching conference. After the presentation, the coach shares the experience with his supervisor.

The coach used the client's drawings in a public setting without previously seeking permission. Whilst the coach believed that sharing these drawings would demonstrate the efficacy of arts-based coaching, presenting a client's personal and potentially sensitive artwork without consent raised some significant ethical considerations.

As we have already mentioned, obtaining informed consent is crucial. The coach should have sought explicit permission from the client before using their drawings. Failure to do so breaches the fundamental principle of confidentiality and compromises the trust established within the coaching relationship. Coaching requires a level of competence in handling the complexities of the coaching process, including the ethical implications of using client-created – even non-descript – creations such as art pieces, for example, a drawing.

In conversation with the supervisor to address this ethical dilemma and uphold the coaching relationship's integrity, the coach reflects on the best course of action and considers the following steps:

1 Apologise and acknowledge the oversight of using the client's drawings without consent.
2 Seek retrospective consent from the client, explaining the purpose and context of using the drawings in the presentation. That involves an honest conversation about the potential impact and the client's comfort level with their artwork being shared.
3 Reflect on this experience and consider the implications of each possible action before making a decision and acting on it.
4 The coach considers these dilemmas an opportunity for professional growth and seeks support through supervision. Learning from this ethical lapse, the coach could update their practices to ensure he/she obtains informed consent before using client materials in public forums.

The case study underscores the importance of maintaining ethical standards in arts-based coaching, particularly regarding the use of clients' creative expressions. Coaches can create a trusting coaching environment by navigating informed consent, confidentiality, and respecting boundaries.

Case study 2: Showcasing trainee coaches' creations

In this case study, during a coach training workshop, the trainer requested to take pictures of the artwork created by trainee coaches. This request was enacted using a consent-to-exhibit consent form. What follows raises questions about the appropriateness of such a practice.

Given the theme of the training – arts-based techniques – it is expected that artistic processes will be used in the training workshop, but the consent-to-exhibit form introduced a layer of ethical complexity. Whilst it enabled participants to choose the fate of their artwork, the nature of the art project – tied as it was to the coaching training experience – had implications for the voluntary and informed participation of the trainees.

During the arts-based coach training workshop, trainee coaches received mandalas and were invited to create imagery individually or collaboratively. The coach trainer asked them to sign the consent-to-exhibit form, providing the option of having their mandalas photographed and exhibited in a permanent installation or retrieving them after the initial exhibit. Whilst most trainees willingly participated, two wanted to keep their work private.

The argument that art exhibited by trainee coaches educates the public, primarily professional coaches, about the possibilities of arts-based approaches, is valid. However, this must be balanced against the participants' preferences and comfort levels. The two trainees' disagreement raised questions about the appropriateness of assuming a collective obligation to exhibit art. Despite the two participants' concerns, all artworks were displayed.

The case study highlights the intricate ethical considerations that emerge when coaches contemplate the exhibition of artwork created during training. Balancing the profession's promotion with the need to assure trainees' autonomy and preferences requires careful consideration.

Questions to consider

What are the key ethical dilemmas in case study 2?

How could the relationships be impacted by the actions of the coach trainer?

What may be the impact on the coaching students by the actions of the coach trainer?

What are the questions the coach trainer could ask of themselves and their students?

What are the pathways of action available to the coach trainer to uphold appropriate ethical standards?

Discussion points

- What competencies and/or capacities are required of a coach educator or coach when engaging in arts in coaching?
- Considering the myriad of art modalities available, how might such competencies or capacities be different or the same in the ethical considerations that arise with each modality in a manner which might not necessarily be anticipated in advance?
- What points in a coaching code of ethics are aligned with arts-based practice? What points appear to be missing?

Suggested resources

Duffy, M., & Passmore, J. (2010). Ethics in coaching: An ethical decision-making framework for coaching psychologists. *International Coaching Psychology Review*, 5(2), 140–151.

Smith, W.A., Passmore, J., Turner, E., Lai, Y.L., & Clutterbuck, D. (Eds.). (2023). *The Ethical Coaches' Handbook: A Guide to Developing Ethical Maturity in Practice*. Taylor & Francis.

References

British Association of Art Therapists. (2019). *Code of ethics*. British Association of Art Therapists. https://baat.org/about/code-of-ethics

AC. (2021). *Global Code of Ethics*. Association for Coaching. https://www.associationforcoaching.com/page/AboutCodeEthics

EMCC. (2021). *Global Code of Ethics*. European Mentoring and Coaching Council. https://coachingfederation.org/ethics/code-of-ethics

Furman, L.R. (2013). *Ethics in Art Therapy: Challenging Topics for a Complex Modality*. Jessica Kingsley Publishers.

Garvey, B. & Giraldez-Hayes, A. (2023). Ethics in education and the development of coaches. In W.A. Smith, J. Passmore, E. Turner, Y.L. Lai, & D. Clutterbuck, (Eds.). *The Ethical Coaches' Handbook. A Guide to Developing Ethical Maturity in Practice* (267–278). Routledge.

Garvey, B. & Stokes, P. (2023). Ethics and professional coaching bodies. In W.A. Smith, J. Passmore, E. Turner, Y.L. Lai, & D. Clutterbuck, (Eds.). *The Ethical Coaches' Handbook: A Guide to Developing Ethical Maturity in Practice*: (36–51). Routledge.

Gerber, N., Bryl, K., Potvin, N., & Blank, C.A. (2018). Arts-based research approaches to studying mechanisms of change in the creative arts therapies. *Frontiers in Psychology*, 9, 2076.

Hammond, L. & Gantt, L. (1998). Using art in counselling: Ethical considerations. *Journal of Counselling & Development*, 76, 271–276.

ICF. (2021). *Code of Ethics*. International Coach Federation. https://coachingfederation.org/ethics/code-of-ethics

Iordanou, C., Hawley, R., & Iordanou, I., (2023). Ethical issues in note taking and record keeping in coaching. In W.A. Smith, J. Passmore, E. Turner, Y.L. Lai, & D. Clutterbuck, (Eds.). *The Ethical Coaches' Handbook: A Guide to Developing Ethical Maturity in Practice*. Routledge.

Iordanou, I., Hawley, R., & Iordanou, C. (2017). *Values and Ethics in Coaching*. SAGE Publications Ltd., https://doi.org/10.4135/9781473983755

Lowman, R.L. (2013). Coaching ethics. In J. Passmore, D.B. Peterson & T. Freire (Eds.), *The Wiley-Blackwell Handbook of the Psychology of Coaching and Mentoring* (pp. 68–88). Wiley Blackwell.

McLean, P., (2023). The psychological contract in coaching. In W.A. Smith, J. Passmore, E. Turner, Y.L. Lai, & D. Clutterbuck, (Eds.). *The Ethical Coaches' Handbook: A Guide to Developing Ethical Maturity in Practice*. Routledge.

Rogers, K.M. (2023). Legal considerations of ethical decision making in coaching. In W.A. Smith, J. Passmore, E. Turner, Y.L. Lai, & D. Clutterbuck, (Eds.). *The Ethical Coaches' Handbook: A Guide to Developing Ethical Maturity in Practice*. Routledge.

Smith, W.A., & Arnold, C. (2023). Ethical coaching and its relationships. In W.A. Smith, J. Passmore, E. Turner, Y.L. Lai, & D. Clutterbuck, (Eds.). *The Ethical Coaches' Handbook: A Guide to Developing Ethical Maturity in Practice*. Routledge.

Smith, W.A., & Clutterbuck, D. (2023). Ethics case studies for coach education and development. In W.A. Smith, E. Hirsch Pontes, D. Magadlela, & D. Clutterbuck, (Eds.). *Ethical Case Studies for Coach Development and Practice: A Coach's Companion*. Routledge.

Stokes, P., Hill, A., & Kelly, K., (2023). Exploring ethical codes. In W.A. Smith, J. Passmore, E. Turner, Y.L. Lai, & D. Clutterbuck, (Eds.). *The Ethical Coaches' Handbook: A Guide to Developing Ethical Maturity in Practice*. Routledge.

Index

Printed and bound by CPI Group (UK) Ltd, Croydon, CR0 4YY

06/12/2024

01802072-0005